About the Author

Sharon Cracknell was born in Yorkshire and has a passion for travel. She has been travelling between work contracts since 1999 and has always wanted to write about her many experiences. The opportunity arose when invited to Australia to house-sit for six months. *Pringles, Visas and a Glow in the Dark Jesus* is her first book.

Dedication

This book is dedicated to my mum whose constant thoughtfulness made my travel memoir book possible...I just wish she was here to read it.

.

Sharon Cracknell

PRINGLES, VISAS AND A GLOW IN THE DARK JESUS

AUSTIN MACAULEY
PUBLISHERS LTD.

A CIP catalogue record for this title is available from the British Library.

ISBN 978 1 78455 747 8 (paperback)
ISBN 978 1 78455 749 2 (hardback)

www.austinmacauley.com

First Published (2015)
Austin Macauley Publishers Ltd.
25 Canada Square
Canary Wharf
London
E14 5LQ

Printed and bound in Great Britain

Acknowledgments

With thanks to Jane Sloan, my fellow Sydney Writers Course student, who gave up so much of her time to proofread my book. Thanks too to Lynn Jackson and David Laughton for entrusting me with their home and cats and for a beautiful garden in which to write, Julie Sugden and Caroline Pinkney for taking the time to read my book and giving me the much needed feedback and to my dad who supports every irresponsible and nonconforming thing I do.

Chapter 1

Arrest

21st December 2004

I knew something was seriously wrong when four policemen entered my classroom and signalled for me to leave with them.

The one who looked to be in charge was shouting at me, speaking fast in wild bursts of Indonesian and sweeping his arms around the classroom then pointing at me. All I could do was look blankly at him and do the two handed shrug gesture, showing him I did not understand a word of what he was trying to tell me.

For once the children looked entertained and interested. Their normally glazed expressions and yawns had transformed into fascination and curiosity as they watched the impromptu show. Their mobile phones are out – this could go viral before I have even left the classroom!

As I follow the policemen out of the classroom my mind is spinning... has someone planted drugs in my bags? Surely I haven't inadvertently committed some kind of crime?... Has a complaint been made against me by a pupil's parent? Questions are reeling around in my head as I frantically try to fathom out why this is happening. My mouth has gone so dry and my tongue feels like sandpaper. My face has turned cold as if someone has placed a damp flannel on it. This must be a mistake. They'll soon realise their error I reassure myself.

The school I am teaching at is in Pekanbaru, which is the capital of the province, Riau, on the Indonesian island of

Sumatra. It has a population of around 1.1 million and most of its money is made from the oil industry. I remember meeting some contractors who worked for the oil giant Caltex who have a big site there. It is also the gateway into Indonesia from Singapore. Most travellers head straight through as there are no particular highlights or attractions to see in the city, unless you include the countless rats that are scurrying around on the roads and pavements or perhaps the raw sewage in the roadside gullies.

Pekanbaru received an award for being the cleanest large city in Indonesia for the seventh consecutive time. The judges must have been either blind and anosmiac (no sense of smell) or they were bribed.

I am led out into the corridor where Oki, the school's finance controller is waiting to speak with me. Oki is also the nephew of the school owner, Alinudin. He is a young Indonesian man in his early thirties with short, black, slick-backed hair and wire rimmed spectacles. He is a small man in height with a very serious nature. More importantly, he is also the only English speaking Indonesian person at the school.

Oki is animatedly talking to the policemen and every so often he points at me. I cannot understand a word that is being said. After several minutes of conversation Oki turns to me and assures me that this is normal.

"Sharon, there is no need to worry as they just want to see your passport".

I scratch my head baffled. "Why?"

"It's just procedure – this is normal" Oki continued "There is nothing for you to worry about".

"I don't understand – has every other teacher in the school been asked to show their passports?"

Oki is now looking even more flustered and blurts "Sharon, you cannot tell the police that you are working here at the school as a teacher. If you do you will be put in jail for five years as you are not on the correct working visa"

Kapow! It felt like a blow to the head. He was right; I was not on the correct working visa. I wasn't even on a working visa. I had entered Indonesia on a 30 day tourist visa – as instructed by the school's Director of Studies.

The policeman then decides he wants to take my photograph – perhaps my hair was looking particularly nice that day I don't know, however, I was forced to stare at the camera for my picture to be taken. It was one of the old Polaroid cameras that spits out a grainy picture with more white framing than photograph. It was not the most flattering photo and under normal circumstances I would probably have asked for another to be taken, but the situation warranted silence on my part.

I could see Oki from the corner of my eye chatting to someone on his mobile phone and he then thrusts the phone into my hand saying his uncle wants to speak with me. I had never met nor spoken with the elusive school owner since starting my teaching contract at the school several weeks earlier. He was like a mythical character amongst all the other teachers. Many tales were told about how he had sacked other teachers because he just didn't like them. Another story was that when a teacher asked to leave his employment contract early the owner was furious and threatened to plant drugs in his bags if he tried to leave! There were also rumours that he was a known criminal with lots of shady practices. To be quite honest we were all a bit scared of these stories and just hoped that we never got on his wrong side. I think I may have screwed that one up today.

I put the phone to my ear "Hello".

"Hello Sharon," said the voice on the phone "This is Alinudin, Oki's uncle. Oki has told me the situation and I would like to assure you that I will sort this out."

I am unsure exactly how he is going to 'sort this out' but that sounded good so far.

Alinudin then said "You must not tell the police that you are teaching at the school. Tell them that you are just observing other teachers and have not yet started your teaching contract."

I am beginning to understand that I am in a very bad situation. This is not England where there are set laws and the worst that could happen is you are politely asked to leave the country. You would probably even get your plane ticket paid for by the UK government! No, this is Indonesia. One of the top three most corrupt countries in the world. Anything goes!

Alinudin continues "Sharon, you could be jailed for five years if you say you are teaching. Do you understand?"

Do I understand?? Now I understand why all my friends were asking me why I didn't go to Spain or Italy to teach. They are closer to home and have proper legal systems plus flushing toilets and drinkable tap water without having to worry about waste disposal contamination.

I agree to lie to the police – what other option do I have? I don't particularly relish the idea of spending five years in an Indonesian prison. I've seen the Schapelle Corby TV movie and the notorious Keroboken prison in Bali where up to 15 inmates share the same cramped, dirty cells with mats on the floor for beds. The toilet a hole in the floor and the shower a bucket of cold, dirty water.

Oki and two of the 'office boys' employed by the school to assist with a multitude of tasks from photocopying classroom handouts to unblocking the generally overused school toilet, were to escort me to the police station. The four policemen straddled their motorbikes whilst Oki and I climbed onto the back of our motorbikes which were being driven by Aris and Slamat – the office boys. I am not sure whether they seriously thought I was going to try and make a break for it en route to the police station, however, they made sure we were trapped either side by their motorbikes. To onlookers we could have been mistaken for 'very important people' with 'police escorts', the reality unfortunately being it was the 'criminals' being guarded by the 'law officials'.

The heat and humidity outside the building was oppressive. Sweat immediately appears on my face like I have just finished my Cindy Crawford DVD workout (believe me, Cindy certainly makes you sweat). It was difficult to breathe in the dense air. It was like being in a sauna. The roads are full of motorbikes and cars speeding recklessly by. Remarkably, even though they all seem to drive insanely, there are never any accidents. They are either very skilled or extremely lucky!

The convoy of motorbikes sets off with Oki and Aris racing alongside me and Slamat. Oki immediately starts shouting across to me, "Let me do all the talking – don't say anything". How ridiculous! He was the only person who could speak English. I could say I was a mad axe woman and I have just killed ten people and they would be none the wiser. I was relying totally on Oki to translate what the police were saying.

Speeding through the streets of Pekanbaru we finally reached the police station. As I walked through the doors I was immediately smacked in the face by a wall of cigarette smoke. Blue swirls of mist sticking to my hair and clothes making me smell like I smoked sixty Benson & Hedges a day. It was an open plan station with a small array of dated furniture that looked like it had come directly from a rubbish skip. Teak seemed to feature quite strongly, together with Formica tables with rusted chrome legs and trims. Retro is very much in fashion nowadays so perhaps it now looks modern. A layer of grime coated most surfaces especially the computer keyboards and monitors where the staff sat chain smoking. Muted light created lots of shadows and dark corners. The room felt heavy and depressing.

A plain clothed policeman sat at the desk near the front door; however, there was nothing plain about his clothes. He was wearing a red and green silk bomber jacket and black aviator sunglasses (with the dim lighting and cigarette smoke I am unsure as to how much he could actually see). Due to the tilting position of his black, curly hair I could only assume that he was also wearing a wig. Saves washing your smoke filled hair every night I suppose. A cigarette was hanging from his lips as he watched me enter the station.

My heart was racing now and I was becoming more alarmed at the whole situation. My internal hysteria increased but strangely all I could think of was that this guy looks like he has come off the set of a 1970s police detective television show.

Where has Oki gone? I spot him in the corner of the room heatedly talking to one of the policemen. Oh God, this is getting out of hand. I am starting to properly panic now as the seriousness of it all sinks in. I could go to jail for what I have done, but it isn't my fault. It is the school's fault for not getting me the correct visa. Oh God, oh God, oh God – this is not good.

The 'interrogation' went on hour after hour. Oki was translating and I loosely use that word as there didn't seem like a lot of 'translating' was actually happening. He did say to me that he had been told that if I am violating the rules of the tourist visa, the sentence would be five years imprisonment. I clearly had 'violated' the tourist visa rules and at this point I could actually feel my liberty slowly slipping away. Who was going to help me? None of my family or friends were here. In fact, they were not even aware of my arrest!

After 3 hours I actually thought my lungs were about to explode. My lips were so dry it felt that they were sticking together like Velcro. I needed water. I was dehydrating. My eyes were stinging from the continuous flow of smoke as the policemen puffed on cigarette after cigarette.

Then through the haze I could see one of the officers walking towards us with two cans of what looked like coke or lemonade. Hallelujah!!! A drink!!! You can imagine my relief after 3 hours. The can was handed to me and my excitement faded slightly as I felt the warm metal against my palm, but a drink was a drink – warm or cold. I pulled off the metal ring and took a big gulp... yuck! It tasted like drinking a bunch of scented flowers. I then looked at the label and saw that it was violet tea. Who buys this stuff? It's gross. I still drank the whole can as I was thirsty and needed to keep hydrated. Who knows how long this ordeal was going to take.

There was a policeman typing my statement. By statement I mean what Oki was telling them in bursts of Indonesian. He could have been telling them I was a secret British agent working undercover for all I know but whatever was being said – it needed to be typed.

The keyboard was so caked in grime that you really couldn't see what letter was printed on each key. The relentless smoking had created a tacky film on every surface making each key stick like glue onto the keyboard then slowly release back up. Power cuts were a regular occurrence in Pekanbaru, so I was praying that we didn't have one now or else we would have restart the whole statement.

We are now approaching our fifth hour at the police station and I am still clueless as to what Oki has been saying to the policemen. I am occasionally asked questions by Oki such as;

"Are you teaching English at the school?"

My answer is "No I am not teaching English" as instructed.

"Are you employed as a teacher by the school?"

"No."

"Are you being paid a salary to work there?"

"No I am not."

Oki finally turns to me with an 'I'm really sorry about this' look on his face and tells me that the police have confirmed that I am a suspect along with his uncle and I will be locked in a cell overnight and every other night until his uncle surrenders himself to the police station for questioning.

I am now shaking like a leaf and my head feels lightheaded and fuzzy – as if I had vertigo. Horror and dread fill my entire body as the realisation of my situation sinks in. I am being arrested and imprisoned and there is absolutely nothing I can do about it. My life at this moment could not get any worse.

Chapter 2

A Teaching Contract

January 2004

To understand how I found myself teaching on a tourist visa in Indonesia I need to tell you about events leading up to my arrival in Pekanbaru.

I had just completed a one month intensive TEFL course (Teaching English as a Foreign Language) at Leeds Metropolitan University and was now qualified to teach English overseas. It was a feat in itself just to survive the course. After being given a list of the 'must have' grammar books for fledgling young English teachers on day one, on day two we were teaching a class of authentic, real-life foreigners! They were from all corners of the world: Chinese, Japanese, Argentinean, Korean, Malaysian and Omani. They were students at the university who had paid £1 to come to the lessons to practise their English. I personally felt that even £1 was a bit overpriced to watch novice teachers stutter and stammer in front of the classroom, hot and deep crimson faces glowing with the embarrassment of it all.

But improve we did with endless nights of writing lesson plans into the early hours of the morning. One lesson plan that sticks in my mind was using the subject of Che Guevara as the context of the lesson whilst teaching active and passive verb tenses. Che Guevara? Was he Spanish? Was he the good looking one with the beret? So, in order not to look even more of an idiot, I spent all night researching who Che was. I mean, come on, I had an Argentinean girl in my class. She surely will have learnt all about Che at school and be correcting all my facts should I not get them right. The research paid off and I finished the lesson having avoided awkward and political questions.

Beaming with pride we all qualified from the class and were proud owners of TEFL certificates, wondering where in the world we were going to end up.

Now I needed to find a teaching post overseas. I initially looked at a school in Viseu, Portugal and applied for a teaching position there. I was kindly told by the agency that they are only considering teachers with experience at the moment. Would I be interested in Poland?

I then applied for a post in Naples, Italy... application declined. Thailand... application declined. You apparently, by law, need to have a degree to teach in Thailand – subject irrelevant as long as you have one.

I then had an interview in Manchester at the English First offices on Chorlton Street in the city centre. English First have a large network of schools worldwide, their main locations being China, Russia and Indonesia. English First is a brand name which offers franchises to local individuals/businessmen. This allows them to use the English First name (mainly for the school front, text books, teaching aids, etc.) for their school, which is run and owned by the local individual and not English First. Fortunately they appeared very interested in me and my questionable teaching skills.

I was immediately drawn to Indonesia as a destination. Russia was too cold. China was slightly appealing but the pull of South East Asian food did it for me. All those spices and flavours – lemongrass, chillies, lime, galangal – yum, and of course, Nasi Goreng, that lip-smacking Indonesian fried rice dish. My decision was made.

My details were taken by English First and distributed amongst their various schools in Indonesia. I just had to wait to be contacted by one of the school managers who were known as Director of Studies. I was thinking Bali would be nice. All those lovely beaches and palm trees. Then I received an e-mail from the Director of Studies at the English First school in Pekanbaru.

So not quite the idyllic beach setting that I had imagined but it was a person interested in employing me as a teacher. My spirits were lifted.

His name was Gary and he wrote that he had been travelling and working for almost 30 years. He described Pekanbaru as 'a sleepy little town compared to Jakarta or Bali and it was very beautiful in many areas'. How lovely does that sound? Things were looking good. He wanted to speak with me and gave me his telephone number for me to contact him.

Over that summer we spoke on the phone and swapped numerous e-mails. We became buddies. Gary was American and he was employed as the school's Director of Studies – he was basically the school manager.

He told me all about the school – they had a media/computer lab with 9 computers, living costs – a dozen eggs cost only 20 cents, public transport – only 20 cents per ride, or I could buy a second hand motorbike for only $14 dollars. My monthly salary would be a whopping 5.5 million Rupiah which sounds a lot of money but at that time the exchange rate was 9,200 Rupiahs to the American dollar so my monthly wage was, in fact, less than $600. However this, apparently, put me in the high earning bracket in Indonesia. He sent me photos of contented, smiling staff and pupils - everyone looked so happy. I couldn't wait to start!

Gary told me that my first three weeks at the school would be spent observing the other teachers, sitting at the back of the classrooms watching and getting a feel for the teaching methods used at the school and to learn about the content of the text books being used by the pupils. I would not be given any of my own classes until this orientation period ended.

Perfect. This teaching job was sounding pretty awesome to me. Not only do I get to go to an exciting and exotic country to teach English, I am being mollycoddled and handled with care. Being the novice teacher with no previous experience I will be protected and sheltered by the other teachers until I am fully equipped to perform as a teacher at the school. I will definitely be the envy of all the other TEFL graduates when I tell them about this teaching offer.

I was given specific instructions by e-mail to fly via Singapore and not Jakarta. I am to stay overnight in Singapore at their recommended hotel and the following day I am to purchase a ferry ticket to take me across the water to an Indonesian island called Batam. When I arrive at the immigration in Batam centre, I am instructed to go to the 'visa on arrival' counter and ask for a tourist visa. This will cost me $25 American dollars. I am also instructed not to mention that I am going to a teaching post as they will organise my working visa after I arrive in Pekanbaru via their agent in Singapore. As I will not be starting my actual teaching position for another three weeks, the working visa is not yet required.

Now probably alarm bells should have rang at this point but they didn't. Why should they? I had spent the last four months swapping e-mails with my buddy Gary and the arrangements were very clear and precise. What could conceivably go wrong?

No going back. The flight was booked. Tenants were waiting in the wings to move into my house for the next twelve months. My personal possessions were boxed up and placed in storage. Now it was just me, my trusted backpack and my wheelie suitcase full of the 'must have' grammar books and teaching notes.

Friends and family were so pleased for me. I was getting comments like;

"You've certainly landed on your feet with this job – sounds amazing!"

"How did you manage to find such a good English school to work for?"

"Sounds like you are not going to have any problems teaching there"

Oh the ignorance of it all. They say that it's bliss and it was.

The airport farewell to my parents was particularly emotional this time as I was going overseas for twelve months. My previous airport goodbyes had been for travels lasting only two to three months. Their parting words normally on the lines of "stay out of trouble" and "don't do anything silly" ending with "be careful" which is a bit like saying; don't enjoy yourself, don't do anything that involves a bit of risk and certainly don't do anything hair raising! But I always nodded, dutifully confirming I would comply with their words.

This was different. My Mum who is normally calm and composed suddenly burst into tears and grabbed me, squeezing me tightly. Parting words not needed this time. I am now uncontrollably overcome with sadness. We both know this will be the last time we will see each other for some time. Dads are a totally different breed. He nonchalantly watches us and when we have peeled ourselves apart I get a brief embrace and a pat on the back. Then I leave them standing together arm in arm as I go through customs. I do the final turn around to look at them and wave before disappearing into the hub of the airport.

I am on my way to Indonesia to start my new teaching career.

Chapter 3

Arrival in Indonesia

4th December 2004

I followed my written instructions diligently and spent my first night in Singapore. The land of many "Don'ts". Did you know that Singapore has some of the strangest laws and the sentences are pretty harsh compared to western countries? I'll give you a few examples of the really odd ones.

Flushing of public toilets – you will be fined if you are caught not flushing the toilet after using it. Police officers do random checks. How embarrassing would that be? Being arrested as you walk out of the toilet cubicle due to the policeman watching you not hearing the flush go!

Chewing gum – Due to chewed gum being stuck on pavements, subway stations and cars the Singapore government banned the sale of chewing gum. The law has now relaxed so you can now chew it – just not buy it. My advice would be to bring some gum with you.

No walking around your own house naked – If you are caught walking naked in your own home then it is considered indecent and a form of pornography. Not quite sure how they enforce this law?

No spitting – in order to maintain Singapore's reputation for cleanliness spitting is illegal. If you are caught spitting you will receive a substantial fine. How would the Chinese cope in Singapore? Every man and his dog spits in China.

But none of this concerned me. My body clock was a mess. Singapore is eight hours ahead of the UK. I had just lost eight hours of my life. I was exhausted from the flight and the anticipation of my new teaching job. I just crashed in my dark room dreaming of happy, smiling pupils.

The next day I caught a taxi to the World Trade Centre, which is where the ferry terminal is to get across to the Indonesian island of Batam.

Now, alarm bells should have rung again I know... my next instructions were to buy a return ticket to Singapore. Why a return ticket? I wasn't intending on going back for at least 12 months. Did I question this? No, of course not. My entire faith was in my buddy Gary who had arranged my new life teaching in Indonesia.

Having arrived by ferry to the island of Batam I then dutifully made my way to the immigration centre and went to the 'visa on arrival' counter and purchased my tourist visa for a bargain price of $25 dollars. I then purchased my flight ticket to take me from Batam to Pekanbaru on the Sumatra island.

Hurray... after fifty minutes of flying over a small bit of ocean I finally arrived at my destination Pekanbaru.

I am approached by a tall, stocky bald man with dark piercing eyes like pieces of coal in a snowman's face.

"Hello Sharon" he drawled "I'm Gary. Pleased to meet you finally"

Gosh! This was my buddy Gary. Director of Studies.

"Hi Gary. Good to meet you at last and put a face to the voice and the e-mails".

But what a face. I was not expecting my buddy Gary to look like he did. His American twang had made me imagine him to look like Matthew McConaughey or Bradley Cooper. Instead I was looking at a larger and taller version of Dr Evil from the Austin Powers movies.

The intensity of the heat hits me straight away as we exit the airport. My face instantly has a wet layer of sweat as my body swiftly reacts to the humidity.

It's starting to get dark as the taxi speeds away from the airport down the busy, congested road. There are hundreds of people lining the streets, possibly heading home from a day's work. Car horns were blaring everywhere. Gary told me that most drivers hit their horns at least every 30 seconds. An Indonesian man even told him that it makes his car go faster. I would like one of those horns for my car as my accelerator does seem pretty useless at times.

Gary had to shout in order for me to hear him over the noise of the traffic and the CD stalls on the roadside blaring out their music fare. There were piercing whistles of the traffic police trying to control the copious amount of cars and motorbikes. Conversation was difficult.

It was dark by the time we reached the school which, to my shock, was heaving with people. It was after 6pm. Why were all these people still here? Children were screeching and adults were shouting at their kids in an attempt to quieten them down. The reception area was a hub of chatter. We had to fight our way through the throng of people. Conversation was out of the question.

Introductions were made to the young Indonesian women who were sitting behind the reception counter. I recognised some of these women. They were the happy, smiling people in Gary's photographs. They were still smiling which was a good sign.

I followed my buddy Gary into his office which was like entering the Golden Temple in Amritsar, the famous Temple in India where the streets outside are full of frenzied tuk tuk taxis and berserk car drivers. The petrol fumes are overpowering and the noise deafening. Then, as you enter the Temple grounds there is a calm and serene aura. A tranquil atmosphere surrounds you as you are transported into a calm and soothing world. This was also Gary's office. Calm. Quiet. Peaceful. Nice.

My bubble is then burst as Gary started to explain about the school's staffing issues and the constantly increasing pupil numbers.

"Sharon, it is so manic here at the moment. Student enrolment has doubled in the last month! We have had to add 12 new classes."

I didn't like where this was heading.

"We now have nearly 500 students and not enough teachers" he continued.

Oh no. This was not sounding good.

"The current teachers are flat out with extra classes to teach. We are all relieved that you have now arrived to ease their workloads."

What?!!!

"I'm afraid that the agreed three week observation period is going to have to be scrapped. I have prepared a timetable of your own classes... starting tomorrow."

He slid a sheet of paper across the table. Oh my God. What just happened? From the outset I had been assured that I would not be thrown into the classroom to teach. I was to be protected and sheltered by the other teachers. I was not supposed to teach in the first three weeks. What happened to sitting at the back of the classroom? Observing and watching. NOT teaching. I have never taught at a school before, only when I taught the students who paid £1 to be practised on by amateurs.

What about lesson plans? It takes hours to write them. Well, for a novice teacher like me it does.

"Hang on a minute", I say to Gary, "this is not what we agreed. I should be getting my three week induction to the school, not a timetable full of classes to teach."

Gary (who, by the way, is definitely now not my buddy) looked very sheepish as he slid the class timetable even closer to me. "I'm really sorry to throw this on you when you have only just arrived. I have no choice. There are just not enough teachers for the amount of students we have taken on. We need you to start tomorrow".

Well, that was that. What could I do? I had rented my house out to strangers for twelve months so had no home to return to. I had travelled thousands of miles for this job. I had no other option but to accept it.

That night I frantically wrote lesson plans for the classes in my timetable. No time to relax and meet the other teachers. I also discovered that instead of a comfortable house shared with other teachers, I was being ostracized and sent to a guesthouse. No room at the inn apparently. This guesthouse was to be my "home" until proper teacher accommodation has been found for me. The words 'piss up' and 'brewery' sprang to mind.

Chapter 4

Life in Indonesia

After my initial shock I am soon submerged into life as a teacher in Indonesia. There was no other option, it was make or break. I plunged myself into writing lesson plans and teaching classes. The fact that I was in the country on a tourist visa didn't cross my mind. My focus was exclusively on teaching.

Indonesia has the largest Muslim population, home to around 12% of the world's Muslims followed by India, Pakistan and Bangladesh. That equates to about 209 million people. Islam is the predominant religion in Indonesia and 87% of the population are Muslim, 8% are Christians, 3% are Hindus, 1% are Buddhists and the remaining 1% are Animists.

As you can imagine, with this percentage of Muslims there comes a lot of mosques. Every morning at 4 o'clock I am woken by the call to prayer. This is broadcast at extreme high volume over loudspeakers which are usually mounted outdoors on tall minarets. Some mosques have amplifiers that are powerful enough to be heard as far as three miles away. You can imagine how piercing that sound is if you are only a few doors away.

Surprisingly, even with the high Muslim population, every store and roadside stall sells beer! Who drinks this beer? It can't be the 87% of the population who are Muslim. Is it the 8% of Christians? There are about 25 foreigners in town, five of which are teachers at the school plus Gary, Director of Studies. The remaining foreigners work for Caltex, the giant

American oil company. They all live in the 'Caltex Village' about one hour north of Pekanbaru. You occasionally see them on the streets but not very often. They are not hard to spot with their white skins. Perhaps it is they who are contributing to the consumption of all the beer that is on sale?

There is a huge shopping mall in the centre with lots of different levels full of shops and fancy boutiques. It even has a 3 star international hotel! With Christmas approaching the mall has a giant tree in the middle decorated with red and gold shiny baubles. Deep red velvet bows are draped on branches with fairy lights twinkling like stars around the tree. I assume this is for the 8% of Christians too. Father Christmas is also there in his bright red suit and fur lined hat. It is all very surreal.

It is nice to visit the shopping mall if only to escape the heat and humidity outside. The humidity hovers at around 80% making it feel like it is raining when, in fact, it is purely the water vapour in the air making your clothes soaking wet. The air conditioning was cooling, reducing the discomfort temporarily.

There is road kill everywhere. Not your usual hedgehog or grouse. No, road kill here is rats. They are everywhere. It's like the Pied Piper has come to town. They run along the gullies at the sides of the road, which is also home to open sewage. But this is clean – according to the judges giving out awards for clean cities in Indonesia.

The guesthouse was a twenty minute walk from the school, the pavements filled with children on their way to school. They always shouted to me "Hello Miss", and "where are you from?". That was if their grasp of English was fairly good, unfortunately, if not, it was "Hello Mister". It seemed like every minute a child popped up by my side and flashed a huge smile before saying "Hello Mister. Where are you from?" I had to walk at a very slow pace in order to avoid having to wring out my clothes at the end of the walk. The humidity was tough. Saying that, it was actually a nice way to start the day – the best part of the day in fact.

It was preferable to the scooter ride I initially received in my first week. Slamat, the senior office boy, would pick me up from the guesthouse and I would ride on the back of his scooter. Slamat would be wearing a helmet (sensible guy with wife and kids) whereas I was not offered any form of head protection. I had to ride bare-headed – and pray.

His scooter had no wing mirrors, but who needs those when you have a horn? Not only does the horn make your bike go faster, it also lets other drivers know where you are. You see, no-one has wing mirrors. They are not a requirement of an Indonesian driver. The horn is sufficient. Traffic lights are also pointless. Drivers pay no attention to their colour. Red or green? It's irrelevant. It is the horn that will guide you through the traffic lights. If you honk enough times and show no cowardliness or fearfulness you will get through without being hit. It was impressive, their skill. Or stupidity. Not sure which. But it ensures no accidents or injuries. All the same, hanging onto the back with no helmet was pretty terrifying. Especially hair-raising was the right turn at the huge junction on the way to the school. I had to close my eyes for that part of the journey.

What wasn't quite so attractive on my walk into school was the orang-utan I had to pass. The poor thing was shackled to an entrance porch of a house. The metal chain was probably only a few feet in length. It always looked so forlorn and melancholy. I wanted to be brave like Dian Fossey who fought in Rwanda to save the mountain gorillas from poachers. I wanted to free the helpless orang-utan and release him back to the wild. But how could I? Where would I take him? It was very sad.

The stares were also hard to deal with. I felt like I was part of a freak show with the constant staring. It was like I was the elephant man with ugly deformities. The reality was I was just a white foreigner, but I stood out because of that. Stare after stare after stare. Everyone stared at me. If this is what it is like to be famous then I would prefer to stay anonymous.

The school was always a hive of activity. Not surprising considering student enrolment has doubled in the last month and at least twelve new classes have been started. Still, there are not enough teachers even with me on board. The workload was intense. It was overbearing. Being the novice teacher, my skills were still questionable and writing lesson plans took me forever.

My increasing workload was shocking. I was teaching every day from Monday through to Saturday. Three days of those days I was teaching classes solidly from 3.45pm until 9pm. Five minute breaks between each class. Those five minutes were spent frantically searching for my next lesson plan. When not teaching I was writing lesson plans. My buddy... no, not anymore... my nemesis, Gary, alias Dr Evil, is wickedly inflicting all this work onto me. Who had time to think of unimportant things like visas? It was the last thing on my mind. My mind was frazzled. Muddled. It had been stripped of any thoughts other than passive/active verbs, simple present tense, simple future tense modal verbs, comparatives, collective nouns, adverbs and prepositions. Then there were teaching techniques to remember... elicit and sweep and zoom. Visa? Not a thought.

There were three other full time teachers working at the school. Kate and Cheryl (pronounced as 'ch' and not 'sh') were two English girls, both aged 23. Rumour has it that Cheryl married one of the office boys after leaving the school. Maybe it was true love but the cynic in me does wonder if she was doing it for someone to run her errands. Or clean her toilet.

Then there was Neville. Lovely, laid back, mellow Neville. He was a 57 year old Kiwi. A gentle man with white curly hair and kind eyes. When he was concentrating his small, metal rimmed glasses would perch on the end of his nose. He was a compassionate, soft-hearted man who was always helping others. He had recently converted to Islam. He casually informed us that his new Muslim name was Usman. For new Muslims it is not required to change your name unless your name implies a form of disbelief or aggression. However, many new Muslims do choose to change their name to mark their new life after joining the Islam faith. Usman is what Neville chose as his new name. Be that as it may, I could not call Neville Usman. Neville was Neville. I was struggling just to remember when and where my classes were. My brain did not have any capacity to take on name changes at this stage.

There was also a Scottish guy, David, who was the senior teacher. He had worked at the Pekanbaru school for over two years. That soon ended after I arrived as he was shipped off to the English First school in Medan. Staffing issues apparently. Sound familiar?

Lastly, there were two part time teachers. Patricia, an Indonesian woman who needed to earn extra money while studying to become a doctor, and Susanna who was Slovakian and had moved to Pekanbaru with her husband Russell who had a contract working for Caltex. I hardly saw Patricia or Susanna due to their small amount of teaching hours. God I wished I was part time. It might have given me the chance to have a life outside of the school.

In spite of my workload I did get invited to a birthday party. Hurray... a night out to a party! This was exciting. I didn't care that I had lesson plans to write. I didn't care that I had bloodshot eyes with what could only be described as 'suitcases' under my eyes through lack of sleep. I didn't care that the party was for a 15 year old or that most of the guests would be teenage girls. It was a party! With food and drink. Other people. I had no idea of the girl's name. Irrelevant. It was a party.

She was a student from one of Cheryl's classes and all the other teachers had also been invited. The venue was The Aryaduta Hotel. Wow... what a venue! Think ostentatious. Lavish. Extravagant. Then multiply this a thousand fold.

The reception lobby was covered from floor to ceiling in opulent marble tiles with huge flower arrangements placed next to the reception desk. They brought a splash of colour to the area and a beautiful aromatic fragrance to all who entered.

We were led to the party which was outdoors next to the pool. This was no ordinary pool. This was the 'Aryaduta Hotel Lagoon Style Pool'. It was spectacular. It curved around the palm trees like a painter's palette. The spotlights in the pool extracting the intensity of the turquoise water which was shimmering as if it were the ocean lit by the moon. It was stunning.

Palm trees were everywhere, draped in fairy lights which were twinkling like stars. Tables and chairs had been arranged around the whole lagoon. It was like a tropical island, I could have been in Hawaii. The tables were full of people. Hundreds of people smiling, laughing and chatting. This was hard to take in at first. It was such a contrast to the pollution and dirt outside. It was surreal. Was I dreaming? Was I going to wake up and find myself in my tiny, creaking bed at the guesthouse? I had to pinch myself. The last week was now a distant memory as we sat at one of the lagoon tables.

There was a table near the entrance full of food fit for a king. Food was my only reason for picking Indonesia as my teaching destination. Hot and spicy food. I was drooling at the mouth. Not a good look together with the bloodshot eyes and giant bags, no – suitcases, under my eyes. I didn't care. In front of me was an array of dishes. Vibrant and colourful food. I could smell the intense flavours.

Tasty meat skewers served with a satay sauce and rice cakes, fried chicken pieces, beef rendang, lamb curry and, of course, Nasi Goreng. There was grilled fish complete with eyeballs and fins, juicy king prawns marinated in garlic and spices. There were breads, dips, sauces... it was a feast.

We tucked in. I soon faced my first stumbling block. The left hand. Among Muslims, the left hand is reserved for bodily hygiene and considered unclean. Nothing religious or cultural. It's just what they do. Thus, only the right hand is clean. This is the hand that should be used for eating. Tricky. Even for someone who is right-handed. I have no idea how left-handed people cope with the 'unclean hand' when travelling.

For a right-handed novice like me this proved very challenging. My initial selection from the display of food was a giant king prawn. Bad choice. With hindsight I should've gone for the piece of fried chicken. At least I could have held that in my right hand to lift to my mouth. But no, I chose the prawn. The prawn that needed to have its shell removed. I was determined to meet the challenge. Firstly, I clamped the prawn down with a spoon in my left hand. That is allowed before you question this manoeuvre. If you eat with your fingers, you use only your right hand. Utensils can be used in your left hand. The only utensil available was the spoon. With the prawn clamped down by the spoon I endeavoured to pick off the shell with my right hand. Tricky.

It kept sliding on my plate and skidding onto the table. Onlookers from other tables started looking at me disdainfully. I chased the prawn around my plate again in a desperate attempt to get the god damn shell off. I was receiving more disapproving looks. I could feel my cheeks heat up with embarrassment. Blushing, I had one last futile shot at the prawn and then gave up. I had failed. The spoon was ineffective as a clamp. The prawn had won. I went and got myself a piece of fried chicken instead.

Next, the customary singing of Happy Birthday. I still can't remember the girl's name. Let's call her Rachel. The opening bars of the universally recognised tune started and the crowd began to sing... "Happy birthday to you, happy birthday to you, happy birthday dear Rachel, happy birthday to you". Then they sang it again. And again. And again. And again. It was like Groundhog Day. The record had stuck. Kate and I started with a fit of giggles. They must have sung it at least a dozen times. We could've been celebrating Rachel's 16th birthday if they had continued singing it for much longer. It was very peculiar. But funny.

Later it was karaoke... it was a very late and repetitive night.

I also had a brief respite from teaching children which was on a Thursday night. Adults. My weekly salvation. This remission from kids was very much welcome and I always looked forward to teaching this class.

Their English was amazing. I was in awe of their proficiency in grammar. Even with my "must have" grammar books and TEFL certificate, my knowledge was secondary to these guys. They were the Aston Martins and I was the Ford Fiesta.

I had to think on my feet. Stay mentally agile. Focus.

I was determined not to look an idiot in front of my adult students. Embarrassing myself in front of the kids didn't really bother me. But adults? Now that was a different kettle of fish.

What a strange idiom. A kettle of fish. Where on earth did that originate from? Could it be that fish looks a mess when boiled in a kettle? I suppose we will never really know. The long pan used for boiling whole fish is called a fish kettle – we had one at home not much used – it went to the charity shop.

For what was to be my final adult class, even though I did not know this at the time, I chose the subject of the lesson to be 'Crime and Punishment'. How apt was that? Maybe I should do horoscopes. Unbelievable, quite frankly. My imminent arrest within days not yet known and here I am about to learn all about the Indonesian 'legal' system.

The adult students were very animated about this subject and a very interesting comparison of Indonesia versus England was emerging. An interesting and frightening comparison.

Bagus, a law student, was adamant that when he finished his studies he was going to join the police force. Very commendable I thought.

"Is that why you are studying law?" I asked.

"Oh, no. I am studying law to be a solicitor but you can make so much more money being a policeman".

"So, in Indonesia policemen earn substantially more than, say, a lawyer or a barrister?"

"For sure. Policemen take bribes every day. It's a perk of the job. Backhanders are paid for anything and everything. It's how the system works here".

My wide-eyed astonishment and disbelief made the whole class laugh in amusement, my naivety clearly showing. This is when all the alarming stories began, which included intimidation, corruption, threats and extortion to mention but a few. So these were the 'fringe benefits' included in a policeman's salary.

Bagus was thrilled with my crime and punishment theme and eagerly went on to tell me more stories. "I have been stopped by the police numerous times whilst riding my motorbike. They tell you that you were speeding. You know that you weren't but what can you do? Unless you want to be put in jail for disagreeing with a policeman and 'speeding' you just do what he says."

I was stunned by this revelation. My ignorance highlighted even more. I had no idea it was this bad in Indonesia. I thought it was places like Mexico and Brazil that had corruption within the police force.

Fired up, Bagus went on to tell me that the policeman then just puts his hand out which basically means pay him. He will close his hand when you have placed enough notes into his palm. This then goes straight into his own pocket. Fringe benefits. The money is his to keep. No questions. This is why Bagus wanted to join the police force. The bribes and backhanders will enable him to live in a nice house and provide for his family.

This insight into the corruption and unscrupulousness of the law system in this country disturbed me. I distinctly remember thinking at that time, I hope to God I do not get into any trouble with the police while I'm here! You could say that at least I was informed and not totally oblivious to the rotten legal system here in Indonesia.

Then, four days before Christmas Eve, Gary summoned all the teachers to his office – the sanctuary. Gary was most certainly no longer my buddy. My initial impressions at the airport had materialized. He was Dr Evil. Not only in appearance, but also personality. He had become my nemesis. His goal – to dominate all teachers and to rule the school.

Tightly squeezed into his office Gary launches into his rehearsed speech. "The school is in trouble. Big trouble. I want to be frank and honest with you all".

Well, that would be a first. I was all ears.

"Alinudin has been stealing money from the school's funds and all the profits made have now gone. He has disappeared. So has the money. We have no funds left to continue running the school".

There were gasps from all the teachers. Puzzled, blank expressions all round.

Neville – still can't revert to using his Muslim name of Usman – questions Gary "So if you can't continue running the school does this mean it's closing down? If so, when?"

"Yes, I'm afraid it does. The school will be closing on the 23rd December. We have no choice."

"But what about our jobs?" blurts out Kate.

"I will certainly be contacting all the other English First schools in Indonesia to try and find other teaching positions for you. I can't promise anything but I will try my best. Your jobs here at Pekanbaru will be terminated after lessons have ended on the 23rd December.

We all stood there dumbfounded. Overwhelmed with what we had just been told, my teaching position to be snatched away from me. I had only arrived in Pekanbaru at the beginning of December and would now have to leave. We were all praying that Gary would find us alternative teaching posts at other schools.

Alinudin, the owner of our school, was based in Medan. Medan is 287 miles north of Pekanbaru. To fly there it takes just one hour. He also owns the franchise of the English First school in Medan. But now he had vanished. The school's money vanished with him. He was also a wanted man by the police. A criminal. He was evading arrest for many counts of fraudulently drawing cheques from five different bank accounts.

Can you believe this? We were all employed by a crook. A thief. A common fraudster. This was turning into like something out of a John Grisham novel.

We were all stunned by this news and just hoped that a solution was found to keep the school open or that teaching positions would be found for us at other schools. I was, after all, homeless. I didn't want to be jobless as well.

Then I was arrested.

Chapter 5

The Second Arrest

21st December 2004

We had been at the police station for most of the day and Oki had just told me that I am a suspect along with his uncle. I was to be jailed overnight and every other night until his uncle surrenders himself to the police.

The 'statement' that had taken nearly five hours to be typed during my interrogation was now complete. Oki thrust the document into my hand and ordered me to sign it.

I cannot understand a word that is written! The Indonesian alphabet may use the same letters as the English alphabet; however, it is a completely different language. It does not use the same words. I am being forced to sign a document that I am clueless as to whether it is my actual verbal statement or a distorted version confirming I am guilty of being an illegal worker at the school. My heart is beating wildly. It is so loud it feels like my whole body is vibrating with each beat. Surely everyone must be hearing it? I am shaking violently, the statement shaking like a fan in my hands.

"I can't sign this! I have no idea what it says". I was determined not to sign the 'statement'. I've seen the TV soaps and dramas. JR Ewing passes Bobby a document saying that it is routine oil business paperwork when in fact he is getting his brother to sign away his share of the Ewing Empire. Bobby loses everything. All he did was sign a document.

This was all Oki was asking me to do. Sign a document. I would be worse off than Bobby by signing this document. I could be signing my life away. To be imprisoned for five years with no parole. No visitors. It could even state solitary confinement.

No, no, no... I was not going to sign the statement. Then Oki tells me that if I do not sign the statement, I will be jailed anyway. Oh. That ruined my plan. If I sign it is probably a prison sentence. If I don't sign it is an immediate prison sentence. I looked at the pen being offered by Oki.

This was not good. My mind was screaming 'no don't sign it... you have no idea what it says'. But with a sinking feeling I knew I had no option. The alternative was immediate incarceration. This was not a game of monopoly. I did not have a get out of jail free card.

Oki was trying to reassure me that the statement was confirming what I have said: I am not a paid a teacher's salary; I am not teaching at the school; I do not have an employment contract with the school.

I was drowning. No-one had provided me with a life jacket. As much as I really didn't want to sign the statement, I resigned myself to the fact that I would have to. It felt wrong. I am one of those annoying people that read the small print. You never know what clauses are hidden in there. Here I am signing a document that is in a foreign language! I cannot read a word of it! Not good. Not good at all.

I reluctantly took the pen out of Oki's hand and quickly signed the statement. Oh God, what have I done? Well, it was done now. No going back.

The policeman then plucked from his desk what looked like a file. Oh my God. This was my 'criminal record'. I could see the unflattering photo of me inside the manila folder. The signed statement was placed inside. I now had a criminal record including mug shot and statement. Until that day I had not even received a parking ticket or a speeding fine. Now here I was a convicted criminal with an unflattering mug shot and a police file. Both with my name noted.

I think at this point the policemen had run out of things to do. They were bored. They had arrested the suspect, taken the suspect's mug shot and typed up the suspect's statement. What else could they do? I know, why not get her to empty her bag?

Yes, the next episode was the bag. Oki had been speaking to the policeman since the completion of the statement and was now looking uncomfortable.

"The police want to see what's in your bag. They have asked that you empty the contents onto the table".

Oki continued "They are just playing with us. They think it's funny".

What?! Funny? Did I look like my sides were splitting from the amusement of it all? I was desperately trying to recollect what was in my bag. I know the usual handy items that were in there; tissues, mints, phrase book, purse, pen, boiled sweets and then I remembered the one additional and very significant item that was in the bag. My English First employment contract. The legal document confirming my official placement as a teacher at the school. Confirmation of my place of employment. The salary I would get paid to be said teacher. Shit. How the hell do I get out of this one? Shit, shit, shit. I am in deep shit. Oh my God. I have spent the last five hours denying my employment as a teacher. This contract undoubtedly confirms the opposite. Panic kicks in. My heart is pounding off the scale.

"Oki, surely this is unnecessary? Why on earth do they want to see the contents of my bag? Do the police think I am concealing some kind of weapon? This is a joke".

Oki talks fast and furiously to the policeman. The shake of his head and defeated look gave me my answer.

Reluctantly, I tip my bag upside down. Its contents tumbling onto the desk like an episode of Ready Steady Cook where the contestant tips their bag of groceries onto the table. Gasps of delight at to what yummy food items they have to cook with. My gasp will be of horror when they see my employment contract. I see the offending item immediately under my tissues and phrase book. My heart is racing. I am struggling to breathe. I think my heart has stopped beating.

The policeman goes straight to the contract the incriminating piece of evidence. Of course, he can't read it! It is written in English! I could say this is a shopping list or a diary. How would he know? Oki is agitated. He also sees the contract. He starts talking fast in Indonesian to the policeman, wildly gesturing with his hands. The policeman is shaking his head from shoulder to shoulder. He is clearly in disagreement with Oki. He then places the contract as evidence in my manila criminal folder. Exhibit Number One – the employment contract.

It appeared that the police were now happy with the evidence collected that day. They told Oki that I was free to go but under no circumstances was I to try and leave the country. They wanted to question all the other teachers and Gary tomorrow morning.

Poor little Oki looked exhausted. His day of translating (I use that term loosely) had taken its toll. With bloodshot eyes and sunken shoulders we walked out of the police station. Free. For the moment.

Back at the school we all gather in the staff room. Myself, Neville, Kate, Cheryl and Oki. What has happened has shocked us all. We are stunned. Speechless. Overcome with emotion and anxiety. It appears only one teacher is here on a legitimate working visa. The others are on a 2 month business visa. Why? I am the worst offender being on a tourist visa.

The true story unfolds as Oki yields to the pressure of infinite questions from all of the teachers. Oki looks sheepish as he admits things are not good at the school.

"This is very embarrassing for me. My uncle Alinudin is wanted for questioning by the police. He has been drawing cheques fraudulently from five different accounts"

"So what does this have to do with Sharon being arrested?" asked Kate.

"This is where it gets complicated. My uncle has also been stealing money from the school. This is why there are no school funds left to run the school."

Kate is still baffled as we all were. "I still don't get what this has to do with Sharon?"

"Gary's wife has also invested her own money into the school. She is furious that my uncle has stolen her money too. As a consequence she contacted the police to let them know that a teacher is working at the school on a tourist visa. This will be regarded as another offence against my uncle. She was desperate to put further pressure onto my uncle to surrender himself to the police."

That was a blow to the head. I was being used as a scapegoat. A chump. A patsy. A schmuck. Call it what you want. It wasn't good. I was the sacrificial lamb for revenge on the owner.

Gary's wife was Indonesian. They married in October. Newlyweds in fact. She was from a wealthy family which were allegedly linked to the Indonesian mob. I have no idea how true this is. I'm not saying her family were involved in organised crime or employing hit men, however, her family certainly did have money and were very affluent in the area. She was one angry and resentful woman. Revenge on Alinudin was her priority. She wanted him arrested and imprisoned for what he had done. She didn't care what innocent person she used to accomplish her goal. Revenge is sweet, they say.

23rd December 2004

The next day my lessons were cancelled and all the other teachers were taken to the police station for questioning I assumed, about their own personal visas. Due to my lengthy interrogation yesterday, Oki was told by the police that I would not be called for questioning today. Instead I was summoned to the police station to witness the other teachers being interrogated.

Ironically, finally I was observing and watching the other teachers. This is what I should have been doing since my arrival in Indonesia!

When I arrived back at the police station, Neville, Kate and Cheryl had been separated and were seated at different desks like sheep being penned in different parts of a field. I was directed to a seating area that could only be described as some sort of viewing gallery. It had been fenced off but was facing the other teachers. It really did feel like I was the audience and the teachers were the actors getting ready for 'curtains up'.

The mood at the station was a sombre one. The intensity of bewilderment and anxiety had reached its peak. The atmosphere was heavy with anticipation. I could see that Oki was already seated in the audience section. Then I spotted Gary in the audience seating. Where had he been? Where was he yesterday when I was arrested and interrogated? Why did he not contact me yesterday? Buddies should be there for each other shouldn't they? But of course, we are not buddies anymore. He was Dr Evil. My nemesis.

Who was the woman sat next to him? A tall, slim, dark skinned lady. Clearly Indonesian. She had her hair cropped short in a pixie cut. Her face elongated with black piercing eyes, like a vampire, and tight pale lips – which in my eyes depicted a cruel and selfish person. Her hard expression showed me that she was determined to succeed with her mission. Alinudin must surrender himself to the police. Pay his penance. Punishment was imperative. This was 'the wife'. Gary's wife. The police informant.

She looked hard as nails. Picture Glenn Close as Cruella De Vil from '101 Dalmatians' or Meryl Streep as Miranda Priestley in 'The Devil Wears Prada' – the icy stare. The wife had mastered it. She was a pro.

There was also an additional member of the police force, a woman whose specialist skill was speaking the English language. An English speaking policewoman had been brought into the station especially for today's interrogation. That must have been a relief for poor Oki. His translation skills no longer required by the Pekanbaru police force. I did have my doubts about his 'translating' skills anyway.

To my horror, the focus of today's interrogation of the other teachers was me and only me! No questioning about their own dubious visas. As a member of the audience I could hear the questions being directed at Neville.

"How long has Sharon worked as a teacher at the school?"

"How many classes does Sharon teach each week?"

"Is Sharon receiving a salary the same as you are for teaching at the school?"

I was freaked out! What was happening here? Why was I the focal point of all the questions? Why was I being targeted? All the other teachers had inappropriate visas for working in Indonesia too.

Gary and his wife were seated only a few feet away from me. I demanded he explain to me what on earth was happening. There followed a heated discussion which included Gary saying "You shouldn't have lied yesterday. I have told all the other teachers not to lie today. It was wrong of you to lie."

My blood was curdling. I was outraged. This, from the man that promised me a three week orientation when I arrived. To be sheltered and protected by the other teachers during this induction to the school. I was seething. I was now seeing Gary for what he was. A slippery, sly and untrustworthy character.

Gary went on to say "the police just want to get Alinudin to come to Pekanbaru police station and give himself up. He is wanted for various scams and fraudulent cheques. Now he is also wanted for the illegal employment of staff at his school. By bringing all the other teachers into the station for questioning, Alinudin will have no choice but to come out of hiding."

There you have it. Me and Alinudin. Two peas in a pod. Both suspects. Illegal employee and illegal employer. Bloody marvellous.

Gary and Cruella managed to slither away at some point earlier in the day. Like two snakes in the grass. Everyone else had to endure another seven hours of questioning and interrogation. I was in the makeshift viewing gallery. Observing. It felt like I was on trial. The teachers were the prosecutor's witnesses. I was the defendant with no legal representative seated in the dock. Alinudin was the other defendant in the case who had skipped bail and gone into hiding. It all felt like an episode out of Law and Order or Ally McBeal.

I needed to change my statement. It was the nail in my coffin. It was a lie. A BIG, fat lie. The immediate versus probable imprisonment offered yesterday gave me no option but to sign it. No brainer in my books even for a patsy like me. But now I needed to change it.

After two hours of pleading, begging and practically being down on my knees imploring the police to let me change my statement they did. I have no idea why. I don't even care why. Maybe something was lost in translation? Actually, Oki was my translator which could explain their leniency. Oki probably offered them my 'personal services' for the next week or that my family were newspaper tycoons and powerful within the world press. I didn't care. I was allowed to change my statement. Without immediate imprisonment. Phew.

When we finally walked out of the police station I had accomplished two things that day. Firstly, I had changed my statement to reflect to the truth. I was a teacher at the school and paid a salary to teach. Secondly, I still had my passport in my pocket despite numerous attempts by the police to retain it until the matter had been resolved, which was when Alinudin handed himself into the police station. Oki's promises allowed me to pull off these two important things.

I planned to get the hell out of this godforsaken country as soon as I could. I didn't plan to hang around to be put into jail for five years. No parole.

It was a sleepless night. The door to my room at the guesthouse barricaded with my trusty backpack and wheelie suitcase full of my "must have" grammar books. In addition I had dragged across the door a chest of drawers and an occasional table (retro of course). This was Indonesia; the police could come at any time during the night to arrest me again. I was taking no chances. My passport was under my pillow, close to my head. I was fully dressed and ready to run if needed. There are no rules in this country.

23rd December 2004

I survived the night! Hurray!! My makeshift barricade was still intact. I pushed my hand under my pillow and was comforted by the feel of my passport pages ruffling against my fingers.

The walk into school was the same as any other day. I passed the children on their way to school. "Hello Mister! Where are you from?" Past the helpless orang-utan chained to the entrance porch. The endless stares.

As I entered the school there was an air of uneasiness and suspicion. Not a child in sight as the school was now closed. I began feeling all jittery again as the nervousness kicked in again. Something wasn't right. As I walked past reception I could see Neville, Kate and Cheryl sitting in the staffroom. We had all been summoned to the school that morning but no-one knew why.

There were raised voices coming from behind Gary's door. Oh God. What was happening now? Had the police some back to arrest me? Or arrest us all? That would be better for me. At least I wouldn't be on my own. Had Cruella managed to convince the police that we were all guilty? Banished to a jail cell for five years?

Then the door swung open. Oki came out first. Poor Oki. His face looked tired and drawn. His clothes a dishevelled mess as if he had slept in them. Then Gary, Dr Evil, sauntered out of his office. I am now wise to his calculating and deceitful ways. Sly and cunning like a fox. God, how I really loathed him now. Buddy turned baddie. Then another man appeared in the doorway. A middle aged man of medium height with a stocky build. His thinning hair was scraped back on top of his head. Dark skinned and dark haired, clearly Indonesian. He was smartly dressed in a grey suit and tie (especially smart compared to the rest of us who had not slept a wink). The way he walked exuded confidence. Maybe even cockiness. I knew straight away that this man was the elusive Alinudin. Owner of the school, uncle of Oki.

I was daunted and relieved at the same time. This was the man that had helped put me in this lousy position but the fact was he was probably the only one that would get me out of it. He was my jailer and my possible saviour. My light and dark. The yin to my yang. Alinudin strode straight into the staff room with a smile that said 'I'm here now, no need to worry yourselves'.

"Hello. As you have probably guessed I am Oki's uncle, Alinudin. The owner of this school. I am so sorry that we are meeting under such distressing circumstances".

His English was immaculate. I was feeling immense resentment towards this man. Why has it taken him so long to come out of hiding and show his face? Did he not realise I had been arrested twice?

"I want to reassure you that I am taking immediate steps to get this misunderstanding sorted. I know the Chief of Police and many of his cousins who are in very high ranking positions within the police force. The reason you have been arrested is because I don't have a 'contact' at the Pekanbaru police station. I will be going to the station this morning to sort out a contact. It all works very differently in this country. Sharon, I give you my personal guarantee that I will clear your name with the police".

I am not sure what to think. I am certainly not reassured. A scam artist and fraudster wanted by the police is giving me his word? I just hoped he still had some of the school's money to pay the appropriate bribe.

24th December 2004

It's Christmas Eve. Still no news from Alinudin. The bribing of the police officers at Pekanbaru station must be taking longer than expected. They probably can't even see the money through all that thick smoke.

Alinudin had gone back to the police station to continue his 'negotiations'. But as the day progressed into evening it was clear his 'negotiations' were not advancing. My plan to make a run for it and hop on the next available plane was dashed when it was made clear that I would be arrested before I even got to board the plane. Unfortunately, I was unable to blend into the crowd here in Pekanbaru. My white skin, blue eyes and curly blonde hair was a stark contrast to the native dark skin, brown eyes and straight brown hair.

In desperation I tried contacting the English First Co-ordinator based in Jakarta. He was the co-ordinator for the whole of the English First chain of schools in Indonesia and had already been made aware of the illegal activities being practised at the Pekanbaru EF school. His role was to assist all English First employees with any problems or disputes. I felt that 'problem' was a severe understatement. This was a critical and desperate situation. Extreme. Problem does not accurately illustrate the deep shit that I was in. This deep shit situation needed some urgent attention. Major shovelling.

The lady on the phone at English First HQ in Jakarta dismissed my pleas. The Co-ordinator was now on holiday as was everyone else. It was Christmas, she reminded me. Everyone had started their Christmas break. There was no-one there to help and I should ring back in two weeks. She then wished me a Happy Christmas.

Two weeks??? I could have served 14 days of my five year sentence by then. 336 hours. 20,160 minutes. This woman was clearly not grasping the gravity of my situation. I begged and pleaded with her to organise some help for me, but like a scene out of Little Britain the lady stonily insisted "computer says no".

Poor Oki. He was now receiving the brunt of my despair. I was inconsolable. I desperately wanted to leave Indonesia with its perverted laws and profiteering. The country's whole legal system was rotten to the core.

Oki rang his uncle. He really didn't know what to do. He just took instructions from his uncle. After a long conversation with Alinudin on the phone arrangements were made to smuggle me out of the country fast, while at the same time evading arrest.

Can you believe this? I am about to break the law again! Only this time knowingly. I am a willing participant to the plan. What choice did I have?

The proposal was for Alinudin to 'escort' me to Pekanbaru airport where he would pay the appropriate bribe to the airport police. We would then both alight an airplane. Destination Batam island. Disembark Batam island. We would then secure a taxi ride to the boat terminal. I was to approach the Customs and Border desk to obtain the appropriate Indonesian exit stamp in my passport. Alinudin would be standing by to make a bribe should this be required. I was to board the next boat to Singapore. Alinudin would stay on Batam island for business purposes.

Wow. Mission impossible was at the forefront of my mind. Incredulous.

Rendezvous 9am tomorrow morning. Pekanbaru airport.

Chapter 6

Escape

25th December 2004

I felt nauseous. I debated whether to open the car window in case I felt the need to vomit. Susanna, the part time Slovakian teacher and her Caltex employee husband, Russell, were driving me to the airport. They were accompanying me as eyewitnesses and their task was to ensure I got onto the plane safely. When all was said and done, Alinudin was a criminal wanted by the police for various scams and many counts of fraudulent cheques and I was endangering his operations. I had visions of him wanting to wipe me out, kill me to shut me up. I could see the headlines:

'Teacher slayed over school's funds...', 'Batam island bloodshed...', 'English Girl Working Illegally Brutally Killed'

Nevertheless, I boarded and disembarked the plane with no attempts on my life. Alinudin was actually quite chatty on the plane, wanting to give his side of the story. He denied all knowledge of the practises being employed by the school which are;

All teachers should be given the 3 week induction and training. No tick there.

During this time the correct working visa should be obtained from their agent in Singapore. No tick there.

There should be no teachers working on a 30 day tourist visa or a 2 month business visa. No tick there.

The reason the working visas were not being obtained was the cost. Working visas were expensive and Gary wanted to save money to make more profit from the school. His wife also wanted to be a partner of the school. I was a pawn in their power struggle.

Well this patsy was not hanging around to see the outcome. After surviving a taxi ride from Batam island airport to the boat terminal, I queued at the Customs and Border desk to exit Indonesia. As the official studied my passport my stomach was churning. I felt sick again. I couldn't breathe. He then studied my face and I tried to crack a smile. A casual 'hi, yes this is me' kind of smile. My dry lips cracked from the movement. I was sweating profusely, my face clammy from pure terror. I had to get that exit stamp. Freedom or jail.

Alinudin stood in the background chatting on his mobile phone. Was he calling his hit man? Or his cleaner? You know, those people that clean up murder scenes. His eyes kept darting around as if he was expecting someone to rush over and foil our plan. Furtive glances were made in my direction.

It seemed as though a ridiculous amount of time was being taken by the official who was scrutinising my passport. Something was wrong. Oh my God. He knows who I am. What I have done? I glanced over to Alinudin who now looked agitated as he spoke down the phone. What was happening? Where was my exit stamp? I look again at the official. I examined his face for any clue as to what he was thinking but his face was like a stone. No hint or trace of what was going through his mind.

After what seemed like hours, but was only minutes, the official stretches over the desk for his stamp. My heart is racing. Go on. Pick it up. Pick it up. Pick up the god damn stamp. He grasps the stamp by the handle then waits. Why doesn't he move the stamp from the ink pad onto my passport? Come on... do it. Do it now! After one final examination of my face, at which point I had stopped breathing, he pressed hard into the ink pad. Not breathing, my eyes fixated on the stamp. He then flicked my passport open at a random blank page and brought the stamp thudding down onto my passport. Hurray!!!! I had the exit stamp. I felt like jumping in the air and whooping with joy. I so desperately wanted to grin from ear to ear but controlled myself. The stone-faced official had not yet passed me back my passport. Then, like a painter inspecting his craftsmanship, the ink stamp imprinted on my passport was surveyed by the official. What was wrong with this guy? Just give me back my passport. Finally, with one last hardened look at my face, the official handed me my passport. Assignment completed.

Alinudin came to my side and wished me well on my journey. As he apologised for the arrests and police interrogations I endured he placed one of his business cards into my hand. "Sharon, it is so sad to lose you this way. Good English teachers are hard to find".

Good English teachers? He obviously hadn't seen the vacant looks on the faces of the children as I fumbled my way through each lesson and the stuttering and stammering due to my lack of experience. Nor had he seen the glee on their faces when their time to pray was imminent and the resulting race to escape the classroom, the Prayer Room a more appealing destination. And the desperation oozing out of my every pore as I tried to control the children and keep them keen. If he had seen my 'teaching skills' he would have seen how 'good' they were.

"I would really like for you to come back and teach at my school in Medan" he continued "There is a job for you there if you want it".

The offer was remarkable. Did he seriously think I was going to return to Indonesia, as a wanted criminal, to teach at "my accomplice's" school? I was speechless. I was certainly not tempted by his offer but I was also careful and 'respectful'. "Thank you so much. That is good to know. I will be sure to keep your business card safe and if I do return to Indonesia to work as an English teacher again you will be the first person I will contact. Thank you, thank you very much". I grovelled. I wanted to keep him sweet. I was still standing on Indonesian soil. Alinudin turned and disappeared into the throng of people.

I looked at my exit stamp in my passport. And again just to make sure. I now sat at the ferry departure gate waiting for the next boat to take me to Singapore. I looked at my exit stamp again in case I had imagined it. Yes, it was still there. It was an hour before the next boat departed.

I rang my parents from my Indonesian mobile phone that I purchased on the black market for a bargain $40 US dollars. My poor Mum and Dad, they last received a phone call from me the day after my second arrest which was horrifying for them. It went something like this...

"Hi Mum. Hi Dad. It's me... now I don't want you to worry, but I seem to be caught up in something... I've been arrested twice... but don't worry... I'm back at the guesthouse now. They've let me go. It's all to do with my visa... or should I say, lack of working visa. That's the visa that I should have."

Of course this brought the inevitable reactions.

"Oh my God Sharon. Are you alright? Is Gary helping you get this sorted? Are you eating properly? When did you last eat a proper meal?"

This was my Mum's response. No matter the how grave or serious the situation, my Mum would always require confirmation of my food intake. Now this may bring you to think that I have had previous eating disorders, anorexia perhaps, or that I was undernourished. I was none of the above. I was a healthy specimen with no eating disorders. In fact, I have never been on a diet in my life. Not once. It must be a mother thing. They feed you whilst you are in the womb. They continue to feed you milk as a baby, then solids throughout your entire childhood into adulthood. That instinct to ensure their child is fed must never leave them.

My mum was always experimenting on us kids. Broadening our horizons with new things such as Ox's tail, rabbit stew, lentil bake – you name it we have tried it. Our dinner plates always an unpredictable revelation.

I remember one day, after school, my mum dished up a pile of tripe! Yes, I'm not just implicating at a rubbish meal, I mean literally a pile of tripe. That 'edible' offal from the stomachs of various farm animals was served up. It didn't look good. My plate was filled with this white, rubbery mass with an ugly honeycombed membrane wrapped around the flesh. The mantra in our house was "you can't say you don't like it if you haven't tried it". Thus try it we did. Attempts at chewing it were futile as it bounced off your teeth shooting around your mouth like a pinball machine. It was like trying to chew an old tyre. After much moaning and gagging my mum succumbed to our protests and admitted it was 'bloody disgusting'. It ended up in the dog's bowl where it stayed, uneaten. Even the dog spurned the offending offal.

Dads are a totally different breed. My Dad's reaction to my phone call was "have you tried ringing the British Embassy in Jakarta yet? You must make them aware of your situation. Do you want me to contact them for you? What exactly did they say when they arrested you? Do you still have your passport? Can you leave the country? I will do some research to see what can be done".

My dad works closely with logic. If something is illogical my dad believes there will be a reason for this. He will go to the nth degree to analyse a situation or problem and bring 'sense' to the 'illogic'.

When I go travelling to different countries my Dad will buy a map and diligently follow my route, mapping all the places I stopped. He will research every place and e-mail me to relay details about the place, its history and sights to see. Who needs a Lonely Planet guide when you have a Dad like mine? I just refer to the 'e-mail travel dossier' when approaching a new destination to find out the highlights and must-see places to visit.

My travelling also seems to bring out the competitiveness in my dad. Many years ago he was in the Merchant Navy and has visited hundreds of ports all over the world. He likes to do a country count every time I return from travelling to see if I have 'caught up'. His perpetual hunger to win even resulted in him having a major heart attack during a game of badminton. Opposing player: me. Score: 2 games to nil... in my favour. This antagonised my dad to such a degree that he had a heart attack from his efforts to change the scoreboard. Following emergency surgery, thankfully he has now fully recovered and is pestering me for another game of badminton. He's still determined to win.

I reassured them on the phone that all I had to do was step onto the boat. Exit stamp now safely in passport. It was agreed that I would ring them again when I had reached Singapore and found myself a room for the night.

The ferry was clearly owned by the Singaporean side. It was immaculate. All the hundreds of seats stain free. The floor unblemished. Flushing toilets and toilet paper signalling the step back into civilization. No stares. I was anonymous again. Hurray!

The Singaporeans love their karaoke just as much as the Indonesians. The ferry had two big televisions attached to the wall facing the seating area. The passengers' faces were glued to the screens as they watched people with cheesy smiles dancing. Song words lit up in sequence to the song lyrics to assist the amateur singers to keep in time to the music. I remember Backstreet Boys and Vengaboys being particularly popular during the ferry crossing. But no-one sang. Not even a hum-a-long. The onboard entertainment was evidently not entertaining enough. It was not as if the lyrics were too troublesome... 'we like to party, we like, we like to party, we like to party, we like, we like to party'... who could go wrong with that?

One hour later we arrived at Singapore World Trade Centre to be greeted by lots of policemen with sniffer dogs. I looked at my trusty backpack and wheelie suitcase filled with my 'must have' grammar books. Oh my God. The rumours. Alinudin. He had threatened to plant drugs in the bag of another teacher. Did he plant some in mine? Am I about to be greeted by a sniffer dog and have it sit by my side licking my hand, an unmistakable indication to the policeman that I am indeed carrying drugs?

I clambered off the boat and debated whether or not to leave my trusty backpack and wheelie suitcase full of my "must have" grammar books. I could buy a whole new wardrobe of clothes in Singapore. Not so sure about grammar books but would I need them? I am no longer a teacher. Then as quickly as I had thought of the idea, I dismissed it. That was stupid. My name was written in all the books and even a photocopy of my passport was in my trusty backpack.

The cute little sniffer dog was busy at work sniffing at everything and everyone he passed. You could see people stiffen up as the little puppy approached them for a sniff. Even with nothing to hide I have always found it entertaining to watch grown adults be intimidated by a cute furry dog with big floppy ears. But today was my turn. I know I repeatedly refused Alinudin to 'help me with my bags'. I knew what he was supposedly capable of but money talks. He could easily have paid a backhander to a poorly paid airport worker who needed money to feed his family. Drugs could have effortlessly have been slipped into my bags. I felt as if I was going to vomit. My stomach was churning with apprehension, fear making my hands shake like jelly as the dog approached me. At least a Singapore jail would be much cleaner and orderly than an Indonesian one I thought to myself. They had flushing toilets too. After a quick inhale of me and my bags the dog and its handler walked on. My stomach started to settle as the panic subsided.

Several hours later I had found a room. I had always thought of Christmas Day as an occasion when mums and dads together with children and grandchildren get together as a family. At home not in hotel rooms. Every hotel was fully booked. I think I must have found the last available room in the whole of Singapore. Then it dawned on me, of course, not many people in Singapore would be celebrating Christmas Day. Over a third of Singaporeans follow Buddhism and Taoism. The rest of the population is a mix of Muslims, Christians, Hindus and also 'others'. Thrown into the 'others' categories are Jews, Sikhs and even Zoroastrians.

Did you know that Zoroastrianism is one of the world's oldest monotheistic religions? In English that means a religion that believes there is only one god. For over 1,000 years Zoroastrianism was one of the most powerful religions in the world. It was the official religion of Persia, now known as

Iran, for many years. It was founded by Prophet Zoroaster in ancient Iran approximately 3,500 years ago. It is now one of the world's smallest religions. They worship in fire temples, as light represents god's wisdom. Their god is Ahura Mazda the supreme god. Wise Lord. God of Wisdom. Fire is the only way they can control light and to ensure continuous light to worship they have fire.

So for all you Mazda car drivers out there, now you know where the brand name derives from. The car manufacturer also sees Mazda as a symbol of 'automotive culture' and it also 'incorporates a desire to achieve world peace'. This is quoted on the Mazda website. So, hope they haven't taken it to the next level and incorporated fire temples within the car engines. You could be in for a nasty shock when cruising down the motorway!

With my room booked I hailed a taxi to take me to the hotel. As vehicles have wing mirrors, the horn is used purely for emergencies or a call of frustration. All taxis are also metered in Singapore. There is none of the fare haggling before stepping your foot inside the vehicle. The ensuing "you cannot be serious sir that price is double what it should be. I'll pay you half". Eventually, when you could have probably already walked to your destination, the price is agreed.

There was none of this in Singapore, the land of "don'ts". After living and working in a country with no apparent laws and where money talks, where raw sewage runs down the sides of the roads giving off putrid smells mixed with petrol fumes and food stalls, where horns blared constantly in a battle to get through traffic lights and junctions, piercing eardrums until they vibrated with pain, it was a huge relief for me.

And there were no stares! To this uniformed, orderly country where the pavements are spotless and not a piece of litter or chewing gum to be seen. With wing mirrors a common feature on cars which are being driven at the requested speed limits where you can actually smell fresh air instead of rancid odours. No stares. Not even a second glance. Everything and everybody seemed brighter and more colourful. Happiness filled my entire body and I immediately felt refreshed. The tension drained out of my body as if there was a magnet under my feet drawing the stress and strain into the ground. My shoulders physically dropping as my body started to relax. The feeling was exuberating. I felt buoyant. My spirits lifted. I relished in the strict rules and regulations that surrounded me in Singapore. I wanted to understand the rules of the land. To be told I cannot do this and don't do that. It was exhilarating. It felt safe.

After paying the correct taxi fare I checked into my room. 'Happy Christmas Sharon' I thought to myself. This was the best Christmas present ever. To have escaped a five year prison sentence and successfully flee a corrupt and lawless country. It was amazing. To be in what I would now class as a lush hotel room in Singapore. It had a window, television, a bed with a quilted bedspread that looked like it had come off the set of 'Little House on the Prairie' and the best luxury of all... a flushing toilet with the added extravagance of three ply toilet roll. I was in heaven. My room even had a phone. It was palatial. I rang mum and dad to let them know I had successfully avoided jail and had found a room for the night.

"Hi it's me. I'm okay. I made it to Singapore without being arrested. There was a sniffer dog at the Singapore boat terminal which did concern me, but I'm ok. Nothing was put in my bags. And I got myself a room at a nice hotel."

My mum's immediate reaction to this was "Shhh. Don't say anything else Sharon. You don't know who is listening in on our conversation. Shhh. Stay quiet."

The whole terrible saga had tipped my poor mum over the edge. Gone was the sane and reasonable mother who would be the first to tell me to stop being a drama queen. Replaced by an irrational and unbalanced woman who now believed our phones were being tapped in an effort to catch me, the criminal. My dad, forever sensible and logical then interrupted to assure my mum that no-one was listening to us. Singapore's Secret Service had not put a tap on the hotel phone and my room was not about to be raided. With my mum's fears eradicated I went on to tell them I had decided that rather than fly home I was going to Australia. Why not? I had no home to go back to. No job to go to. Why not turn a bad experience into a good one? My mind was made up.

It didn't take long to find an Aussie mate who was prepared to take me in. Even with my criminal record. Things were looking up. I just needed to find a flight. How hard could that be?

26th December 2004

Boxing Day. A Sunday. Orchard Road. A major shopping area for Singaporeans and tourists alike. A never ending road full of boutiques, shopping malls, cinemas, posh restaurants, fast food joints and most importantly airline offices and travel agents.

Orchard Road seemed never ending, but it is in fact a 2.2 kilometre boulevard, the retail and entertainment hub of Singapore. Every brand name is sold on this street. Gucci, Prada, Armani... there is also all the high street names... Topshop, Dorothy Perkins, H&M. The boulevard is lined with trees and plants. Fountains shooting water into the air and cascading down like beautiful waterfalls. Everywhere is so clean and vibrant and colourful. Bright neon lit shop fronts twinkling and beckoning you to enter and purchase their merchandise. Wonderful smells of aromatic herbs and spices floating in the air enticing you to eat their food... lemongrass, ginger, tamarind, chillies and coconut to list just a few. This is infused with the western influences of Pizza Hut, Kentucky Fried Chicken and McDonalds. It is a shopper's and eater's paradise.

But it was not for me. The latest dungaree shorts and tartan leggings would have to wait. My mission was to find a flight to Australia. But none of the travel agents were open. It was Boxing Day, who in their right mind would be trying to book a flight during this festive season? Well, this patsy wanted one. I needed to get as far away from Indonesia as possible.

After a couple of hours searching for travel agents and then finding they were closed, I surprisingly found that the Singapore Airlines offices were open! Hurray! Flight booked.

Singapore Airlines are in my opinion one the best airlines in operation. The flight attendants, known as the 'Singapore Girls', are so gracious and hospitable. They glide around the aircrafts in their sarong two piece outfits – a long wrap around skirt down to their ankles which limits their gait to more of a shuffle. The matching top is a simple round neck, three quarter sleeved and fitted around their petite waists. Small red and purple oriental flowers cover the whole outfit. They are so elegant with their warm tiny smiles and obliging manners. They are forever gliding up and down the aisles with water for the dehydrated passengers. Who have, no doubt, taken advantage of the free alcohol thus tipsy and thirsty and destined to end up drooling on the shoulder of the person sitting next to them as they nod off in a semi-drunken state. The tray of food which normally smells disgusting and tastes of plastic is packed with Asian delights. The aroma of fragrant herbs and spices when the foil is peeled back is amazing. It even tastes like proper food!

Compare that to American Airlines. The flight attendants look like they are competing in 'The Apprentice' for a job with Alan Sugar. They are dressed in stiff navy power suits and red neckerchiefs with starched, crispy white blouses. Their outfits immediately make a statement. Don't mess with us or else. We mean business. Dog eat dog. Water seems to be on rations and if you ask for more they make it clear they have more important tasks to attend to. When flying with American Airlines a few years back, the flight attendant accidentally spilt a whole plastic cup of fresh orange juice all down my front. I had another seven hours left cramped in my tiny economy seat. No change of clothing in my hand luggage. The flight attendant didn't apologise, but just passed me a rationed handful of serviettes with a look that said "what's your problem?" She then went on to instruct me to "take on a picnic mental attitude on this flight, you will find the whole experience more enjoyable"!! With those words of wisdom she continued pushing her trolley down the aisle ready for the next victim – her stance clearly stating "don't mess with me". The food was basically a McDonalds Happy Meal served up on a plastic tray.

So, with my flight to Australia purchased, I made my way back to the hotel via the MRT Singapore's train system. It is by far the cleanest public transport system I have ever travelled on. None of the usual litter items such as read newspapers, empty take-out coffee cups or scrunched up sweet wrappers. Certainly no offending chewing gum that is so annoying when it has been freshly chewed and sticks to the sole of your shoe, the only way to remove it is to pull the disgusting wet gunk with your fingers. Not one graffiti artist has been on the train to make their statement. Not a tag, not even a tiny scribble.

Back in my hotel room I flicked on the TV just for some background noise more than anything. I had tuned into the English speaking news channel and could not believe what I was hearing. Oh my god. This is horrendous. The newsreaders were saying that there had been a major earthquake that had hit the Sumatra Island of Indonesia at 9 o'clock that morning. That would make it 8 o'clock Indonesian time. The extent of the damage and death count not yet known but it was serious. The earthquake was huge. Even possibly off the scale. It was sending shivers down my spine just hearing this. My eyes were as wide as saucers as I continued to listen. I felt physically sick. They kept saying northern Sumatra but they had no idea at that point as to the exact location. Pekanbaru is pretty much smack bang in the middle of the Sumatra Island. Were my friends and fellow teachers, Neville (known as Usman), Kate and Cheryl okay? Was the school still standing or has it crumbled to the ground?

Later that day the sombre newsreaders were saying that thousands of people had died. The damage created by the earthquake affected not just Indonesia, but Sri Lanka, Thailand and India as well. They were talking about tsunamis. What the hell is a tsunami? It sounded Japanese to me. A sushi delicacy. I had never heard of this word. It is in fact a Japanese word meaning "harbour wave". "Tsu" means harbour and "nami" means wave. It is basically a long high sea wave caused by an underwater earthquake or other underwater disturbance. The devastation was horrific. The only reason Singapore was not affected by the earthquake and subsequent tsunami is because of the Indonesian archipelago which acts as a barrier, protecting the country from such events. Also, the shallow water around Singapore makes it impossible for killer waves to create any destruction. In theory, the largest tsunami that could possibly affect Singapore would only be a maximum height of half a metre. This miniature 'tsunami' would not even register with the Singaporeans. It would just look like a stormy day. Or good surf.

I was ignorant to the quake vibrations as at that time I was travelling on the MRT, underground, in a tunnel. The train vibrations against the track made it impossible for me to even feel the quake. I was oblivious. I have no idea of the harrowing disaster happening only a short distance (in world terms) from where I was.

Weeks later the degree of devastation was revealed. Over 230,000 people were killed in a single day in 14 different countries. Some people are still missing to this day. It was one of the most destructive disasters in recorded history. The third largest earthquake ever recorded with a magnitude of at least 9.0. The largest two being the 1960 Chile earthquake and the 1964 Alaska earthquake measuring 9.5 and 9.2 respectively.

The magnitude of the earthquake in Pekanbaru was 8.6. The English First school shook violently but remained intact. Neville, Kate and Cheryl were unhurt. Fortunately, there were no deaths in Pekanbaru that day as a direct result of the earthquake.

The school did eventually close its doors for good eight months later in August 2005. An e-mail from fellow teacher Kate confirmed this news. It did re-open after the Christmas debacle but it appears Alinudin had spent all the stolen school funds. He had had to sell his car to make ends meet. You reap what you sow.

I spent a glorious three months in Australia visiting friends and travelling around the country, basking in the fact that I was a free woman. The threat of a prison sentence well and truly behind me I found my mind kept wandering back to events at the school. The arrests, the earthquake, the tsunami. I am not entirely sure I could ever repeat the challenging and thought-provoking events I had experienced in Indonesia. Not that I want to experience being arrested again but I was working on a plan.

Chapter 7

A Plan

The plan didn't really materialise until a few years later. I continued my nonconformist existence, travelling the world in between work contracts. The work bit not quite so nonconformist but it had to be done to fund my lifestyle.

I needed a gripping and exhilarating challenge. Something to push me physically and mentally. Like being arrested and smuggled out of countries. Just missing earthquakes and tsunamis. But in a more controlled environment. The nights were cold and dark back in Old Blighty. Doors closed and curtains shut I flicked through the television channels in an attempt to find something remotely interesting. The section of programmes was lousy. Some would say diabolical. A typical night of TV would firstly involve a soap drama. Eastenders, which was full to the brim of glum and gloom, was one of those soaps that made you want to slit your wrists with compassion for the characters suffering or actually made you feel good that your life was so much better than theirs. The incredulous storylines have included the killing of an evil pub landlord – where he got whacked over the head with a bust of Queen Victoria on Christmas Day – a desperate push to get the biggest audience. Then there was conniving Janine Butcher who pushed her husband off the edge of a mountainside for his money, and don't forget nasty Nick Cotton. He returned to the soap pretending to be a born again Christian only to try and kill his 'Ma', Dot Cotton, with a portion of poisoned cottage pie. Is this supposed to be real life? Do people who live in the East End of London live like this? Constantly worrying about someone trying to kill them? Reluctant at dinner time to eat what is put in front of you in case it has been poisoned?

Then you have the other side of the coin – Coronation Street, based on the Mancunian cobbles. Characters on the street include Haley, born as Harold, with her trusty red anorak. The first transsexual person to be portrayed in a British soap. Her partner, stuttering Roy Cropper and his trusty beige anorak. Train enthusiast and cafe owner. A knickers' factory that seemed to employ every resident of the street. Deirdre Barlow arrested and jailed for bank fraud after falling for a bogus airline pilot. The newspaper coverage of this 'unjust imprisonment' was beyond belief. A campaign to 'free Deirdre' was led by the major tabloids. Good grief! Did they not realise that this was just make believe? Not a documentary? This was a made up story known as a script for TV. When Tony Blair, the UK Prime Minister at the time, declared 'the nation is deeply concerned about Deidre' I really thought that Britain had gone mad. Maybe he had eaten too much beef during the mad cow disease period?

The programme selection after the prime time soaps consisted mainly of repeats of Midsomer Murders, Taggart and Doc Martin or documentaries telling us how fat the UK population is becoming. Bored with television I picked up a travel magazine that had arrived in the post a few days ago. The pages fell open and there in front of me was an amazing picture of a huge mountain with a white, snow-capped peak and blue skies with wispy clouds like candy floss surrounding the top of the mountain. Mount Kilimanjaro. The highest mountain in Africa at 5,895 metres. It looked awesome. Absolutely spectacular. I read on. It was telling me that even though Mt Kilimanjaro is one of the world's largest mountains it doesn't take any technical skills or specialist equipment to climb. This sounded like something I could tackle. No expensive gear to buy. No training courses to attend.

It went on to say that even so it is not an easy feat. It is mentally and physically exhausting. A challenge, I thought. I had been there before and survived in Indonesia. It was just what I needed. The article said that even professional athletes have underestimated how difficult it would be to climb Kilimanjaro and it turns out to be one of the hardest things they had ever done in their lives. This was it! This was going to be my plan. My mental and physical challenge. To climb Kilimanjaro. No training needed.

The article continued to advise readers that you must train vigorously prior to attempting a climb. Three times a week for three months prior. The best training would be to strap a heavy pack on your back and go hiking. It also recommended you to visit the gym regularly. What a load of hogwash. I was fit enough.

My two senses, smell and taste, had taken me to Indonesia. The enticing South East Asian oriental herbs and spices were irresistible. Another sense. Sight. My sight of this incredible mountain was luring me to Africa. I wanted to see it with my own eyes, not through someone else's camera lens. I started to make a plan.

To my horror, before I even had time to plan, a group of celebrities also decided to climb Kilimanjaro in aid of Comic Relief. The most implausible assembly of famous people that were obviously in the need of some fresh publicity were trying to steal my glory. Almost ridiculing my forthcoming climb of my life! For goodness sakes – there was Chris Moyles included in this flock of stars, an overweight, beer swilling and cigarette smoking Radio One DJ. Cheryl Cole, the glamorous ex 'Girls Aloud' all girl band singer who was more accustomed to wearing zebra print three inch platform shoes than a pair of Gore-Tex lined walking boots. TV presenters Denise van Outen and Fern Cotton were the blonde-haired beauties that should get the ratings up for the BBC and encourage the UK male population to dig into their pockets for Comic Relief. There is now talk that the charity invests in managed funds that in turn invest in alcohol, firearms and tobacco companies. A contradiction perhaps to their 'commitment to helping people affected by conflict' and 'working to reduce alcohol misuse'. Not sure that investing in the companies that supply firearms and alcohol will help their cause.

Unbelievably, all the celebs made it to the top. I had hoped that at least a few of them wouldn't make it, if only to make me look better when I conquered the mountain. Even Chris Moyles made it. With my spirits dampened slightly and my swagger certainly abated, I continued my planning.

I chose the Marangu Route out of the six established routes. It takes only five days to ascend and descend making it reputedly one of the toughest routes and the most dangerous to your health. This is mainly due to the severe lack of time to acclimatise resulting in the probability of successfully reaching the top quite low. Ha! The celebs did the Shira Route that took them eight days. This eases the physical effects of high altitude dramatically due to the longer acclimatisation period. But what about the poor cameramen, the ones who heaved all the equipment up the mountain to film the impressive achievement of the celebs? In reality half a tonne of broadcasting equipment had to be carried up the mountain to capture all the celeb 'moments'. They allegedly had one hundred porters and two doctors with medication and syringes to immediately alleviate any nausea or high altitude sickness they experienced. There was an entourage of security guards, not sure who was going to go to the effort of climbing Kilimanjaro to steal Cheryl's hiking boots, but security was apparently needed. Then there was another thirty or so film crew members to ensure that a slick production was achieved. My swagger makes a quick recovery as I continue to finalise my plans which had now expanded to include several more weeks discovering East Africa.

Chapter 8

Kilimanjaro

Marangu Hotel is a beautiful hotel on the foothills of Mt Kilimanjaro. A plethora of white painted cottages with red painted verandas sitting in a charming garden, it has immaculate lawns with pathways leading to each cottage. These gardens have clearly received loving care from a green fingered labourer, as tropical flowers with vibrant colours; purple, red, yellow line the paths leading to the manicured grass. Exotic trees provide shade from the harsh African sun within the twelve acres of lushness in this colonial setting. It even had a croquet lawn. The main hotel building, built in the early 1900s, brought further charm and elegance to the surroundings. A family run hotel oozing hospitality and homey atmosphere. Then there was the magnificent view from the garden, the snow-capped mountain with wispy white clouds floating around the crater top, like a Christmas cake with brandy custard dribbling over the sides. This is exactly like the pictures I saw in the brochure – Mt Kilimanjaro.

The pre-climb briefing took place the night before we set off to conquer the mountain. It scared the hell out of me. After the meeting I just wanted to jump back on one of the daily flights to Amsterdam. I could lie to my friends. Who would know? I could just lie low for the required five days and reappear having 'climbed' Kilimanjaro

The trek organiser, Desmond, was frank and honest. "The Marangu route puts the biggest strain on your lungs and respiratory system as your body doesn't have much time to acclimatise. But I have to tell you, our success rate to Uhuru peak is seventy percent. The ones that don't make it are usually stopped by the extreme effects of acute mountain sickness known as Altitude Mountain Sickness (AMS). It strikes people randomly. You can be young and fit and still be struck down by it." Oh dear. I think I would have preferred a head in the sand approach personally. He was being too thorough with his descriptions and warnings for my liking. He was ruining the fun of it all.

Thirty percent of climbers don't even make it to the Uhuru peak, the highest point of Kilimanjaro. This is very worrying. What if I am in that thirty percent? Fitness levels are irrelevant he said. I would be the laughing stock back home. I could just hear the comments... "Well, can you believe Chris Moyles managed to reach the summit but Sharon failed?" Or, "she was a fool to attempt such a feat." This was a massive worry. My street credibility could be in ruins. Desmond then went on to tell us even more gruesome altitude facts. "AMS can develop into what is known as high altitude cerebral oedema, HACE for short, or high altitude pulmonary oedema HAPO. These are life threatening and can kill you. These oedemas are a build-up of fluid on the lungs. The symptoms are the same as AMS, headaches, nausea and vomiting. Dizziness, loss of appetite and insomnia are also some of the effects of altitude sickness".

I am feeling a bit nauseous myself now. Perhaps I am starting to feel the effects of acute mountain sickness already? I mean, we were already at 1,600 metres above sea level just sitting in the briefing room. I could die on this mountain. How was I going to cope at 5,895 metres? Another 4,295 metres above me?

He continued, "there are only around ten deaths a year on the mountain and when you consider that approximately 40,000 people attempt to climb Kilimanjaro each year then this is a very low statistic".

I really didn't want to hear about deaths or statistics. Is this statistic supposed to reassure me that I will survive? I am starting to think that perhaps the five year Indonesian prison sentence was a much better option.

Desmond went on to describe in detail the severe effects of pulmonary oedema, which were ultimately shock, respiratory failure and organ death from lack of oxygen.

But here came the catch... you can't really tell the difference between acute mountain sickness and pulmonary oedema. The effects are exactly the same! So even if you have a crushing headache and are puking every three seconds how do you know to turn back? You may just have acute mountain sickness and could actually carry on. Turning back could be a mistake. But if you continue climbing and have pulmonary oedema you will die. You won't even know your mistake then, as you will be dead. Silver lining I suppose.

There is a drug, Diamox, which Desmond said can help alleviate the altitude sickness. However, there is another catch; the side effects of the drug are identical to the effects of altitude sickness: nausea, dizziness, vomiting and headaches. But if you are lucky and have no side effects from the drug, you still have to deal with an overactive bladder as Diamox makes you excessively urinate. Not an easy feat when you are on the side of a mountain in temperatures of -15 degrees Celsius.

My four fellow climbers who had initially appeared relaxed and happy now looked panic-stricken. An uneasy mood came over the briefing room. The five of us contemplated what we were about to take on. I had paid for this opportunity to die on a mountainside. What was I thinking? I should've just stuck to the Yorkshire Dales or the Lake District. Scafell Pike is the highest mountain in England at 978 metres above sea level. No chance of dying from acute mountain sickness climbing that one. But no, I had to fly thousands of miles to Africa to climb its highest mountain.

It took Desmond over two hours to complete his 'Kili' briefing by which time we were all mentally making notes of the loved ones we needed to send e-mails to that night. Just in case.

There were five of us attempting the Marangu route. With me was Irmi, a 58 year old German woman who had lived in Australia for many years. She had clearly adopted into a laid back Aussie, however, she still hadn't lost that German efficiency which came to light during the trek. Irmi was the ultimate driving machine.

Edward was a 49 year old company director from Belgium. His greying hair made him look older than his age, however, his red hiking books helped create a more contemporary look. His clipped, almost abrupt accent made him sound like he was constantly issuing orders. He wanted to climb Kilimanjaro before he turned 50 which was only 4 months away. Could be the last thing he did.

Tara was 38 years old and from Canada. There were numerous red maple leaf flags sewn onto her backpack, God forbid no Canadian wants to be mistaken for being American. Tara was a stocky, red faced girl with a distinctive pink streak dyed into her hair. She boasted of her many triathlons that she had competed in and generally how sporty she was. I guessed Tara would be the first to the top – she may be the only one to reach the summit. While the rest of us battled with respiratory issues and possible organ failure.

Kate, 29, was a fellow Brit. A Southerner, but I didn't hold that against her. Kate had arrived in flip flops with a backpack full of beachwear and summer outfits. Not a waterproof or walking boot in sight. Luckily for her the Marangu Hotel had a mammoth building packed from floor to ceiling with walking gear. Water bottles, gaiters, gloves, boots, jackets, it was jammed full of items left by climbers over the years. It was impressive. If only I had known about this 'loan facility' I would have come with nothing too. I could have saved myself a tidy sum. Kate clearly wasn't as stupid as I initially thought. After raiding the store and sending my 'just in case' goodbye e-mails it was soon the morning of the start of our climb.

Day One
We all assembled at 9am sharp in the hotel courtyard where we met our porters and guides. I felt a bit like Cheryl Cole and the celebrities at this point. For the five of us wannabe 'Kili' climbers there are ten porters and guides plus the chief guide, Fetaeli. Eleven crew versus five wannabe 'Kili' climbers. It felt uncomfortable. The thought of those poor boys trudging up the mountain with my changes of clothes, body wipes, sleeping bag, plus all our food for five days – breakfast, lunch and dinner. Me, I just carried my modest daypack containing my snacks and water for the day together with my waterproof jacket, hat and gloves. At least we didn't have doctors and bodyguards I suppose.

Fetaeli wasn't Italian as his name may suggest. He was a big African man with wide, piercing brown eyes. He wore corduroy trousers with a chequered lumberjack shirt under his zip up fleece. The only thing Italian about Fetaeli was his walking boots. He wore a good pair of 'Asolo' boots which I assume he picked up from the 'outdoor store' at the Marangu Hotel. He carried a very small day pack with a very big umbrella which doubled as a walking stick. His English was flawless. No lessons needed from a redundant English teacher. Fetaeli was the Chief. He was the man in charge. He had a good sense of humour with a lovely twinkle in his eye. He was a Kilimanjaro veteran.

From the Marangu entrance gate to the Kilimanjaro National Park it took only three hours to walk to our first set of sleeping huts. The hike was through lush rainforest with trees overhanging the pathways. Altitude? Not a problem. I wanted to bound along the track but Fetaeli kept barking "pole pole" urging us to walk at a ridiculously slow pace. It felt like a funeral march. Pole pronounced "poe-lay" is Swahili for slowly. They say the faster you climb in altitude the greater the chance you have of getting acute mountain sickness. But I felt fine. The slow pace was excruciating. Irmi "the ultimate driving machine' was beside herself. She was having none of it. "I cannot stand this slow pace, we need to vauk faster" she pronounced as she sped off.

The first mountain huts at Mandara were an 'A' framed wooden affair. They looked like they had come from a Swiss alpine ski resort. The walls inside were slatted wood that looked a bit like a Swedish sauna room. It certainly didn't feel anything like a nice hot sauna. It was freezing. Thin mattresses lay on wooden 'beds' which were basically shelves at long sides of the 'A'. A third 'bed' was higher up on the end of the 'A'. It was cosy.

There was a big 'A' frame hut which was the dining hall. All the walkers congregated in the big hut to sit at long tables and benches to eat their evening meals. Wow – what a meal. Soup for entree followed by a substantial main meal and hot beverages to finish. Unfortunately there was no wine on offer, but considering the list of ailments that were about to be inflicted on my body I thought water would be the best liquid intake for this journey. I was envious though of the two grey-haired German guys seated further down the bench. They had a bottle of red wine with their dinner. Who carried the bottle? The poor porters had enough to carry. I later saw them smoking, not sure their lungs would endure any more smoke inhalation after today. It will be difficult enough to cope with even breathing in air.

Day Two
Sleeping at 2,700 metres wasn't too difficult. The usual two or three night time toilet visits which are normal for me were just a tad trickier when you have to creep out of a hut in the pitch black and grope your way to a smaller hut which I was hoping was the toilet – not my next door neighbour! I woke ready for another day of walking. Today was a climb in altitude of 1,000 metres. Easy. We gained 840m yesterday so how hard could another 1,000 metres be? Our wake up call, not that we needed it, was Fetaeli banging on our hut door barking "wake up!" Outside our door one of the porters had left us a plastic washing up bowl of hot water to wash our hands and faces. I really did feel like just pouring the whole bucket over my head but I resisted realising that this manoeuvre would not gain me any friends. Instead I dug out my dependable Nivea

wipes from my sack of belongings and proceeded to perform my body wipe wash. This was a tricky procedure with lots of writhing and contorting. My body twisted and tangled a bit like a Houdini show. I managed to master numerous positions that I had no idea I was capable of in order for me to get the Nivea wipe under my clothes and around the majority of my body. Boy did I smell nice after that show.

The trek today was much steeper than yesterday's steady incline. Gone were the beautiful trees overhanging the wooded pathway, replaced by meadows and rocky valleys. Giant Senecio trees that looked like double ice cream cones. The thick brown trunks stretched far up in to the sky, then dividing into two, three, four or five platforms. This was where the 'ice cream' sat. Lots of flat green leaves, almost cacti-like in appearance sprouting out of the cones in a big round ball. Moorland heather speckled in between the rocks and Senecio trees.

Breathing was getting increasingly harder but still manageable. We were all revelling in the fact that we were still capable of sucking air into our lungs knowing that this would soon be pretty difficult. We reached the Horombo huts which were even better than the Mandara accommodation. Again they were 'A' shaped wooden huts but with little verandas outside each one perched on the side of the mountain. Super Tara, the Canadian athlete who competed regularly in triathlons, was struggling. To be honest she was out of breath on day one, which to me screamed 'UNFIT'. Gone was the constant crowing about her athletic prowess. In fairness I don't think she had the capability to speak due to her never ending puffing and panting. Her red face was even redder. She did, however, manage to whine and grumble in between her wheezing. "I don't think I can do this" she panted "I think I am having problems with my lungs. Serious problems. My breathing is irregular".

That night, Super Tara was in a frenzy. She was crying hysterically insisting there was something seriously wrong with her lungs as she was struggling to suck in air. "This is not normal. I can't breathe properly I can't go any further. I must go back down tonight. I have to go now! I am going now! Does anyone have a flashlight I can borrow?" We tried to calm her down and explain that we were all feeling the effects of altitude. I don't think she had quite grasped the concept that air was thin at altitude.

Kate was on a constant trek to and from the toilet hut as the Diamox took hold of her bladder and squeezed. She was also suffering from a bout of diarrhoea which was unfortunate for the queue of people behind her waiting to use the toilet. It was a case of rolling up your trouser legs and breathing through your mouth when entering the rustic latrine.

Day Three
3,720m. Tara made it through the night, her midnight mission to run back down the mountain thwarted by myself and Kate. When I say run it was metaphorically. Tara was no more capable of running than I was of teaching English.

Having performed my Houdini act with my dependable Nivea wipes I headed to the dining hut to be greeted by a plate of bacon and eggs! These eggs had been carried up the mountain by one of the porters. I feel another Cheryl Cole similarity moment. This porter had a baby formula milk tin swinging from the side of his backpack which, unknown to me, contained a dozen eggs nestled in handfuls of straw in a primitive attempt to not break the eggs. It worked! He did not break one egg! I bet he was the champion egg and spoon racer at school.

Today involved endless trudging uphill. We had another 1,000 metres to ascend. Gradually all vegetation disappeared as we lumbered into what looked like we had stepped onto planet Mars. The ground was so dry and barren with big boulders strewn across the dusty plain; the landscape open and windswept with big rolling clouds above us. My head was pounding. It felt like it was going to explode as I battled against the wind and rain. It was desolate. Oh my god. My head throbbed so much. The agonising pain behind my eyeballs was so intense. It was like someone was stabbing my eyes with pins. I could see Kate in the distance with her head down, back hunched in quiet determination to keep going. Her feet shuffling slowly one foot then the next. It was gruelling. We could see our destination ahead, Kibo hut; a cold cement block which was to be our resting place prior to the final climb to the top. The hut looked so close yet it took another three hours of torturous trudging to reach it. Even Fetaeli had ceased barking "pole pole" as he too battled the elements, his umbrella now acting as a shield against the harsh conditions.

Kibo hut was a stark, drab, concrete building, a reject from a communist-era country. The bleak and desolate backdrop did nothing to help the grim setting. After reaching the hut the temperature dropped fast and we were all soon in our thermals lying in our bunk beds thinking about the climb to the summit. We all tried to sleep, but with an 11.30pm wake-up call for the final ascent it was an impossible task.

Day Four...just
4,703 metres. Midnight. We were now dressed in every piece of clothing available in our woven sacks. We looked like we were at a weight loss boot camp with our bodies bulging and clothes straining from the outrageous amount of layers. I had increased in size from a petite 10 to a size 20.

This was the highest point in my life that my body had ever walked to. I had felt a great achievement at reaching 4,200 metres during the Inca Trail that took me to the Machu Picchu ruins but this was on another level. My head was splitting and my eyeballs felt like they were going to explode. Breathing was difficult. You suck in what you believe to be a sizeable amount of air and what you get is a whiff. A smidgen. It's like your lungs are failing. Fully loaded with our 'Kili Survival Kit' which comprised of three water bottles, one with a strap to loop around your neck and hang under your many layers of clothing to prevent freezing. A pocketful of broken biscuits as you must keep your energy levels up during the final ascent. The biscuits are broken to enable a quick manoeuvre from pocket to mouth without having to hold or bite the biscuit. Lastly, head torches to light up the path as you climb. Water, food and light, the essentials. I did wonder that perhaps the 'Kili Survival Kit' should also include an oxygen tank, stretcher and qualified medic but I kept this idea to myself.

Super Tara was in a state at this point. She kept ranting "I won't reach the top. I know I won't. I can't breathe. How on earth will I climb the mountain anymore if I can't breathe now?" Her crimson face glowed in the dark like a beacon under the scrutiny of our head torches.

Irmi, the 'ultimate driving machine' insisted "Vee need to start vauking!"

Edward had a look of steely determination on his face. His 50th birthday was looming. He was going to make it to the top even if it meant the cancellation of his birthday celebrations due to hospitalisation.

Kate had managed to control her bowels and we were excited. We were also apprehensive about the possibility of being in the thirty percent of people who don't make it to the top. We did not even entertain the thought of the ten or so people a year that die attempting to climb. Actually, being in the thirty percent who fail to reach the summit is probably a harder pill to swallow. God damn it... Chris Moyles made it to the summit. How hard can it be?

We all set off up the slope, our boots crunching on the loose, slippery shale, rasping noises all around as people struggled to inhale the thin air. One step forward, two steps back, one step forward, two steps back. This was the motion as we zigzagged our way up the mountainside. In front and behind me were the headlights of other climbers bobbing up and down like a string of fairy lights draped up the mountainside. The black sky was clear and you could see hundreds of twinkling stars. It was a pretty surreal moment. But I am now focused on Edward's red booted feet in front of me. "Pole pole" barked Fetaeli. I have no other gear but slow at this moment in time. Edward is swinging his walking sticks like he is in a majorette show and whacks me in the arm.

"Votch my schticks!" he commanded. "You are vauking too close to me!"

"Sorry Edward" I mumbled with my head still down, eyes focused on his red boots. Oh my god. I couldn't get enough air into my lungs. My head was splitting so much it was excruciating. I tried digging into my pocket for some biscuit pieces but my hand was too big. I peeled off the three layers of gloves and quickly dived into my pocket. I grabbed a handful of what were now biscuit crumbs and threw them into my mouth, leaving behind what looked like a Hansel and Gretel trail. People might be thanking me later for this ingenious crumb trail. I felt nauseous. The biscuit crumbs were not agreeing with me. I started retching; a dry hacking retch that made my stomach feel battered and bruised as if I had been in a fight with Lennox Lewis. Oh god, my lungs. I cannot suck air into my lungs. Where is the god damn air? The oxygen deprivation was crippling me!

Fetaeli had his eye on me. I'm hunched and shuffling along the shales, wheezing like an old woman and retching like a teenager who has drank too many alcopops. Strands of my unruly hair had poked out from the sides of my beanie hat and had now frozen due to the well-below freezing temperature on the mountain. Crumbs of what I believe to be Bourbon and Nice biscuits were stuck to my face and neck. I bet Cheryl didn't look anything like this when she was climbing the summit. Maybe it's because she's 'worth it' and I'm clearly not.

In a flash Fetaeli is beside me with one of the young local guides.

"Sharon, this is Heaven, one of our experienced guides. The altitude seems to be affecting you so I have asked Heaven to stay with you all the way to the summit. OK?"

OK? Of course it's OK. I felt like I was dying a slow, painful death. If someone, especially with a name like Heaven, is going to look over me then I certainly wasn't going to argue.

Oh hell, maybe he thinks I have the beginnings of high altitude pulmonary oedema? Am I dying? What was it... ultimately shock, respiratory failure and organ death from lack of oxygen. But it seemed no-one else thought I was dying and Fetaeli sent me on my way with my new guardian, Heaven.

Through the snow I shuffled and staggered with Heaven's watchful eye on me, as I vomited regularly onto the clean, crisp snow. It was a messy sight. Patches of steaming, lumpy, orange vomit sank into the pure white snow. My biscuit crumb trail was turning into a vomit trail.

The water drinking stops were a lengthy affair. It involved many stages. Stage One: Peeling off the three pairs of gloves. Stage Two: Eventually getting a grip of my jacket zipper to open and reveal the unfrozen water bottle. Stage Three: Fumbling with the water bottle to get the cap off. Finally I could take a glug of water. Then it was back through stages three to one. After a gruelling six hours we reached the top. Gillmans Point. 5,685 metres. Hurray!!! I had reached the top of Kilimanjaro. The sunrise had already been and gone with Heaven reminding me to look up and take a photo. I could hardly function at this point never mind negotiate a camera with all its fiddly buttons and dials. My fingers felt like they were developing frost bite in a ridiculous attempt to capture the moment on camera. I just wanted to get up there and back down without dying.

My guardian, Heaven, then kindly reminded me that we were not yet at the highest point. To get to Uhuru Peak which, at 5,896 metres, is the highest point on Kilimanjaro it was another two hour trek through snow and ice. This revelation made me throw up some more with Heaven patiently waiting. Patting my back in an attempt to make the vomiting cease he posed his important question: "OK Sharon" he then pointed up "do we go up or do we go down?" His eyes implored me to say yes even though at this point I was convinced I was dying from pulmonary oedema. I feebly pointed up towards the sky. More really to indicate the other Heaven above where I would shortly meet my maker, rather than to continue up the mountain. But Heaven cheerfully took this gesture as my approval to continue climbing so off we went. The last two hours were brutal. We were walking along the rim of a volcanic crater which is covered with ice and snow. One wrong step or skid on the ice could send you tumbling into the crater. This happens every year to some 'wannabe Kili climbers'. At this moment in time it was debatable whether this was the preferred option of dying which I was convinced was going to happen. My headache was intensifying and my eyeballs were stinging from the brightness of the sun reflecting on the snowy mountaintop.

The euphoric feeling when we made it to Uhuru is hard to describe. Apart from the fact that I was still breathing – just, the combination of the physical demands on my body and the mental strain to keep positive when the fatigue and then self doubt emerge is a challenge. To overcome the self-doubt and punishing demands on your body is such a gratifying experience.

I bumped into Irmi, Edward and Kate on my way up to the 'Uhuru signpost' and we all hugged like old friends. All of us beaming from the exhilaration of the whole experience, or maybe I should call it an ordeal. Super Tara was no-where in sight. Perhaps she turned back. I had no idea and I just needed the last few steps to reach the summit.

It all happened so fast. Heaven and I reached the 'Uhuru Peak 5,895 metre signpost' and waited for a group of buoyant climbers to pose for the all-important photo. We then took our stand in front of the infamous signpost and did a cheery smile pose for the poor guy that I accosted to get my photo taken with Heaven. We also did a thumbs-up pose which was pretty insane as thumbs-up was the last thing I was feeling like! Then, when I actually started to take in the spectacular 360 degree perspective from the 'roof of Africa', Heaven grabs me and urges me to descend immediately.

"Sharon you must leave now. We need to descend fast. The lack of oxygen to your brain is very damaging."

We then started our rapid descent, soon catching up with the others. Kate and I were practically running down the loose shale, our feet sinking into the loose stone, sliding and skidding like a pair of lunatics. This was better than drugs! The rush of oxygen back into our brains made us giggle like school girls. Everything was so funny! We were high as kites!

It was insane but we revelled in it. My dogged headache miraculously gone! Hurray!! It was a long trek back down to the Horombo huts where we stayed on day two. I got a sadistic pleasure in passing 'wannabe Kili climbers' who were clearly suffering from the effects of high altitude. Ha! I had accomplished my challenge. My glory still slightly tainted by the fact that Chris Moyles had also reached the summit.

Day Five
A hop, skip and a jump back through the meadows and rocky valleys; past the giant Senecio trees and heathery moorland, through the rainforest with the canopy of trees overhanging the track and back to Marangu Gate, the official entrance to the Kilimanjaro National Park were five 'wannabe Kili climbers' now proud owners of certificates confirming they are no longer 'wannabes'. Super Tara did make it to Gillmans Point but couldn't climb any further. She did indeed receive a certificate to confirm she reached the summit but not the 70 kilometres of walking and climbing to the highest peak. It seems that once you have climbed Mt Kilimanjaro you are in the 'know' and it is now fashionable to call it 'Kili'. Therefore, I have extreme pleasure to confirm I succeeded in climbing to the summit of Kili! Was it worth it? Yes, I believe it was even though I felt I had nearly died during the final ascent. To conquer such an epic climb under immense mental and physical pressure is a big achievement in my book. So well done Cheryl and Chris, even with your doctors and portable toilet.

Chapter 9

Chimp Tracking

My African adventure had started with such an awesome experience that I wondered whether it would be possible to match such an exploit. My next journey was to take me from Marangu to Nairobi and after a couple of lazy days lolling in the beautiful lawned gardens of the Marangu Hotel, my taxi had arrived to take me to Moshi where I would hop on the bus to Nairobi.

My taxi driver was a cheery guy who loved to chat about his beautiful home and Tanzania the country. His taxi was a rusted old Chevrolet Impala painted in a tan brown colour, or maybe that was just the layers of dirt and rust. The taxi ride should have taken only 45 minutes; however, as we bounced along the bumpy road a policeman at the side of the road beckoned the taxi driver to pull over. My friendly, smiling driver was not smiling anymore. As he parked up I started to think, is this because of the driver; did he do something wrong? Or is it me? Had my name been given to the police again? I am actually panicking as I know from experience how quickly a person can be arrested without any clue as to what offence has been committed.

They start a heated discussion and the driver was instructed to open his boot. I was starting to feel a little uneasy as the intense exchange between the two men continued. Eventually, my dejected taxi driver digs into his pocket to pay the policeman some bank notes. It's everywhere! All over the world backhanders are being paid to police officers. It scares me to think how the entire world revolves around illegal payments.

We eventually drive away and my taxi driver's smile and cheery disposition returned as he explained to me the problem. "There are many police checkpoints on Tanzanian roads that are specifically there to check your vehicle for a fire extinguisher. Every taxi driver should have one but they don't. The manufacturer has increased the price of the extinguishers so much that none of the drivers can afford to buy one. When the police were made aware of this they increased the number of checkpoints". My driver told me that it was cheaper to pay the backhander to the police than it is to buy a new fire extinguisher. How insane is that? I was just praying that there were no potential fire hazards with the taxi before I reached my destination.

Forty minutes later I am at the bus ticket office in Moshi. Ticket purchased, I boarded the shuttle bus to take one of the worst bus rides of my life. The main road to Nairobi was clearly still in its planning stages. It was a rollercoaster of potholes the size of Wales and rubble was strewn everywhere to add some extra bumps. With the nonstop jolting it felt like my organs had been thrown into a blender; one lung, kidney and heart smoothie coming up.

Having survived the rollercoaster bus ride I am seated in the nominated hotel meeting room in Nairobi ready to unite with my fellow travellers. I have chosen to use Intrepid for this leg of my African journey as they are specialists in overland adventures which seemed to fit my agenda in Africa. With the room now full the man at the front of the room, who was incessantly sniffing, introduced himself as Victor, the trip leader. He seemed pretty distant as he rambled on about campfires and bugs.

"It is Intrepid policy not to have campfires. You may not realise this but lots of live insects live in dry logs. If we used these logs for lighting campfires we would be murdering all the insects. It is Intrepid policy not to harm living insects, so, by not lighting campfires they can be conserved. It may seem a bit strange to you all but it is our strict policy not to kill insects".

By now all the paying passengers are getting restless in their seats, bewildered and perplexed by what Victor is telling us. We weren't interested in grasshoppers and beetles. We wanted to know about gorillas and lions. We had signed up to see giraffes, buffalo, mountain gorillas and leopards. Bugs were not on our list of 'must see' creatures.

A few days later, having taken in the scenic Kenyon surroundings and the breath-taking views of the Rift Valley, we entered Uganda. Our mission: to see wild chimpanzees. I was taken aback by how green and lush Uganda was. Different shades of green foliage everywhere. Uganda is a landlocked country bordered by Kenya, Southern Sudan, Rwanda and the Democratic Republic of the Congo. Embarrassingly, this is yet another African country that was ruled as a colony by the British in the late 1800's, however, Uganda gained independence from Britain on 9 October 1962.

Since then there have been so many intermittent conflicts and power struggles. The country's leader, Milton Obote was toppled by dictator Idi Amin in 1971 who brutally ruled Uganda with the military for the next eight years and carried out mass killings to ensure his power. Obote returned as President in 1980 and was then ousted again in another coup in 1985. And so it goes on. The most recent civil war against the Lord's Resistance Army has again resulted in thousands of deaths in Northern Uganda and over 1.4 million people displaced from their homes. Other humanitarian issues prevalent are child labour, slavery and torture, just to name a few.

The most recent controversial news to come out of Uganda was President Museveni's new anti-gay bill that increased the punishment for homosexual acts to include the death penalty. Due to global opposition to this outrageous law the final bill put into place in February 2014 had the death penalty replaced by life imprisonment. Life imprisonment? How bigoted is that legislation? I take it Elton John will not be including Kampala as a venue on his next world tour?

What about all the other monstrosities happening in the country? Is new legislation not required for them?

My focus, however, was not on history or politics as the Intrepid truck trundled along the scenic roads, it was the chimps; those entertaining hairy, human-like animals that eat bananas and drink cups of tea in the PG Tips tea television commercials. Our destination was Kibale National Park, Southern Uganda, 300km west of the capital, Kampala.

On arrival at the National Park, before we embarked in chimp tracking, we were split into groups of five. I was with three Aussies and a Canadian. Fenella and Georgie sounds like a supermarket clothing brand name but they were, in fact, nurses from Sydney travelling together for five weeks. Fenella was like an Aussie version of Pamela Anderson with long wavy blonde hair, a golden tan and a voice that made her sound ten years old. I assume the sweet little voice was her calming patient's tone that had taken a number of years to master.

Georgie on the other hand had more of an Audrey Hepburn look with dark long hair and pale skin. Her fashion trademark was a trilby hat like Schapelle Corby wore when she was released from prison. They both always looked so clean and fresh. Their manicured hands and feet were immaculate. I needed to get some tips from these girls to improve my 'tent hair' look and grubby fingernails.

Rachel, also an Aussie, was quiet as a mouse. A tiny, petite woman who seemed so frightened and fragile, which was unfortunate for me as she was my tent partner. Her skills at pitching and dismantling a tent were limited.

Then there was Ali, a no-nonsense Canadian girl who was an outdoorswoman, into her kayaking and hiking. Again, her maple leafed backpack clearly indicated her Canadian roots.

Our chimp tracker for the day was a local guide called Julian. Most African men seem to have old fashioned English names and I cannot say why. Is it to do with colonialism? I am assuming they also have an African name that has meaning and represents their roots and traditions. A more likely reason for the English names is to assist the intellectually challenged tourists in actually remembering and pronouncing their names correctly.

Julian was a very articulate young guide and proceeded to give us information about Kibale National Park and the star attractions, the chimps.

"Kibale National Park is 795km squared and is one the last remaining tropical forests in Uganda" said Julian.

This was all very interesting but what we really wanted to know was what our chances were of seeing the cute human like creatures Julian continued, "There are almost 1,500 chimpanzees here at Kibale which makes it the largest population of endangered primates in East Africa. You have a ninety five percent chance of spotting them".

Ninety five percent! That's high. We all looked at each other in acknowledgement of this high percentage, beaming from cheek to cheek. Julian went on to tell us that they nest up in the trees so it is unlikely for us to see any on the ground. Oh dear. The trees in this National Park looked awfully high. Even if we did spot one it could be just that. A spot!

Julian then instructs us to pull up our socks and tuck our trousers into them. We all dutifully bend down to follow his instructions now looking like we have walked off the set of 'Last of the Summer Wine' with our 'Compo' style bottoms. Fenella and Georgie were not looking quite so glamorous now. Apparently the forest has a lot of ants on the ground which can easily get up your trouser legs and can be rather painful when they start to bite your flesh. Especially if there is an army of them!

Julian then leads us into the forest to track the chimpanzees. We have to keep quiet as we tramp through the foliage searching for the elusive chimps, looking up to the roof of the trees rather than the ground. This way of walking is unquestionably ludicrous as we are stumbling around, tripping on tree roots and rocks, unaware of where or what we are placing our feet onto. We were in line, one behind the other and every so often Fenella would turn around and grin at me to show her excitement, as talking had been prohibited whilst chimp tracking. I returned the silent communication with a big cheesy grin of my own indicating I felt the same way. We had been traipsing through the forest for what seemed like ages when Julian held up his hand to halt the procession.

There was a chimp on the ground! Then in a flash it was gone. Damn it. Julian fastened his pace, his cortege of novice chimp trackers close on his heels. Julian had suddenly veered off the established track and we were now grappling with wayward branches and vines to fight our way through the forest. The hand of Julian rose again and we all halted in a clumsy collision, our hearts racing with the prospect of a chimp encounter.

"Do you hear that drumming noise?" whispered Julian. In the distance we could hear a beat like a muffled drum. "That's the chimpanzees communicating to each other". He pointed to one of the many large, root-exposed trees. "They are hitting these tree buttresses with their hands and feet to communicate. It is like a telephone for them to let their family know their location. They could be over a kilometre away". The rapid beating got louder and louder. I had never heard anything like it before. The forest seemed to tremble from the vibration of the drum beat. My own body trembled from the magnitude of the drumming, booming through the forest. Fenella's jaw dropped as she turned to look at me, her eyes the size of saucers. The beating was now at full volume, penetrating the whole forest... and our eardrums. The tree canopies seemed to shake in tune with the beat. Then the drumming stopped. The chimps had finished phoning home. Next came a soft "hoo, hoo, hoo, haa, haa, haa".

"This is their vocal communication to their community members to bring their attention to potential danger or food sources" Julian informed us.

The "hoo hoo hoos" increased in volume, building up to a crescendo of screams. The screaming got louder and louder and louder. It was so ear-piercing at the climax of the screaming that I had to put my hands over my ears. At this point all our jaws had dropped as we stared at each other in awe at this incredible experience. It sent shivers down my spine. I had never experienced anything quite like it. The volume of the chimps screaming was remarkable. You don't hear them doing this in the PG Tips teabag television commercials do you?

The screaming gradually died down to a soft "hoo hoo hoo" again, eventually stopping altogether. We all just stood there in wonderment at what we had just heard. It was astonishing.

Julian, clearly pleased by the chimps' show, beckoned us to continue tracking. He was close to spotting some chimps, I could feel it. As Julian craned his neck he pointed up into the trees and there they were, two chimps sitting up high on a branch watching us. Then three, then four. Julian pointed out a mother chimp with her baby clinging onto her chest. He was so cute with his wide, startled look, shrinking even more into the safety of his mother's chest.

We were all mesmerised by these human like hairy creatures. Their facial expressions and gestures so uncannily like humans, but seeing that they are the closest relative to humans then this should be no surprise. Our necks were straining under the constant craning backwards to get a better sighting of the chimps. As if bored by our stares the chimps start to swing from tree to tree across the forest canopy. They are so agile. The accuracy in which they caught a stray branch or vine and catapulted themselves onto another tree was remarkable. The swishing and rustling movement was so loud, as the weight of their bodies crashed into the foliage. Some branches looked so precarious it appeared uncertain whether or not they would fracture and break from the strain.

What seemed like an age gazing up to the treetops watching the chimps our time was up and we eventually had to return to the established track which took us back to the National Park headquarters.

Our training was complete. We were now primed, or so we thought, to go tracking again but next time it would be for the mountain gorillas in Rwanda. Since seeing Sigourney Weaver play Dian Fossey in the film 'Gorillas in the Mist', I had a desire to come to Rwanda to see the giant creatures in their natural mountain habitat for myself; to see the legacy of Dian Fossey and her work to save the endangered gorillas.

Chapter 10

Gorillas in the Mist

Rwanda has had a violent history with many conflicts and one of the most horrific mass genocides ever seen. This all took place whilst the rest of the world just stood by and watched it happen.

The original inhabitants of Rwanda were the Twa Pygmies who were joined by the migrating Hutu tribes people – then the Tutsi. For centuries Rwanda then existed under the Tutsi monarchy until the late 1800's when colonial Germany took control. This was lost during World War I when the country was placed under Belgium administration. The Belgians then effectively turned the Hutu-Tutsi relationship into a class system. The minority Tutsi were favoured over the Hutus and given all the power and privileges, while the Hutus were subjected to slave labour and a peasant like existence which deteriorated over the years. In 1957, the Hutus urgently demanded some form of radical changes, then, in 1959, following the death of their ruler, Mwami Matara III, the Tutsi-tribes people seized power and started killing Hutu leaders. This led to an uprising within the Hutu population resulting in a campaign of Hutu violence against the Tutsis. This ethnic conflict escalated to extremity when, in 1994, President Habiyarimana was assassinated. The Hutu leader, who had been in power for 21 years, was allegedly killed by extremist Hutus as part of a plot to blame the Tutsis, thus giving the government a reason to rid the country of all Tutsis. But this theory has never actually been proved. The bloodshed that followed was one of the worst humanitarian crises the world had ever seen.

In just a period of 100 days the Hutus had brutally murdered approximately 800,000 Tutsis using not bullets, as they were pricey, but machetes, clubs and knives. Due to all Rwandans having an identity card labelling them Hutu, Tutsi or Twa, the government could seek them out, door to door, and kill them. Even the thousands of Tutsis who sought sanctuary in churches were found and murdered inside the holy buildings themselves.

As the Tutsis were hunted and brutally murdered, the world just stood by and watched. No aid was offered. Not by one single country.

As the Intrepid truck entered Rwanda we were all very much conscious of the brutal history and suffering endured by the Rwandan people. We even visited the Kigali Genocide Memorial Centre in the capital city. The centre is actually built on a site where up to 250,000 genocide victims were buried in mass graves. It's a heart wrenching place. Video clips of Rwandans telling their personal accounts of horrific loss and suffering. Did you know that even after the genocide the killing of Tutsis continued in the refugee camps in Zaire? That is if they didn't die first from the cholera epidemic that also swept through the camps.

As we make our way onto Ruhengeri, which is approximately 220 kilometres from the Parc National Des Volcans, our solemn moods lift and are replaced by the thoughts of big, black, furry gorillas. These animals are no chimps. They are much larger and they are ground based animals. There will be no craning of necks to see these giants. No racing through wayward branches and vines, getting ripped to shreds for a glimpse. No, this will be a close up and personal encounter – we hoped.

Our accommodation in Ruhengeri was a dormitory at a local church mission. The building looked like an old American motel, a flat single storey building with doors leading into each dormitory in the shape of a 'U'. There was what looked like a vegetable patch in the middle but it could possibly have been weeds. The dormitory was a large room which had twelve bunk beds that precariously swayed and squeaked with the movement of just your little toe. It was very clean but I wouldn't have expected anything less; as the saying goes 'cleanliness is next to godliness', and this was a church mission. The first night was a hive of activity in the dormitory as we all unpacked, my trusty backpack still my loyal travelling companion. Finally, the last plastic bag rustler had finished what sounded like a major overhaul of their whole backpack contents and the lights went out. There was a lot of squeaking and clonking noises as people adjusted their positions in a futile attempt to get comfortable on their chosen bunk bed.

One of my travel companions, Ali, then starts laughing, "Guys you are not gonna believe this! Check out the back wall. Can you see it?"

It sounded like a freight train racing through the room as everyone moved in sync, the bunk beds creaking and clunking under the strain of their manoeuvres, to look at the wall. There, high up near the ceiling, or maybe I should say heaven, was a glow in the dark Jesus looking down on us. Perhaps we should have made the sign of the cross or said a prayer but we just laughed. It was so unexpected and the fact that the church mission had thought of placing a Jesus on the wall for visiting guests to see all day and all night just tickled us. Actually, I have to admit no-one even noticed Jesus when it was daylight. After the uncontrollable giggling and laughing died down and we all said our goodnights again, I did say a little prayer to the glow in the dark Jesus to ask if he would ensure that we saw lots of gorillas in the Volcanoes National Park.

The next day was an early start as we needed to be at the Volcanoes National Park entrance before the 'tours' began at 7 o'clock. The Intrepid truck was having a rest so we were being transported to the entrance by jeeps. The Volcanoes National Park merges with three countries; Rwanda, Uganda and the Democratic Republic of the Congo, and derives its name from the impressive chain of Virunga volcanoes. There are mountains all over Rwanda and it is so green and lush everywhere. This is where Dian Fossey studied her beloved gorillas and one group in particular, the Susa group who live high up in the mountains. Ali, the no nonsense Canadian, and I had a pact that when the park rangers assigned eight people to each gorilla group, we would put ourselves forward for the long trek to see the infamous Susa group. No nonsense Ali was up for the task. We were not just going to put ourselves forward but, if needed, throw ourselves at the ranger's feet or chain ourselves to the 'Susa' jeep. Whatever it took we were prepared to do it.

With our secret pact cemented, we hopped onto one of the jeeps that had arrived at the church mission to take us to the park entrance. We were excitedly chatting to the three elderly Canadians that were travelling on the Intrepid truck with us. They were all retired, in their sixties and wanting a bit of adventure. Good on them is what I say, but there is no way I am getting into the same gorilla tracking jeep that they choose. However adventurous they are there is no chance of the rangers picking three old aged pensioners to do the long, hard trek to see the Susa group. An English girl, Hannah, was also in the jeep. I had had some decent conversations with Hannah, however, she did have a tendency to be over zealous with her camera which had created a lot of animosity and embarrassment to the whole group, with local people waving their fists at her in fury at her incessant photo taking. No consideration given as to whether these people actually want or like their picture being taken.

The entrance gate to the Volcanoes National Park had a big metal gate with a giant gorilla statue at the side. The statue was made out of metal and the detail that had been etched into the creation of the gorilla's face and body was exceptional. Ali, Hannah and I decide this is a good photo opportunity, if nothing else, we could tell people that this was a real life gorilla if we didn't actually see any live gorillas as the statue was so life-like. In turn we clambered onto the metal gorilla to pose for our 'gorilla' pictures. One photo taken of me looks like I was doing something indecent to the gorilla as I clung onto the shiny surface trying not to slide off. Not one for the album. Hannah and Ali also mounted the gorilla for the 'just in case' photos. Hannah then starts jumping and hopping like she's standing on hot coals.

"Oh my god. I'm being bitten all up my legs. Ouch!! Ouuucchhh!!! It's really hurting. I've got frigging ants all over me!" Then, like a viral disease spreading through the air, Ali started shouted "Shit shit! Get off you buggers!" Then I saw the ground moving with hundreds of red ants. I quickly jumped to safety from the little biting pests. Hannah and Ali were jumping around slapping their legs in a desperate attempt to squash the little buggers. Perhaps my prayer to the glow in the dark Jesus had saved me from the wrath of the ants? Poor Hannah and Ali had to dance, skip and hop to the nearest toilet to strip off their clothes to rid themselves of the hundreds of ants that were devouring their legs.

As we congregated around the Headquarter's entrance buildings we tried to stand near young, athletic looking people in preparation for the gorilla group selection. Then Victor, the insect loving Intrepid leader, calmly strolled over and told us that whoever was in the jeep with us on the journey here would be in our gorilla tracking group. What?! No way! This can't be happening. Ali looked at me in horror. "But the three older Canadians have made it clear to us that they do not wish to do a long trek to see the gorillas. Man, this sucks!" Victor gave us a sheepish look and shrugged as if to say 'looks like you will be doing a short trek to the nearest gorilla group'. Our hearts sank. Clearly my prayer to the glow in the dark Jesus did not work with gorillas. Just ants. A ranger came over and started to tell us about the gorillas.

"There are 19 families of gorillas in the Volcanoes National Park, ten of which can be seen by tourists. The remaining nine are accessed only by scientists and researchers. A maximum of 8 people can visit each gorilla group per day spending a maximum of one hour each visit. Due to gorillas being so genetically close to humans there is a risk that we can infect them with human diseases." He went on to show us photos of the different gorillas in each of the families including the Susa group.

"The Susa group is the most famous gorilla group as this is the one studied by Dian Fossey. This family is the hardest to trek to as it tends to habitat in the higher part of the mountain. Our trackers have confirmed they are located about a four hour uphill trek away from the park entrance. This challenging trek is only suitable for fit, experienced hikers. There is a lot of dense undergrowth and much bending and crawling will be needed to get through the bamboo forest. Then there are the nettles to get through to where the gorillas have stopped. It is extremely strenuous."

Ali and I glanced at each other with a knowing look. We both knew we had to get into the 'Susa syndicate'. At this point we were prepared to thump, kick and even kill, to get ourselves into this trekking group. The ranger continued as if teasing us with more Susa titbits.

"The Susa group is very impressive with a family size of 28 gorilla members including 3 silverbacks. It was the largest group before it split into two. The group used to have 42 members. The oldest known habituated gorilla is also in this group. Poppy was born in 1976 and is from the very original group of gorillas that Dian Fossey studied."

He then showed us all a picture of Poppy; a brown haired elderly gorilla. There were photos of other Susa members ranging from babies and juveniles to young males and silverbacks. The Susa family looked so cute. I had to see them in their furry flesh. Perhaps not eye to eye as direct eye contact is perceived as a threat by the gorillas, or a challenge. He then went on to warn us of the arduous hike that will take us over 2,800 metres (9,300 feet) to see the Susa group which will impact on breathing and can be a major challenge to persons not accustomed to higher altitudes.

Ha! I think my recent high altitude experience should be enough training for me to handle this negligible height. I personally was more concerned about disgruntled silverbacks feeling threatened by our presence, wanting to protect their fellow gorillas no matter what it took.

Finally, he got to the gorilla group assignments. My lips had gone dry and my heart was pounding with the suspense of the Susa selection. Ali and I had at this point actually held hands in readiness to make a run together to the 'Susa syndicate' spot. Looking around we could see other Susa groupies getting ready to sprint when the ranger called out. It was tense. At that moment in time nothing else mattered apart from getting into the 'Susa syndicate'.

"I would now suggest that the fittest people come forward to the long trek to see the Susa group".

In a flash, Ali and I darted to the front at the same time as ten other people. No-one was budging. Four people had to go. The atmosphere was tense. It was going to take an army to persuade me and Ali to move. "Don't move" whispered Ali. Our stance clearly indicated we were not going to be ousted from our position in the Susa syndicate.

"There are too many people. Four of you will need to move to another group" declared the ranger who was seemingly oblivious to the Susa battle that was taking place right under his eyes. We all stood there, our feet firmly planted on Susa ground for what seemed an age. "Quickly please. Can four people move to another group" insisted the ranger. Ali and I looked at each other silently cementing our pact again. Phew! At the last moment four people begrudgingly dragged themselves to another group, not before casting a hateful glance over the Susa champions. Hurray! My prayer continues to perform. Thank you glow in the dark Jesus.

The Susa champions set off in our quest to seek out the Susa group. Included in the elite group along with myself and Ali were Fenella and Georgie with their trousers tucked into the socks again due to the ever encroaching ants. Hannah with her third eye – and I don't mean her ability to see what might be –I am referring to her actual camera lens. Then there was also a married couple from England that I remember from his tall height and the fact that his head seemed to keep appearing in all my gorilla pictures.

The initial trek was a very gentle thirty minute walk uphill through fields of farmers crops which led us to a forest cordoned off by a small dry stone wall. There, waiting for us, was a tracker dressed in full army combat clothing carrying a rifle. There was a small gap in the wall which was the very modest, but official entrance, to the Volcanoes National Park. Our ranger then told us how we should meet and greet our furry friends.

"The gorillas are extremely passive and shy creatures. They rarely attack humans but if a disgruntled gorilla approaches you, should stay still and refrain from looking directly into the eyes of the gorilla".

He is now looking at eight increasingly concerned faces. The male silverbacks, which there are three of in the Susa group, can weigh over 200 kilograms, that's 30 stone. Standing on hind legs he can be up to 1.7 metres, the equivalent to 5 feet and 6 inches. A playful swipe of their arm could kill you outright. This was serious stuff. The ranger's walkie talkie then crackled and hissed into life and, after a brief interaction with his handset, he tells us that the gorillas are on the move.

"Don't worry. There are two trackers with the gorillas as we speak. They will follow the gorillas to their next location. You will see them today. No problem." the ranger assured us. "Let's continue".

We forged ahead, through the tiny dry stone opening into the forest. This was not your usual forest full of trees, this was a bamboo forest. This grass is one of the fastest growing plants on earth. It can grow to heights of over thirty metres. It was very challenging having to bend and crawl under giant stems, our backpacks getting tangled with the wayward shoots. Our reactions needed to be quick in order to duck and dive in an attempt to avoid getting smacked in the face by a branch or even worse, a bamboo shoot. The bamboo forest was so dense that not much light could filter through. The forest then gave way to the lush, green mountainside, but to our horror, the lush vegetation was giant nettles. They were enormous! Talk about Roald Dahl's 'James and the Giant Peach', this was 'Sharon and the Humongous Nettles'. They towered above our heads, the leaves the size of hands, ready for the sting.

"Oh gosh!" gasped Fenella "I've never seen nettles this big before!" Fenella is from Australia where celery sticks are as long as your arm and capsicums are the size of heads, so, if she thought they were big then they must be very big indeed.

The ranger and tracker had come prepared with machetes to hack through the nettles and make a very rustic path for us to use, but, however hard we tried it was impossible to avoid getting stung by the giant weeds. The African sun beat down on us as we clambered through the dense vegetation, stumbling on vines and roots as we made our way up the increasingly steeper slope. "Gosh, this is tougher than I thought it would be" I said to Ali as a giant nettle swings dangerously close to my eye. "I know. Gee, these nettles are really stinging me. With the ant bites and nettle stings I am gonna be a wreck before I've even seen a bloody gorilla" replied Ali, while dodging a wayward branch.

The three men who had spent the night tracking the gorillas appeared before us in the bush, squatting next to their rifles. The ranger, after speaking with the trackers, beckoned us further into the bush and then right there in front of us were a group of gorillas. It was unbelievable. There was no chase. No craning of necks to try and spot them in the trees. They were just there, right in front of us having a relaxing afternoon in the sun. There must have been around a dozen gorillas. Some were snoozing, others were snacking on pieces of bamboo. The kids were playing in the grass, tumbling and rollicking, their antics being carefully watched by their doting mother. A couple of juveniles were swinging on a vine, passing time on a sunny afternoon. We were stood just a few metres away, watching all of this unfold. It was inconceivable that here I was stood in the Rwandan mountains sharing my afternoon amidst wild gorillas. They were so human like with their facial expressions and bodily gestures, but not surprising seeing that ninety eight percent of their DNA is identical to that of humans.

It was all so peaceful and surreal. The gorillas accepted us standing feet away from them as if we were guests that had been invited to an afternoon gorilla picnic. Anyone for bamboo stick? Perhaps a piece of crunchy bark or juicy stem? Their brown eyes inquisitive but gentle. The juveniles were playful, like toddlers, and had mischievous glints in their eyes. It was as if they were daring us to come and play with them. I so wanted to play with them. Ruffle their fluffy black fur and tickle their stomachs to make them laugh even more. They were so cute. I wanted to stay with these gentle giants forever. Suddenly my gorilla picnic bubble burst as a silverback stood up on his back legs and made a loud burst of short deep guttural noises. He puffed out his chest which was over a metre in size and beat it with his open hands making a loud hollow thud that seemed to echo around us. The male silverback is the biggest and heaviest of all living primates. This show of aggression was somewhat worrying considering we were only a few feet away from him. One of the trackers began making a similar guttural noise but a longer throaty sound, a much calmer tone.

"The tracker is communicating with the silverback and letting him know we are his friends and not a threat" whispered our ranger.

I wasn't totally convinced that this small man, squatting in the foliage making grunting noises, was going to control a wild, disgruntled gorilla. The male silverback is the leader of the group who is in charge of protecting the group members from predators or rival silverbacks. I got the distinct impression from his chest slapping and teeth baring gestures that we had been placed into the initial category of predator. The tracker continued to grunt whilst crouching in the bush, playing with bits of grass as if he was bored by the whole conversation with the silverback. My heart was pounding off the scale. Did anyone here know how to control a wild silverback gorilla?

The silverback was now on all fours doing the knuckle-walk which does sound like he was performing a cheesy eighties dance move but this is their actual walk. All the pressure is on his hand knuckles with his fingers rolled into his hand. He was making a beeline for us. There was no question that his intention was to approach us. The predators!

Oh my god. Who was controlling this situation? Where have the rifles gone? Our tracker then said "there is nothing more I can do now". What?! There is nothing more he can do? He had a rifle for god's sake. Why hasn't he got it ready? Who is controlling this situation? "Keep still and you must not look him in the eyes. This is very important. Do not look him in the eyes" instructed our ranger who was now not looking quite as self-assured.

The silverback was now right in front of us. I believe at this point I had actually stopped breathing. We were now a bunch of trembling imbeciles wondering why on earth we had chosen to track down wild gorillas. Who in their right mind wants to stand in front of a dozen gorillas who are the biggest and heaviest of all living primates? The silverback swaggered past us all within inches of our bodies. His shoulders the size of footballs and his arms like tree trunks. Muscles bulged from his body like a hairy version of Popeye. Even his forehead looked like it had muscle growth, or perhaps that was just excess hair.

Once the silverback had aired his show of dominance to each of us he then sauntered back to his troop, his head held high as if to say 'it's alright ladies. I have shown them who is boss'. Our ranger then explained, in what I can only describe as a relieved voice, that this was just a bravado display by the silverback to demonstrate to his troop that he can protect them.

The silverback had now slumped back down onto the floor looking like the dominance parade had worn him out. With the power display over, the juveniles had returned to their latest pastime which was grooming. This is where they inspect each other's hair; their fingers burying deep into the fur and parting clumps of hair to scrutinise each tiny area. Picking out what looked like imaginary specks but were in reality probably dead skin or parasites.

All too soon our hour chilling with the gorillas was up. It was heart wrenching to leave the gentle giants. I just wanted to cuddle up with the baby gorillas and stay the night. Exhilarated with our gorilla encounter we skipped back through the humongous nettles, bamboo forest and modest dry stone wall official park entrance to the farmland and then onto the park headquarters. That night back, at the church mission dormitory, we were all excitedly chatting about our exploits with the gorillas and our near death experience with the angry silverback. After lights out I whispered a little thank you to the glow in the dark Jesus. I reckoned that as it worked last time there was no harm in trying it one more time, so I also cheekily sneaked in another prayer for us to see the 'Big Five' on the next part of our African journey. Thank you glow in the dark Jesus.

Chapter 11

Uganda...again

As we crossed the border back into Uganda I felt a tinge of sadness leaving Rwanda and its beautiful lush countryside. The mountain gorillas were fascinating to watch and it was an honour for them to allow us to occupy their territory. The macho silverback was an added adrenalin bonus to the gorilla spectacle, however, I do shudder to think what could've happened if he genuinely perceived us as predators. The newspaper headlines would've been 'Eight tourists infringe on gorillas provoking silverback into attack' or 'Eight tourists dead as a silverback protects his family from predators... they should've known better'. It would be just like the Indonesian teaching saga 'English teacher jailed for working on tourist visa... she must've known it was illegal'.

Uganda is just as lush and green as Rwanda. Every tourist who ventures into Uganda will no doubt visit Jinja which is where the Intrepid truck was heading. Jinja is comparable with Queenstown in New Zealand or Victoria Falls in Zimbabwe. It is the adrenaline adventure capital of East Africa. Instead of white-water rafting on the Zambezi you raft in the grade five rapids on the river Nile.

It is also famous for being the location of the source of the Nile River. This sounded like it was going to be an amazing sight to see, I mean, the Nile is the longest river in the entire world! After arriving in Jinja we headed out to see this natural wonder. There are two main rivers that form the River Nile; the White Nile and the Blue Nile. The White Nile is much bigger and Jinja is where it all begins. Expectations were high. This was going to be an incredible natural phenomenon but as we approached we did wonder if we were actually at the right spot.

"Is this it?" mumbled Ali who, being Canadian, is no doubt used to seeing some spectacular rapids and waterfalls during her hiking and kayaking jaunts. Fenella and Georgie also looked extremely unimpressed, their Aussie roots expecting a big water show as everything is big Down Under.

"Are we at the right spot?" asked Fenella, "should we check with someone?"

What we were looking at was a regular river with a mini rapid and a few trees dotted here and there. I could've been looking at the River Thames or perhaps the River Aire in Leeds after a bout of rain. I would not have believed we were facing the source of the River Nile had it not been for the plaque rooted in the ground nearby that clearly stated the words *'This spot marks the place from where the Nile starts its long journey to the Mediterranean Sea through central and northern Uganda, Sudan and Egypt.'* Slightly dejected, we decided to locate the other 'source' of the Nile, the Nile Special Lager, which is brewed in Jinja and was much more satisfying than looking at a river.

That evening, while sipping even more source of the Nile Special lagers at the campsite bar, we were introduced to three young lads who were labelled as 'international rafting guides'. They looked like they had just arrived from a surfing session at Bondi Beach, flicking their sun bleached locks, their trousers seemingly a few sizes too big as they hung from their hips revealing the elasticated bands of their Calvin Klein underpants. Is this really necessary? Surely it must be a pain to be pulling up your trousers all day in an attempt to ensure they don't fall to your ankles? To have the crotch and backside sagging halfway down your legs and practically dragging along the ground must be bothersome. The 'international rafting guides' clearly obtained their international status by being Australian and of course, there was the token Kiwi, but I can never tell the difference in their accents. I keep getting told by Australians that their accents are nothing like New Zealanders who they say talk in clipped, short tones. It is like me asking an Australian to tell me who is from Leeds and who is from Manchester just by listening to a couple of sentences. It is impossible to a foreigner. If I asked them to differentiate between a Mancunian and a Glaswegian then that would be noticeable beyond a doubt. For one thing you would not be able to understand a word of what is being said by the Glaswegian. It wouldn't be unreasonable for an Australian to think that a Glaswegian might be from another non-English speaking country altogether. A shot in the dark guess could end up being a remote place somewhere in the middle of Inner Mongolia. The cool dudes then gave us an in depth talk about the hair-raising rafting on offer in the spectacular White Nile at Jinja, one of the world's top spots for grade five white water rafting.

"Guys, get ready for the most exhilarating white water rafting you have ever experienced. Man it is the dogs" cooed one of the international rafting guides.

"I'm so pumped" exclaimed sporty Ali "it sounds awesome! I will definitely be putting my name down for that". Personally, I am not very competent at extreme water activities, or any form of water activities to be honest, which I blame on a childhood full of ear issues. With grommets thrust into my ears from an early age it made swimming virtually impossible. A grommet may sound like a cartoon dog with a friend called Wallace but these were like miniature plastic cotton reels surgically placed in your ear drum to help maintain normal middle ear pressure in your ears. A hole through the centre of the reel allows air through to your middle ear but it also lets water run straight in which can cause infections. I remember trying to use swimming earplugs that clearly a wannabe Dragons Den contender had the ingenious idea of making, which was a shaped like the inside of an ear and was about as effective as an inflatable darts board. This meant I was no Michael Phelps and my swimming skills were as questionable as my teaching skills. This was why I chose one of the alternative adventure activities on offer that did not involve the risk of being thrown out of a raft and engulfed by rapids or even worse, death by drowning. I chose quad biking as this undoubtedly did not involve any form of water torture and my feet, well, technically my wheels, would be on firm ground.

Fenella and Georgie also chose the all terrain vehicle (ATV) safari having likewise decided that their rafting survival skills were paltry and insufficient for the Nile rapids. Two other Intrepid travellers, Charlotte and Graham, had also chosen the quad biking. They were a couple from Devon who were very unassuming and spoke in that lovely West Country accent that was so warm and welcoming. Like an idiot I did test out my West Country accent on them by saying "I'd like a pint of Scrumpy Jack please" which they politely said wasn't bad for a Yorkshire lass. I did regret the outburst and made a mental note to myself not to be such a jerk and to ensure that I needed to rectify their opinion of me which at that time must've been along the lines of 'what a moron'.

The following morning, after breakfast, we boldly walked down the street to the quad biking headquarters to begin our off-road adventure. The fearless five go forth. We were met by a very tall, bald headed man who looked like he would struggle to even fit on a small quad bike never mind drive one. There was basically an accelerator and a brake on the automatic ATVs which pleased me no end. Anything more complicated would have got me all flummoxed and muddled, which I would liken to trying to assemble IKEA furniture or finding a document that has gone 'missing' from the computer. After being nominated a quad bike each we were then taken to be dressed appropriately. The garment we all had to wear was a camel coloured boilersuit which felt, and looked like, it was ten sizes too big for me. The black helmets were the old fashioned type that looked like they had raided a tenpin bowling alley and swiped all the tenpin balls for them to be sliced in half. It even had the 'finger holes' positioned on the crown of your head for ventilation. Then, looking like we had just stepped out of a book, 'Biggles Learns to Quad Bike', we were provided with metal rimmed goggles, which in all likelihood made us look more like Despicable Me Minions than Biggles. The final touch was a black bandana to tie across our faces in what ended to be a futile attempt not to get dust in our mouths and up our noses. We ended up looking like a bunch of wannabe robbers! Thank goodness our overalls weren't blue or else we would most certainly have been mistaken for Minions.

After a quick spin on the practice circuit, the fearless five bandits were primed and allegedly proficient to enter the outside world on our all terrain vehicles. We raced single file out of the practice circuit onto the dirt road generating a swirling cloud of red dust as our tyres disturbed the settled earth. Our bandanas tied back from the bridge of our noses evidently having no real use aside from making us look like bandits. Our mouths and nostrils now operating like vacuum cleaners sucking in the fine particles of red dust, making our nostrils clogged and our mouths feel like fine sandpaper. We sped through farmland, with crops growing at either side of the track that towered above our heads like Jack's giant beanstalk.

It was all a blur as we sped past the giant crops and tiny villages. Along the riverbank trails following the Nile River downstream to Bujagala Falls which was really a series of rapids rather than an actual waterfall. Our quad bikes were bouncing in all directions as our wheels vaulted from every uneven surface on the trails, which was pretty much every inch of the terrain. Our bodies jerked up and down and snapped from side to side like shaken dice. Charlotte and I were at the back of the convoy. Now this certainly wasn't a race and equally there was no winner, nonetheless, this form of activity brings out the competitive streak in people. There was a grim determination on everyone's face which undoubtedly exposed their desire to 'win'.

Charlotte then gave me a little wave as she increased her speed to inch past me, her pitch, not to be 'last'. I was actually impressed that she had even managed to lift her hand off the handlebar to wave considering the incessant bobbing up and down and hurtling from side to side. In my resolve to curb

Charlotte's lead over me I pressed hard on my accelerator only to have the quad bike stall on me. God damn it! Why was this happening now? There was no clutch work involved. Why had the engine stopped? I could feel myself getting flustered. Panic creeping in at the thought of not just being last but being a farcical last. After a few attempts and many obscenities the quad bike spluttered and shuddered into action. Hurray! The other minions were now specks in the distance. At that moment nothing else mattered. My sole mission: to advance swiftly and rejoin the fearless five. 'Last' was not something I was going to consider. Eagerly I squeezed the accelerator hard forcing my quad bike to surge forwards, the wheels spinning on the dusty track. My obsessive zeal to catch up was so intense, any rational thoughts as to my safety had been eradicated. I had to catch up. I had to. My body was thrown in every direction like a cowboy on a bucking bronco. My hands gripped so tightly to the handlebars I felt blisters forming between my thumb and index finger. The quad bike seemed to be wheezing and groaning as it raced down the track. Charlotte's head was getting bigger as I gradually closed the gap with my erratic driving in my stubborn pursuit to rejoin my fellow minions. This is what it must feel like to be Lewis Hamilton, the Formula One racing driver. Nothing else mattered but 'winning'. Simply not 'losing' would be a respectable result for me.

Was everyone slowing down or was I speeding up? Charlotte's head size was increasing at an alarming rate. To my relief Charlotte's head was not enlarged and she was not suffering from any serious medical condition. She had indeed stopped. Everyone had stopped. This was our designated refreshment stop, a local trading centre for a cold drink. Back home in England a trading centre would probably include a McDonald's, Kentucky Fried Chicken, Argos, Marks & Spencer, WHSmith and other well known branded stores and food outlets. In rural Uganda a local trading centre is three or four shops on the side of the red dirt road. Flat roofed brick buildings, mostly with a layer of faded paint. Weathered slatted wooden doors opened like shutters revealing the shop's ware and fare. Sun bleached posters were displayed on the walls and doors advertising soda drinks and confectionary. Everywhere the yellow and blue logo of the MTN Uganda mobile network was hanging from the sheets of corrugated iron that act as a shelter for the customers visiting the shops.

Ice cold drinks were purchased and immediately guzzled, our throats parched from the copious amount of red dust hoovered up through our mouths and nostrils. The sun was unrepentant as it beat down on our boiler suited bodies. Having taken off our goggles we were starting to resemble a colony of baby emperor penguins with white circles around our eyes where the goggles had protected them from the red dust. Our faces looking very much like we had spent the day basking too long in the sun.

When I wasn't acting like Evel Knievel, performing death-defying quad bike stunts in my stubborn determination to catch up, I could take time to marvel at the beautiful scenery. The landscape was so lush and so green with trees and vegetation everywhere. The stunning Nile River wound through the land like a snake. The vibrant red dirt brought another dimension to the surroundings. Huddled together in tiny villages were small round mud houses with cone-shaped roofs made of straw or banana leaves which were the homes of the locals. We saw children laughing and playing on the dirt paths. Some were playing with sticks and tyres as they raced against each other while trying to control the tyre and keep it rolling by using just the stick. It was very humbling to watch knowing that back home a child's letter to Father Christmas would include a request for an iPad, the latest smart phone and an Xbox games console. Not a tyre or stick in sight unless it came as part of a designer mountain bike or an iPad keyboard stick.

Back at the quad bike headquarters we were all covered from head to toe in red dust with the exception of our white ringed eyes. Fenella and Georgie were no longer the picture of immaculateness. Their freshness replaced by red dirt and helmet hair. I made sure I took a photo of their transformation, if only to console myself on tent hair days and with my permanent grimy fingernails that they can look like grungy travellers too.

Graham, who by the way came 'first', was grinning from ear to ear, clearly delighted with his 'win'. In my defence at coming 'last', I did experience some engine complications which inevitably slowed me down. I graciously acknowledged his victory and swallowed any petty feelings of bitterness as everyone else commented on his outstanding quad biking performance. I did read somewhere that Jinja is the place for the adrenaline junkie and the eco conscious traveller. I agree with the adrenaline junkie statement, who wouldn't? You have the top two thrill seekers dream pastimes, bungee jumping and grade five white water rafting. The quad biking I doubt can be labelled as 'eco friendly' when all we did all day was spit out petrol fumes into the environment. Thankfully, we did not deviate off the trails thus we didn't interfere with the indigenous vegetation. It was an amazing experience to hurtle along dirt tracks in the middle of rural Uganda even if I did come 'last'.

English First School – Pekanbaru, Indonesia

Leader Fetaeli and Kate conquering Kilimanjaro

On the way to the top of Kilimanjaro

Me and Heaven 'thumbs up' at the top of Kilimanjaro

Mountain gorillas in Rwanda

A game of hide and seek in the Rwandan mountains...

Who's the boss…silverback showing his maleness…

The minions quadbiking in Jinja, Uganda (Georgie, Fenella, Graham, me and Charlotte)

Getting into position for ballooning over the Serengeti

Sunrise from the air over the Serengeti

The Serengeti in a balloon

A lion 'hanging' out in the Serengeti trees…

Wrapped up like a parcel on the boat in Zanzibar

Two fish, lifeguard Jake, Ali and me – Zanzibar

Onset of gambling and Pringles addiction on the Everest Base
Camp trek (Cassie, Neil, John and me)

Me finally pointing to the correct Everest peak!

The Pringles stakes are the highest at the actual Base Camp of Everest…

Everest teahouse post earthquake....my glow in the dark Jesus was working overtime...

Missing paths after landslides – Everest Base Camp

A concerned Anouk when landslides damage swing bridges –
Everest Base Camp

Matt performing a bank transaction at the AKB bank in Karakol, Kyrgyzstan

Altyn Arashan 'resort and mountain chalet' Kyrgyzstan

Tashkent 1966 earthquake monument – one of many creative
photo poses…

The colourful minarets and domes of The Registan, Uzbekistan

Catherine, Matt and new friend Zaf at an Uzbek wedding party –
one of many vodka shots!

Darvaza gas crater, Turkmenistan – the 'Door to Hell'

Chapter 12

The Big Five and Two Fish

So it was goodbye to Uganda and Rwanda as we crossed the border back into Kenya. Our close encounters with our furry relatives just a distant memory. Family ties broken as we headed further away towards Nairobi. Or should I say Nai-robbery? Due to the extremely high numbers of attacks by robbers armed with guns and many cases of car-jackings in Nairobi, it has now acquired the anonym, 'Nai-robbery'. It must be hard working for the Nairobi Tourist Board, striving to convince visitors that the armed robbers are harmless and really don't mean to violate or hurt you as they wave a gun in your face. Perhaps they should try a different approach. Reverse psychology maybe? Along the lines of "Sir, your Nairobi experience will also include, free of charge, a confrontation by a man brandishing a gun demanding your wallet and items of jewellery. This is a thrill seekers ultimate adrenaline rush and is completely free of charge. Nothing will get your heart pumping faster than a gun being pointed in your face. I do hope you enjoy your 'Nai-robbery' experience".

Nairobi is where the Intrepid truck was picking up new passengers and Victor, the Intrepid leader, had now fully recovered from his cold and that night performed a much improved meet and greet speech for the new arrivals. Not one mention of campfires or bugs. The following day was an early start heading south across the border into Tanzania then onto the Ngorongoro Crater and the Serengeti.

The Ngorongoro Crater is a spectacular 22.5 kilometre (14 mile) wide volcanic crater and it is the largest unbroken caldera in the world. A caldera is formed from an explosion and collapse of the centre of a volcano, which in turn creates a very big hole. The Ngorongoro Crater is approximately 600 metres (2,000 feet) deep and the crater floor covers 260 square kilometres (100 square miles). In other words it's bloody gigantic! It's crammed full of animals, over 25,000 of them. We were all bubbling with excitement at the thought of driving down into the crater to see all the animals.

The Intrepid truck was having a rest for a couple of days and being replaced by a number of small jeeps. The walls of the crater were very steep and it would be very tricky to manoeuvre a ten tonne truck down the windy track. Ten tonne was a shot in the dark and no doubt totally off base, but my point is they are heavy. We had all packed our overnight daypacks to take into the crater. I had jammed into my bag at the last moment my dependable Nivea wipes knowing I was going to have to perform my Houdini act while in the crater. The Serengeti campsite did have one shower but water was not guaranteed. Never fear, I knew I could count on my dependable Nivea wipes to keep me clean. Well, perhaps 'clean' was an exaggeration, smelling nice anyhow.

Fenella and Georgie looked impeccable in their spotless safari wear. Ali and I were looking grubbier than ever. Fingernails filled with grime and hair looking feral. I made another mental note to get some body maintenance tips from them. Maybe you are just born that way, but I need to know. Note to one's self, Fenella and Georgie's body grooming advice – urgently required.

At the Ngorongoro headquarters the jeeps were lined up ready to go. I ended up in a jeep with Lydia, Shannon and Emma. All three were newbies on the truck from Nai-robbery. Lydia was Australian and a very cool lady. I mean, anyone who wears gold rimmed aviator sunglasses and pulls it off is cool in my book. She had the Erik Estrada 'Chips' thing happening and it worked. She was a nurse and had just finished volunteering at a remote village in the middle of nowhere which was another big tick in my book. Anyone who can look that cool after spending weeks in wooden shack with a bucket for a shower and mosquitoes eating them alive is just short of a miracle. Another note to one's self, get body maintenance tips from Lydia too. Shannon and Emma were another story. They were friends from Australia wanting to see some of Africa. They both initially scared me as they were like the cocks of the school. Everything they said seemed to be shouted and included 'fucking this' and 'fucking that' like it was a required adjective to get their point across. It brought to my mind the character Vicky Pollard from Little Britain, not that they wore tracksuits and trainers, just their hardness and effrontery made me think of the resemblance. Shannon had jet black hair worn long with a perm running through it, a bit like Michael Jackson's 'Dangerous' period. Her hair had the appearance of being constantly wet due to a liberal application of gel each day. Despite this I did soon warm to Shannon as behind the brazen exterior was a genuinely nice person. Emma on the other hand never did reveal another side. She remained impertinent and cocky throughout the journey. She retained her 'Vicky Pollard' status with distinction.

Harry, our jeep driver and guide introduced himself to us. "Hello ladies. My name is Harry and I will be your driver and guide for the next two days". He then grinned at us revealing the most perfect set of white teeth that I had seen in a long time; with the exception, of course, of Fenella and Georgie who had faultless teeth. Another note to one's self. Obtain teeth maintenance advice from F&G also. Not quite as urgent as body maintenance though. Harry continued, "I am the best driver here and I am gonna make sure you see every animal up close. You have any questions, just shout. If you want me at any time to stop the jeep just let me know ladies. You may have spotted an animal that I have not seen or you just want to take a photo of the scenery. I am here to make your experience the best". Harry then rewarded us all with another winning smile. He was The Man without a doubt. If anyone was going to charm the animals it was going to be Harry. Our own Doctor Dolittle. He was going to speak to the animals and use his come-hither look to lure the animals to our jeep.

"Let's go ladies. We have animals to see" announced Harry, as he climbed into the driver's seat. We all jumped into the back of the open top jeep eager to see some animals.

"I like Harry" declared cool Lydia "he sounds like he is gonna be the best guide". We all agreed as we approached the crater rim.

The views into the crater from the rim were breathtaking. It is an extraordinary natural wonder. They say that the height of the volcano, which exploded and collapsed many years ago, was equivalent, or higher, than that of Kilimanjaro. Imagine trying to climb that one? I don't think my biscuit trail would have reached the summit of that volcano before I succumbed to the dreaded high altitude pulmonary oedema. The only heaven I would've seen was the one high up in the sky. The huge bowl created by this phenomenon is now filled with big wild animals... and tourists in jeeps. Yes, the only competition the wild animals have in volume count is the boundless amount of tourists in vehicles visiting the crater. Fortunately for us there were no traffic jams. No tailgating. We hardly saw any other vehicles which meant sightings of just animals and not tourists.

Harry kept us all entertained with his banter. "Sharon, do you know who you remind me of?" asked Harry, flashing yet another one of his cheeky smiles. "No" I said casually while praying that he wasn't going to refer to my tent hair and grubby fingernails then liken me to Worzel Gummidge, the TV scarecrow. "Shakira" declared Harry "your blonde curly hair and your face are just like Shakira". Well I'll be damned. Fenella and Georgie eat your hearts out! God, I wished they were here to hear that. I found myself uncontrollably blushing like a teenager. I'm a grown woman for god's sake; but still, Shakira? I did suddenly think, should the man be driving? If his eyesight is that bad how on earth is he going to see the difference between a bush and a zebra, or a lion or a leopard? "I am naming this jeep the Shakira jeep" declared Harry who was now beaming from ear to ear. Wait until I tell Fenella and

Georgie about this I thought to myself as I tried to give a flick of my 'Shakira' hair, but failing miserably as my tent hair seemed to just stick out in all directions.

As the jeep made its way along the crater floor we saw an array of wild animals; zebra, buffalo, wildebeest, giraffe and warthog, all in close proximity to each other and the jeep. There was a large lake in the crater where the animals congregated. The animals, even though they are wild, seemed used to being pursued by jeeps transporting camera wielding tourists. They gave the appearance of being familiar with their role as stars of the show with the relentless visitors gawking at their every move, snapping away at their cameras in an endeavour to capture the perfect shot. Inconsequential really considering the wonders of editing software packages nowadays.

We constantly saw animals hanging around in groups. Maybe they were catching up with mates and passing on the latest gossip about the goings on in the raunchy rhino household? They certainly looked relaxed, even with a bunch of idiot tourists peering out of the roof of a jeep, like a herd of giraffe heads peering over the tree tops, excitedly taking photographs. We were heading into the Serengeti where animals, jeeps and tourists can move in and out despite the steep crater walls due to the area between the two now being utilised as communal farming land.

As we entered the Serengeti campsite our jaws dropped as to its location. I use the word 'entered' very loosely as there was nothing in reality to 'enter'. There were no boundary walls or fencing to separate the 'campsite' from the rest of the National Park. Not even a piece of chicken wire. We were all exposed to the wild animals we saw on our journey to the campsite. Harry's specific instructions this morning were fresh in my mind as I looked around.

"Ladies, under no circumstances are you to leave the vehicle. You are safe whilst in the jeep as the animals will never try to get into a vehicle. However, the moment anyone steps out of the jeep you are their target. Their pray. You will be seen as potential dinner by some animals".

Oh my god! What about now? Are we fair game now that we are not in a vehicle? A tasty banquet for Mr and Mrs Lion perhaps? Or a delightful feast for the leopard family? We were informed that the wild animals would not approach the unfenced 'campsite' during the day, on the other hand though, night time was a level playing field to the animals. If you left your tent you were fair game. There was apparently a man on guard in a small tower near the 'entrance' of the campsite who was armed with a rifle should things get out of control. I never did see this man and have my doubts as to whether there even was a 'tower'. I think perhaps this was mentioned in an attempt to make us feel safer.

"Lions and buffalo tend to roam around the tents at night," warned Victor "under no circumstances are you to leave your tent at night. Even if you need the toilet you will have to wait until daybreak. The animals do not attack people whilst they are inside their tents but the minute you step out of your tent it's game on."

I wish now, instead of mocking and ridiculing the 'Shewee', that I had bought one for my night surrounded by man-eating lions. The Sheewee, a portable urination device, had been on the shelves of outdoor and camping shops for a number of years now. Pooh poohed by my friends and I, it was a plastic funnel in which a woman can stand and pee into. Although that might be tricky in a tent! Perhaps you could kneel or squat while juggling with the device, hoping to goodness that you had positioned the funnel correctly. Spillage in a tent could create bad tensions with your tent partner, not to mention an unhealthy odour. At the camp meal that evening we all refrained from drinking liquids. The thought of needing to urinate during the night was terrifying, with the grim knowledge that you could be ravaged by a pride of lions or crushed to death by stampeding buffalo.

On account of it being a hot and humid night, Rachel and I decided to lift all the tent flaps, front, sides and back, to expose all the netted air ventilation 'windows'. This allowed any flow of air to enter the tent and also enabled us to look out at the other tents or up to the stars in the sky. Rachel was tiny.

She took up what seemed like a few inches in one corner of the tent when she was sleeping. The top of her head must have just reached my chest. She was the ideal tent partner for additional space inside the tent which enabled extra room for me to manoeuvre and wriggle within my sleeping bag in my futile attempts to get comfortable. The downside to a tiny tent partner was the pitching and putting down of the tent. This was tricky for Rachel. Her arms too short to reach the top of the tent, and the weight needed to press down onto the tent when rolling up was impossible for her. She was not designed for tent duties.

As we settled into our tent for the night, my mind was filled with thoughts of lions and urinating. I don't know which was worse. The thought of lions prowling around the tents in the hope of catching some prey, or, crossing my legs for hours on end until I could wait no longer and have to use the nearest plastic bag as a makeshift Shewee. Then pray there are no holes. Rachel was asleep in minutes. I tried closing my eyes but sleep eluded me as I wriggled around in my sleeping bag. At nearly midnight I could feel sprinkles of water on my face, a pleasant sensation considering the heat inside the tent. Being in a semi-sleep state I initially ignored the increasing sprinkles of rain that were now dampening my sleeping bag and all that was inside the tent. Rachel was oblivious, curled up in a ball like a tiny kitten in the corner of the tent, not a sound leaving her lips. The light sprinkle of rain was developing into a heavy rainfall and we were becoming wetter. Oh my god. What do I do? If I go outside to drop down the tent flaps I could come face to face with a buffalo or even worse a Sharon-eating lion. But we were getting wetter and wetter. Do I risk it? Then I heard rustling from the tent next to me. Great! Someone else was awake and as I peered through the net window I saw that their flaps were open too. This was encouraging. Then I heard the familiar noise of a tent zip. It was Fenella.

"Fenella, Fenella" I whispered through my netted window "is that you?"

"Yes, just dropping the flaps as we are getting soaked in there". Like a whippet she ran round her tent, dropped the flaps and had crawled back into her tent. "Phew!" exclaimed Fenella after zipping up her tent door. "I really didn't want to do that but I made it without getting attacked by a lion". I took a deep breath and unzipped my tent door. "My turn now!" I whispered to Fenella. I ran around the tent grabbing the flaps and throwing them down when I heard shouting. "Someone help me! Please, someone help me!" It was a woman with an American or Canadian accent. I apologise to all Canadians but without a maple leaf to clarify I have no idea of nationality. "What's wrong?" I shouted over to her. "Help me please. Help! Call the ranger" was her response. Ranger? Does she think she's in the Canadian Rocky Mountains? Who is this ranger she is asking for? Is he the mythical man in the tower watching over us at the make believe entrance of the campsite? "What's your problem? Tell me what's wrong" I insisted. How could I help if I don't know what's wrong? "Call the ranger! I need to get out. There are cats surrounding my tent. I need to get out!" she wailed. Oh my god! Here I am standing outside my tent shouting to a woman only inches away and there are lions prowling around. What a dimwit. I promptly threw myself back into my tent. My heart was pounding so fast. My hands shaking from the adrenaline that had just kicked in.

I could hear commotion near the American or possibly Canadian woman's tent which I was pretty sure didn't sound like hungry lions clawing at her tent and ripping it into shreds to get their evening meal. It sounded like a man's voice. Did the mythical man in the tower actually exist? Was this the ranger she so desperately wanted? Knowing the immediate cat danger had gone I snuggled into my sleeping bag and dreamt of toilets; rows and rows of toilets. They were just that little bit out of reach no matter how hard I tried to reach them. A loud trilling noise filled my ears interrupting my focus on catching a toilet. The unrelenting trilling finally roused me from my toilet dream. My alarm clock stared me in the face, flashing and trilling, demanding I wake up. It was 4 o'clock in the morning. Then I remembered, today was the day of my sunrise hot air balloon ride over the Serengeti. My stomach started to churn with excitement as I quickly performed my Houdini act with my dependable Nivea wipes. I dressed and sneaked out of the tent without any movement from tiny Rachel curled up in the corner.

A small group of people had gathered near a jeep which, at 5 o'clock in the morning in the middle of the Serengeti, was without a doubt my ride to the balloon launch site. It was still dark as we set off down the bumpy track, the start of our balloon safari adventure. Steph, one of the newbies on the Intrepid truck had also paid the outrageous amount of money it cost and had joined me on the pricey hot air balloon experience. What felt like putting down a house deposit was actually lower than the cost of visiting the gorillas in Rwanda. I wouldn't go as far as to say it is a bargain-basement activity, nevertheless, it was something I had always wanted to do. Floating in the sky over the Serengeti in a hot air balloon, seeing all the wild animals and grassy plains seemed a much more desirable alternative to Leeds city centre hot air ballooning and seeing the Trinity shopping centre, Leeds train station and the Vue cinema complex.

When we arrived at the launch site it was a hub of activity. Giant balloons lay deflated on the floor like discarded popped balloons at a children's birthday party. Near the vibrant nylon balloons were the burners which are effectively the engine of the hot air balloon. The burner propels hot air into the fabric envelope which creates the lift off and the up and down motion. The direction is determined by the wind. There is no control over where you end up. It is in God's hands. That's why some employees of the balloon company stay on the ground and chase after the balloon by car to see where it lands, otherwise you could be stranded in a very remote part of the Serengeti acting as fair game again. They then pick you up and drive you back to your campsite. Then there's the basket, or if you want to sound like you know what you're talking about, the gondola. This is simply a wicker basket similar to a picnic hamper that you might win at a

Christmas raffle. It's a very simple contraption. Worryingly simple! A balloon, a burner and a basket; surely they need more components? As liquid propane is blasted from the fuel tank to the burner, flames are projected out in a long controlled stream of fire like a military flamethrower. The limp balloons began to bulge as the hot air entered into each of them.

It was fascinating to watch the balloons slowly puff up. The hot air filled the top of the balloon until the whole thing began to swell from the pressure of the air inside. The balloons now resembled bloated whales stranded on an isolated beach. Eventually they began to lift from the floor into the air. Just before the balloons were fully inflated we were taken to the wicker basket to be given our safety instructions. Steph and I sidled up to the basket; up close it still resembled a giant picnic hamper! The inside was divided into eight squares, each with a small ledge positioned halfway up from the bottom of the basket.

A man, who introduced himself as Phil, was our pilot for the hot air balloon flight and he proceeded to run through some basic safety instructions like, "don't hang out over the basket with your feet in the air" and "do not try to climb out of the basket whilst in mid air". Phil was from England which was unbelievable. Here I was in the middle of the Serengeti, about to embark on a hot air balloon ride, and the pilot was from England.

The process of getting into the basket was quite strange. Each section fitted two people. For takeoff we had to climb into a square and lie on our backs with our heads towards the top of the basket and our legs bent at the knees and resting over the ledge with our bottoms touching the top of the ledge. It was as if we had been sitting on a chair and fallen over backwards onto the floor. It was very bizarre and it made Steph and I giggle incessantly. When all passengers were positioned correctly and 'seated' on their ledges, the pilot gave the burner a blast and searing hot flames roared inches away from our heads. The heat was so intense I felt my face turn crimson.

"Oh my god!" I exclaimed. "The flames are burning my head!" Steph agreed. "I wasn't expecting our heads to be so close to the naked flames" she shouted. We had to shout to each other to be heard over the roar of the burner flames. My tent hair, or should I say my Shakira hair was so dangerously close to the flames that it could soon be transformed into a Sinead O'Connor cut. I felt like an astronaut getting ready for lift off with the countdown to commence at any moment five, four, three, two one. All engines running. Commence lift off.

As the giant balloon lifted from the ground all Steph and I could do was grin at each other. Our scorched, red faces were like rising beacons. We tried to talk but the roar of the burner was making it impossible to be heard. The red-hot flames eventually moved away from our heads as the balloon rose into the sky. The wicker basket shook and then rocked as it was pulled from the ground and we became suddenly became upright. Now we were seated on the ledge and not laying on our backs as was our original pose. Giddiness took over as we gently rose higher and higher into the air, the grassy plains below becoming further and further away. The word Serengeti is Maasai for 'endless plains' and that is what we could see as we continued lifting up into the sky. We could see for miles and miles. When the pilot stopped triggering the blast valve for the propane gas it was silent. Not a sound as we silently floated in the sky. It was magical. This is what it must feel like to be a bird. Gliding effortlessly in the clean, crisp air and looking down on the widespread savannah below. Not a power line or telephone wire in sight. Not even any fencing to divide the land, as we knew from the distinct lack of boundary walls at the campsite. The land belongs to everyone. Man and animals. Any cloud that did appear in the endless blue sky was white and fluffy like fresh cotton balls. None of your tainted clouds caused by car exhaust emissions and industrial factories spewing out polluted fumes. No smog hung over the Serengeti. This air was pristine and unblemished.

"Wow", I mouthed to Steph "the perspective is totally different from up here!" On the ground you are limited to seeing directly what is in front of you and nothing further.

Floating in the sky enabled you to grasp just how enormous the Serengeti was. To give you some idea it is roughly the same size as Northern Ireland or Connecticut; around 14,300 square kilometres or 5,500 square miles.

Phil, the pilot, was very accommodating as he effortlessly triggered the blast valve gadget to force the balloon to rise and fall. We were lowered to get a handsome view of two cheetahs and then lifted to witness a herd of wildebeest racing along the ground. Phil explained that this was part of the migration that took place around this time every year. He was even flabbergasted to see the galloping animals. The wildebeest were making their way to the Maasai Mara Reserve in Kenya to follow the rains and the growth of new grass. The Serengeti was now near the end of the dry season and the grasslands were dried out. It was unbelievable to be an airborne spectator to this prodigious event, silent witnesses in the sky. The moving wildebeest were oblivious to our presence and continued their journey across the plains.

The sunrise seemed so long ago as we floated aimlessly in the air. It was strange to think of men in a jeep below chasing after the balloon, jolting and jarring on the uneven trail in their struggle to keep pace with us. I tried to block out any thoughts of the 1989 Alice Springs disaster when two hot air balloons collided in mid-air. The fabric on the envelope of one of the balloons was torn by the collision and it plunged to the ground killing all 13 people on board. In February 2013 there was an even worse hot air balloon crash in Luxor, Egypt that killed 19 people. The balloon caught fire and a gas tank exploded. It was horrific. If that tragedy had happened prior to my Serengeti adventure I would possibly have refrained from this little excursion. I did a quick check of how close the other balloons were to ours and thankfully they were some distance away.

Phil was now looking out for a clearing to land the balloon. He pointed out a moving blot on the landscape which was the vehicle that had been hastily following us. The lookout man diligently not letting us out of his sight as the vehicle scrambled along the grassy plains. Phil began his decent, having spotted a suitable tree free stretch of land. We were instructed to sit back down onto the ledge and hold onto the side ropes as we did for takeoff. It felt like we were slowly floating down for such a long time when suddenly we accelerated towards the ground. Steph and I braced ourselves for the landing knowing that we could rebound several times on the hard ground before ultimately ending up with the basket on its side, recreating our original pose on our backs and our feet in the air. Phil expertly guided the basket to the ground creating only the slightest of bumps. We remained vertical with our bottoms firmly on the ledge and our feet on the floor. Phew. That was a relief. I had been told stories of the wicker baskets being dragged through thorny bushes and trees resulting in all the passengers suffering from lacerations and splinters. Such a gentle landing was a big relief. The conscientious balloon chaser was driving towards us, his task accomplished.

My mind was now occupied with the thought of food. The expensive cost of the balloon safari also included an upmarket bush breakfast with a glass of champagne and a full English breakfast. Perhaps the upmarket prices will have paid for gold plated sausages or diamond encrusted hash browns? The balloon chaser who was still performing his duties drove us all to our makeshift bush 'dining hall' which blew me away. It was impeccable. Set in the middle of the yellow grassy plains, under an acacia tree, a grand rectangular dining table that could easily seat twenty people. A white linen table cloth covered the whole table which was dressed with bone china crockery and gleaming silver cutlery. We were escorted to the table by stewards wearing traditional Swahili dress which were pristine, white long robes known as kanzus. Waistcoats and turbans completed their smart outfits. Steph and I were speechless. After two months of eating from plastic plates and drinking out of brown plastic mugs, while balancing on a fold-up camping stool, this whole bush breakfast experience was overwhelming. We were served champagne in glass flutes followed by huge platters of fresh tropical fruits. Then came the full English breakfast comprising lashings of bacon, juicy sausages (not gold plated as I had thought), eggs, mushrooms and grilled tomatoes. Oh my god it was mouth-watering. After months of cereal with UHT milk or if we were lucky, some porridge, this was heavenly, and to be eating this from grand white china plates too! "Think of all the others now", laughed Steph, in between mouthfuls of bacon, "eating their Weetabix or leftover stale bread from yesterday". It made us laugh even with the knowledge that we would be eating just that tomorrow if we survived another night in the unfenced campsite.

I must mention the opulent bush toilet that had been fabricated for this occasion. Just in case someone couldn't find it in the middle of flat grasslands there had been a little wooden sign erected with the word 'Toilet' and an arrow pointing to a small cream square construction. For the benefit of dumb tourists I guess. The toilet walls were made out of windbreakers, cream in colour and positioned in a small square, similar to a toilet cubicle. There was a hanging sign in front of the toilet; one side read 'occupied' and the other 'unoccupied'. There were only three sides, the entrance was at the 'back' and faced out onto a remarkable view of the Serengeti that you could look at while seated on the exceedingly deluxe portable toilet. I did have a Cheryl Cole correlation moment while using the bush facilities. So this is what it must have felt like when needing to pee whilst climbing Kilimanjaro? I did wonder.

Feeling a bit tiddly after drinking all the leftover champagne and perhaps due to our impoverished appearance and stories of camp meals, the pilot donated a spare bottle of champers to Steph and me. Hurray! We agreed to drink this to celebrate our hot air balloon experience, or should I say, survival, with a select few fellow Intrepid travellers to join us. The balloon chaser's final errand was complete as he delivered us all back to our accommodation. In our case it was in the middle of the Serengeti, a tent, with no protective fence to fend off the wild animals.

Back in the Shakira jeep with Harry and the other girls, the rest of the day was a safari ride in the Serengeti. The array of wild animals was incredible, though there are two encounters that I especially remember. Have you ever seen a lion hanging in a tree? Well, I didn't even realise they hung around in trees until this day. Harry was his usual charming self, flashing his immaculate teeth with every smile and keeping us all laughing when he suddenly veered left. "See the other vehicles?" he asked, "there is something there. We need to get there fast to get a good viewing position". We could see in the distance other vehicles changing direction and racing to see what? What were we racing towards? It was like an episode of 'The Amazing Race' desperately trying to get there first to secure an immunity place on the next leg of the race. "Harry, what is it? What are we racing to see?" asked Shannon, baffled like the rest of us. "I'm not sure ladies. What I am sure of is people have stopped and are taking pictures. It must be something big like a lion or even better, a leopard" concluded Harry. Yes! A cat! That would be amazing and I was safely in the jeep so no fair game rules apply this time. Harry slowed down as we approached the other vehicles. I scanned around and couldn't see anything. Was it a bush mouse or a rock squirrel? Then Harry pointed up to a tree. "There! Look! Two lions. See?" Well I'll be damned.

Hanging from the branches were two female lions, sleeping. They were massive. Their stomachs were flat to the branch with their four legs hanging from either side. Giant floppy paws suspended in the air. Their long tails were also hanging, the black tip like a pendulum swinging from a clock. They had round fluffy button ears and a big black triangular nose, their mouths a thin black line, no doubt hiding a decent pair of gnashers and their eyes also thin black lines as they slept. The sandy colour of their furry coats could be mistaken for Labradors had it not been for their feline facial features and giant paws. After the initial astonishment at firstly actually seeing lions just metres away from our jeep (Harry had secured the best spot for the Shakira jeep) and secondly, lions hanging from a tree, I hastily pulled out my camera. Word eventually spread throughout the Serengeti as jeep after jeep appeared. It ended up looking like an NCP car park. The lions were going nowhere. After a while Harry suggested we should move on to see other animals. We reluctantly agreed and Harry flashed us one of his winning smiles before artfully manoeuvring the jeep around all the other vehicles.

The second and even more memorable moment happened shortly after. The Shakira jeep was ambling behind another jeep when it suddenly stopped indicating to us to stop too. As I stood up I still couldn't see any form of animal. Cool Lydia was also puzzled. "Can you see anything?" she asked while craning her neck out of the jeep. Shannon and Emma were also straining to see something. Then from the front of the jeep, a leopard appeared, sashaying towards us, nonchalantly glancing at our jeep. She gave it an almost disdainful look before strutting alongside the Shakira jeep. My heart was pounding. A leopard! She was inches away from my face. This was a dream. Leopards are rare to see unless you are visiting the zoo.

Like something out of the Cartier Odyssey TV commercial the leopard sauntered down the side of our carriage. Like a peacock on parade. She remained aloof, indifferent to the bunch of camera snapping idiots hanging over the side of the jeep. Look up. Look up. I silently willed the leopard to look up for that perfect portrait shot but she was having none of it. As I snapped away, taking hundreds of pictures of the top of her head, she passed the jeep and strolled up to a nearby tree. Effortlessly she scaled up the trunk and found herself a nice branch to 'hang' from, another moggy hanging from a tree branch. Am I the only person who had no idea that big cats liked to hang from branches of a tree? What if they couldn't get down? There's no emergency number out here. No firemen with long ladders to rescue kitties from trees. Bit of a shame really. A few hunky firemen to guard the campsite wouldn't go a miss. I was not looking forward to a second night in the unfenced wild and made myself a mental note not to drink any more water. Word had got around about the leopard as a traffic jam of jeeps formed behind us. The leopard, now 'tree hanging' as this I now know, is the favourite pastime of a wild cat, was going nowhere. Harry again suggested that we move on and off we went in search of more wild animals.

After a full day on 'safari' and my body now in the late stages of dehydration, I was nestled in my sleeping bag bracing myself for another night in the unfenced campsite. Rachel was already asleep in the corner of the tent, oblivious to the perils of the night. It was a struggle to sleep. It was so hot even with all the tent flaps open and the netted windows exposed. As I fidgeted and jiggled in my sleeping bag I could feel my bladder slowly fill up. Oh no! How could this be happening? I hadn't drunk any liquids since mid-afternoon. This should not be happening. Panic crept in as the thought of leaving my tent entered my head. Visions of lions and leopards leaping from tree branches. Mauling me with their giant paws, their mouths open revealing the razor sharp teeth that were concealed earlier. My bladder strain was getting worse. I was going to have to leave my tent. Fair game. Oh god, this was horrible. Then to my relief there was rustling in the tent next to me. "Fenella, Fenella. Is that you?" I whispered, "Are you awake?" To my relief Fenella was awake. "Yes. I'm desperate for a pee. Do you need to go too? Can we go together?" Hallelujah! Fenella needed the toilet too. Even if there was a gang of lions outside our tents licking their lips in anticipation of the kill, the fact that there were two of us made it much better. I mean, at least I wouldn't be on my own and we would both be mauled together. The jeeps were parked a few yards from my tent. "Shall we just go behind one of them?" I asked, knowing there was an actual toilet we could use but it was way over in the distance. Fenella agreed. "Okay. Let's do it". In unison we unzipped our tents and ran to the back of the jeep and promptly squatted. Indistinguishable between humans or horses as we hurriedly urinated, determined to completely empty our bladders in double-quick time. "My god, it's taking so long to come out!" exclaimed Fenella. Not quite the whippet tonight I thought. Eventually, mission accomplished, we trotted back to our tents and hastily zipped up the openings before any cats appeared. Phew. We made it. "Thanks Sharon. I owe you one.

Night" whispered Fenella. Was now a good time to mention the body maintenance and teeth hygiene tips? I thought, perhaps not. "Good night Fenella".

Sleep continued to evade me that night. The moon shone over the campsite stage like a theatre spotlight. Its beam illuminated the tents and walkways created by the temporary canvas structures. It was no good. I couldn't sleep. My eyes were wide open as I sat up and stared out of the netted door. It was as if night had become day. The moon functioned as a communal torch for all the campers. Down a clear walkway about ten metres from my tent I could see two small round sparkles. They didn't move. As my eyes adjusted to the night, it was clear what the two round sparkles were. The silhouette of round button ears and chiselled jaw line encompassed the two round sparkles. This was undoubtedly a lion. I was mesmerised by the motionless sparkling eyes that seemed to pierce through my netting directly into my eyes. We were having a staring contest. Oh my god. This lion was staring right at me. Could she see through the netting? My heart had stopped, my breathing also. This was eerie. I knew I should have stopped staring but I couldn't. The profile of the lion was so clear from the moonlit sky. The contours of her shoulder blades began to rise and fall as she sauntered towards me. Not one sound was made from her padded paws as they touched the ground. As she closed the gap our eyes were still locked. Five metres separated her from my flimsy netted tent door. What was I doing? Was I mad? What deranged idiot would have a staring contest with a lion? Did a net barrier class as fair game? In a moment of sanity I threw myself back down onto my sleeping bag and lay like a corpse. Was she still there? Could she hear me breathing? My heart beat was like a drum in my ears. Could she hear that too?

It felt like I had been lying stiff as a board for at least fifteen minutes when in reality it was probably only five. Should I sit up to see where she was? Had she gone? Her soundless movement gave me no clue as to where she was. She must've gone. Surely? Yes. She will have long gone. I willed myself to sit up and open my eyes. Convinced the lion was gone I sat up to come face to face with the sparkling eyes, nose to nose with the feline face. The outline of her button ears and chiselled jaw practically pressed against the bottom corner of my netted door as if sniffing her next meal. Oh my god! This was unreal. What had I done? Like a coiled spring I threw myself back down onto my sleeping back. I was fair game. I was convinced of it. What imbecile would challenge a lion to a staring contest? What was I thinking? Should I wake Rachel? What help would she be if she can't even pitch a tent? Believing the tent was about to be ripped open by a giant paw clawing at the canvas, I lay there like a cadaver and braced myself to be dissected by a raging lion. I cursed myself for being such a jackass and silently apologised to Rachel who was still curled up in the corner of the tent, oblivious to our current predicament. I waited and waited. Nothing. I waited some more. Still nothing. I needed to know if death was imminent. Was the lion still there? I know. I'll do it in stages. I gently lifted my head from the ground, straining my neck to peep into the corner of the netting. Phew! No eyes. I gingerly rolled over to check all sides. No eyes. I breathed a sigh of relief.

Sleep was impossible after that encounter but eventually my body did drift into a light sleep. Images of lions filled my head, their eyes sparkling and locked with mine. My lesson learnt from that encounter was not to have staring matches with lions, especially when inside a flimsy tent.

The following morning it was a relief to leave the unfenced and unguarded campsite. Neither the mythical man in the tower nor the ranger were to be seen. After calling in at the Olduvai Gorge where the first known recordings of humans were made, we retraced our route back through the Ngorongoro Conservation area and out of the crater to rejoin the Intrepid truck. Did you know that a skull was discovered at the gorge dating back 1.8 million years, together with footprints of a man, woman and child believed to date back 3.5 million years? Not much more of interest at the gorge unless you are really into palaeontology.

It was sad to say goodbye to Harry and the Shakira jeep as we all boarded the Intrepid truck to head south. As I recounted my confrontation with the lion to Ali, Fenella and Georgie they were shocked to learn that there was an actual lion roaming outside our tents. I had already reported the night's events to Rachel who looked truly horrified and I'm not sure if that was by the thought of a prowling lion by our tent or by my bird-brained idea to have a staring match with the lion. Fenella's immediate reaction was "what if the lion came over when we were squatting behind the jeep?" I hadn't even thought of that scenario. Seems we are all lucky to survive the night at the unfenced campsite which was not helped one bit by my foolish staring games with the wild moggy.

Three days later, after a number of stops en-route, we arrived at Dar es Salaam. Originally named Mzizima, this town started as a small fishing village in the mid 19th century when the Sultan of Zanzibar decided to create a trading centre at the harbour and it expanded from there. It became the capital of Tanzania in 1891 but lost that title to Dodoma in 1973 which is more centrally located within the country. Dar es Salaam is the gateway to the island of Zanzibar, famous for its spices and even more so for the birthplace of Freddie Mercury. After a night camping near the beach and not a kitty cat in sight, we caught the ferry to take us across the water to Zanzibar.

There were around thirty people on the ferry that day. Blue sky, calm waters, it was perfect weather for a boat ride. I was excited. Zanzibar. It sounded so exotic. Known as the 'Spice Island' it brought images of huge sacks filled to the brim with fragrant spices, turmeric, ginger, chilli, cinnamon, star anise and cardamom to name a few. Vibrant in colour; yellows, reds, greens, oranges and all ground to a fine powder. In the mid 19th century Zanzibar was the world's largest producer of cloves and the also the largest slave trading port on the east coast of Africa. It had pristine white-sand beaches and a diver's paradise with incredible corals. Then, of course, there was the house where Freddie Mercury was born and lived in until he moved to boarding school in India when he was nine years old.

As we all clambered out of the ferry we were immediately faced with the Zanzibar Immigration and Customs enforcement officers. Unbelievably, Zanzibar has its own government and strives to be a separate entity from Tanzania. Which it isn't. It's comparable to Scotland and the United Kingdom of Great Britain. Scotland has no wish to be part of the United Kingdom and it also has its own government. However the comparison ends there as there is no immigration and customs enforcement at the border with England. They haven't gone that far... yet.

Everyone was required to produce their passports and get stamped into Zanzibar. As with my Indonesian visa, I had no concerns as I had dutifully paid the extortionate £75 fee and obtained my Tanzanian tourist visa prior to leaving the UK together with my visas for Kenya, Uganda and Rwanda. Conscious of my tourist visa history I diligently investigated the visa requirements for these countries. I discovered that Kenya had an agreement with Tanzania, Uganda and Rwanda to waiver visa re-entry fees if travelling between the three countries as long as your single-entry visa remains valid for each country. This meant that visas were not required if going from Kenya to Tanzania or Uganda and Rwanda and back to any one of these countries for a second time. No problem. Tried and tested at the Ugandan border. The agreement worked. We had all re-entered Uganda from Rwanda on the same visa. No dramas. I had re-entered Tanzania from Kenya on the same single-entry visa. No complications. Everyone was seated on long wooden benches that had been provided outside the immigration office, waiting in line to be 'stamped' into Zanzibar. Victor had gone into the office and was showing the officers the Intrepid truck paperwork. Fenella and Georgie had received their official stamps and were proudly displaying their ink marks when an official came out of the immigration office and shouted my name. Why on earth was I being singled out? I quickly stood up and confirmed, a bit reluctantly, that I was indeed Sharon Cracknell. "Please can you come into the office? We need to speak with you about your visa", instructed the officer. Questions raced through my mind as I walked to the door of the immigration office. Why do they need to speak with me? I paid £75 for my Tanzanian tourist visa. It was valid for three months, which I was still within. What was the problem? As I entered the building I could see Victor seated opposite another stern looking officer. "Please sit Sharon. We have some questions about your Tanzanian visa", the stern officer said as he gestured to a chair next to Victor. His eyebrows were furrowed as he scrutinised my passport. "Your visa is not valid", he declared, "and you have entered Tanzania illegally". Oh no! Why was this happening all over again? I had a visa which I had paid a scandalous £75 for. "Did you enter Tanzania via Kilimanjaro airport in January?" asked the officer, his eyebrows still furrowed as if in a permanent state of puzzlement. "Yes sir", I replied. Perhaps a big dollop of good manners and respect for officials might help my situation. My visa was clearly not favourable with the immigration officer, the reason for which was still not apparent. "Since then, you have visited Kenya, Uganda and Rwanda. Correct?" he asked. "Correct sir," I confirmed. A layer of sweat now covering my face in my nervous anticipation of what I had done wrong and what action they intended to take. Maybe a five year prison sentence? I reckon I would fare much better in a Tanzanian jail than an Indonesian one.

"Then you should have purchased another tourist visa when re-entering Tanzania in February. You have illegally re-entered the country", he solemnly declared. "But I understood that there was an agreement in place between Tanzania, Kenya, Uganda and Rwanda to enable tourists to re-enter on a single-entry visa?" I challenged him. This man knew nothing. He didn't even know his own country's immigration rules. He shouldn't be working in their immigration offices; at least he should get some more training. "Rwanda is not included in that agreement", was his flat response. "That agreement is between Tanzania, Kenya and Uganda only. The fact you have entered Rwanda makes your Tanzanian visa invalid and you are here illegally", he stated. The man was like a dog with a bone. Damn it. How did I miss that? But why was I let back into Tanzania without a new visa? I tried to catch him out with this question but he just came right back at me with, "They shouldn't have let you in". So here I was, an illegal immigrant, detained by an immigration and customs officer on the island of Zanzibar at a pretend 'border' immigration office. How did this happen? Victor was apologising and trying his best to pacify the immigration officer. "We need to refer this case to my boss. Ultimately it is her decision as to what action should be taken Sharon", advised the officer.

Every other Intrepid truck traveller arrived directly to Kenya, consequently, they all had entered Tanzania only once. Me, on the other hand, had arrived directly from home to Tanzania to climb Kilimanjaro and then got the road from hell bus ride that took me across the border into Kenya. This crossing into Tanzania was my second one on the same single-entry visa. Everyone else had their passport stamped and were now waiting for the boss lady to arrive and give her verdict. It took over thirty minutes for her to arrive. My popularity was fading fast as everyone else had to hang around the immigration office. I was strangely calm. I think the thought of a Tanzanian jail compared to an Indonesian jail made it easier. It would no doubt be a much more luxurious affair than an overcrowded cell in Pekanbaru, with a hole in the corner of the cell as the makeshift toilet. It was illogical that I was being detained at a 'make believe' border crossing.

It was all a big show. They debated what punishment should be inflicted on me. Would they allow me to 'enter' Zanzibar', or wouldn't they? Power; control. Some people love it. I have worked with people who have gone to great lengths to 'control' someone or something. They will lie, withhold important information or just blame all their own errors on others. This lady seemed to thrive on the control she had over my situation. Eventually, she allowed me to 'enter' Zanzibar. "We want to maintain good relations with the UK so, with that in mind, I will allow you to enter Zanzibar", she announced. "You may need to pay for another visa when you exit Tanzania". Over an hour wasted at a border crossing that wasn't even a border crossing. It was a big relief though. I was going to have to get my act together when it comes to visas. This was getting hard to endure.

Finally we all left the immigration office and made our way by foot to the old part of the island known as Stone Town. This charming place is a labyrinth of narrow, winding streets lined with rows of tall, terraced buildings that exude faded elegance. Time had taken its toll on the aged dwellings which were all weathered and in need of repair. Some of them were over four floors in height, towering over the confined alleyways, blocking the natural sunlight for the majority of the day. A small number of houses still had the old wooden doors with intricate carvings and embedded brass studs. Wandering the charismatic streets, it was hard to imagine the cruel slavery that used to exist in Stone Town all those years ago. Slaves were crammed tightly into wooden boats called dhows and sent to the slave markets in Stone Town where the Arab traders would imprison the slaves in oppressive underground chambers until they were sold. It wasn't until 1873 that the slave market was finally closed down for good by the British. There is now a memorial where the market once was to remind people of the appalling treatment of the slaves when brought to the markets to be sold. After staying overnight in the beautiful old Stone Town we caught a bus to take us up to the northern tip of the island to, what I can only describe, as a tropical paradise. Kendwa beach. Imagine a postcard depicting your typical idyllic beach; clear turquoise sea lapping onto a powdery-white sand beach and not a high rise building to been seen, only bungalows and chalets dotted on the hillside. It was in these bungalows that we were staying for the next two nights.

Ali and I were excited. We planned to go deep sea fishing the following morning. All we needed to do was find a boat with a skipper willing to take us out into the Indian Ocean in search of fish; big fish! Our first port of call, however, was the beach bar. Donning our bikinis, sarongs and flip flops we shuffled our way to the bar lounge which consisted of a straw roof, open sides and a view to take your breath away. Steph, my fellow hot air ballooner and full English breakfast eater, already had in her hand what look like a glass of Dulux fuchsia pink emulsion but was, in fact, a cocktail with lashings of grenadine and alcohol amongst a list of many other ingredients. Fenella and Georgie also appeared looking like Baywatch beach babes in their tiny bikinis, their bodies like goddesses, toned and firm. Another note to one's self, get Fenella and Georgie body toning tips.

I actually felt like I was on holiday; the safari adventure with lions and roaming buffalo now replaced by beach bars and an exotic ocean facing location. The only wild animals to look out for would be the drunken idiots who have had too many beers whilst sitting in the African sun. That night after dinner, at the restaurant bar, we had been unsuccessful at finding a man with a boat to take us deep sea fishing. We had enquired at the bungalow reception desk but found nothing in our price range. We had also asked at the restaurant and bar. There didn't appear to be anyone that could take us deep sea fishing for less than $600! The average boat charter price was an outrageous $600 for a half day hire which equated to 5 hours. Ali and I couldn't afford that. We could have done another month of travelling with that amount of money!

Ali then got chatting to Jake, an American guy and mentioned to him about our desire to go deep sea fishing. Unbelievably, Jake had just been talking to a man about a boat. The local man was at the bar and had brought up the subject of his boat for hire. He sometimes let tourists use his boat for deep sea fishing and he was free if Jake wanted to hire him. Jake had dismissed the casual offer made by the man as he had no other interested travellers to do it with him. This was our chance. The guy had offered a price of $150. How cheap was that – too good to be true perhaps? We needed to find him, to chat to the man about a boat. It didn't take Jake long to find him. The four of us sat at the bar to negotiate the price. Ali was a good haggler and soon had him down on price. A rendezvous time of 4 o'clock in the morning was agreed. It was already midnight. The skipper of the bargain boat was still drinking beers. Shouldn't he be now heading off home to catch some sleep having got himself a hired boat? He was going to be sailing this boat. Warning signs did flash a little, but the excitement of having a deep sea fishing boat 'hired' soon wiped out any doubts I may have had.

Before we knew it 4 o'clock had arrived and we were scrambling down to the beach to meet up with the skipper and his boat. There were threatening black clouds in the sky and the sea was very choppy. It looked like a storm was brewing and my doubts came flooding back. "Ali, I'm not sure about this", I admitted, "my swimming skills are lacking and the sea looks choppy. What if I fall off the boat?" Ali was having none of it. "Don't be silly, Sharon. You'll be fine. I'm a strong swimmer so if anything happens I will make sure you are okay". I wasn't happy. Water was not my thing. I knew Ali was super fit and had no issues tackling the grade five white water rafting at Jinja, but a choppy sea and me? Not a great combination. A bit like Indonesia and teaching, not a good amalgamation. Jake had arrived just as our man with a boat appeared. The boat was nothing like what I had imagined it would look like. I'd seen pictures of the deep sea fishing boats before, with white sleek curves running down from the tip of the vessel. Thirty feet plus in length with an elevated cabin top to enable the crew to spot the fish for their guests to hook up; equipped with five or so high end fishing rods situated around the boat and some up high like antennas and metal safety railings running along the front 'V' of the vessel. Those boats were rigged up with all the fishing gear needed for a day's deep sea fishing experience, the pristine white top coat on the boat gleaming in the hot African sun, with pictures of the crew wearing spotless white t-shirts and baseball caps while their happy smiling guests proudly held up the giant fish they caught all by themselves. Nope. Not this man with a boat.

Our skipper for the day, whom we met at a bar four hours earlier, was wearing just a pair of black shorts. It was as if he had just rolled out of bed, which he would have done if he had gone to bed at all. He looked like he had just hopped on to his 'deep sea fishing boat' to meet us, his spur of the drunken moment, paying customers. He was a local man, dark skinned with unruly short curly hair, or perhaps that was his 'just got out of bed' look. The boat wasn't white and didn't glisten in the sunshine. It was a wooden affair with faded, peeling paint which I believe the fashionable term is 'distressed', paintwork. It wasn't the only thing distressed at that moment. It did have a cabin but no elevated viewing platform and not a fishing rod to be seen. They say you get what you pay for and I most certainly conceded with that adage. This boat didn't look seaworthy. "Ali", I whispered, "don't you think the boat looks a bit dilapidated?" "Not at all", Ali assured me, "it's just a bit run down, nothing to worry about". Oh my god. Panic was starting to emanate from me as I looked at the black clouds and choppy sea once again. "Ali, I'm sorry but I am not putting one foot onto that boat if he doesn't have any life jackets on board". The thought of the uncontrollable waves slapping against my face, going up my nose and down my throat making me choke as I battled against the vicious waves was making me feel ill already. If I fell into the middle of the ocean I knew I would perish without a life jacket to keep me afloat. "It's ok Sharon", piped up Jake. "I'm a qualified lifeguard. I'll do a check of the life jackets to make sure they are up to standard". Relief surged through me temporarily. He did look the part; athletic, into sporty activities and blonde spiky hair. Our skipper had anchored his boat and beckoned for us to join him on deck.

As we clambered on board I desperately needed to know about the life jackets so I gave Jake a stern look to spur him on to enquire about the lifesaving jackets. "Morning skipper", said Jake. "We're all set for some deep sea fishing but could I possibly check a couple of things with you?". "No worries", confirmed the skipper. "What is it that you need to know?" Jake then ran through some important points; fishing rods – check, life jackets – check. Our skipper pulled out some life jackets from under a wooden seat and to me they appeared to have the same distressed trait that the paintwork had. There were five life jackets in total which Jake, the qualified lifeguard, inspected and confirmed they were useable and in full working order should the need arise. Well, I couldn't exactly still abandon the 'organised' activity without looking like a quitter. Mine and Ali's mutual girlie admiration for each other dissipated in a second. No, I had to stop being a scaredy cat and start to woman up. It's just water for goodness sake. A life jacket would ensure my life would not end via a drowning incident while deep sea fishing in the Indian Ocean.

So, with the safety jacket check complete and the fishing rods on board, we set off. Four hours earlier during the bar negotiations, our skipper promised that a light lunch and refreshments would be provided. However, he clearly had nothing edible in his fridge and unable to shop for food between the hours of 12 midnight and now, it was necessary for him to call into a grocery store at the next bay. This involved anchoring at an inlet a little further along the coast, the skipper wading through the water to the tiny beach, disappearing amongst the trees and vegetation on land to provide to us his spontaneous lunch menu. At this point I believed that perhaps our skipper had second thoughts about the whole boat for hire thing and had deserted us at the nearest port. But no, he eventually returned carrying in a banana box two pineapples and some bottled water. You get what you pay for came to mind again. Holding our 'gourmet lunch' supplies over his head, he waded once again through the water back to the boat, clearly satisfied with his off the cuff lunch fodder.

Off we set, the boat motor distinctly straining from the exertion as it spluttered and gurgled. The stench of petrol penetrated our nostrils and filled our lungs with the intoxicating fumes. The repugnant odour, fused with the severe jarring of the boat against the rugged ocean waves, had already begun to make me feel a little queasy. I focussed on keeping deep breaths but it didn't help. Sucking in more of the overpowering petrol vapours was not helping at all. Ali and Jake were immune to the fumes and continual fluctuations of the boat. I tried to think of anything but the fumes and fluctuations. Our skipper had told us of the big game fish that were swimming around this area for us to catch if we were lucky. There were Yellow Fin Tuna, Wahoo, Dorado, Barracuda and Kingfish (also known as Trevally) just to name a few. Unfortunately, my angling skills had only been tested once while in a small tin boat on the Noosa River in Australia when I was fishing with my housemate, Garry. My line miraculously managed to hook onto a tiny bream fish which was smaller than the span of my hand. We dutifully cooked our catch of the day which was full of bones with a minuscule amount of flesh. So I thought angling could perhaps be a talent that's been hidden all these years.

As it turned out, our skipper had several sets of snorkelling gear, as well as the appropriate fish bait which would allow us to at least tempt the fish to the rod even if we couldn't catch one. This was encouraging. The boat, and I, didn't look or feel as distressed as the sun broke through the clouds. The sea, while undeniably choppy, didn't appear as turbulent or savage as earlier. Maybe it was just the earlier gloomy weather that made the whole situation appear much more intimidating than it was. Glum weather can seriously affect your memory of a certain place or activity, making your recollection a sombre one. Dull, overcast days quell any feelings of cheerfulness and well-being, turning the mood into a downbeat and low-spirited perception. I understand not everyone reacts this way and that I no doubt suffer from S.A.D. or Seasonal Adjustment Disorder, nonetheless, it does factor in my thought process hence the original sentiment. It's particularly unfortunate that I live in England seeing that most days are grey and overcast, making winter a very depressing time. Actually, make that summer too. My perception now revised I started to relax and actually enjoy the boat ride as we made our way further into the middle of the Indian Ocean. There was not another vessel in sight. Snorkelling was the agreed first activity of the day and our skipper, having sailed out for a couple of hours, now stopped the boat.

Lifeguard or not, there was no way I was entering the water without a life jacket on. I realised my tough Overlander image would no doubt be quashed by this request and Ali's impression of me would alter dramatically, however, I knew my limits. Choppy waters, which can even be described as savage in my book, were not a challenge to me. I considered it foolish. Jake was clearly not impressed by my request for a life jacket, the lifeguard in him secretly appalled by my lack of swimming skills, but I threw the first jacket over my shoulders, arms through the armholes, ready to zip up and secure the simple yet ingenious lifesaving apparatus. Oh no! The zipper didn't zip. What use is an unzipped lifesaving jacket? Its lifesaving properties completely eradicated by an inoperative zipper. That's okay I thought. There are four more jackets. But it was like Groundhog Day. Jacket after jacket the zippers failed to operate. There was no lifesaving qualities to these jackets. I may as well have a bag of bricks tied to my feet for all the good one of these jackets would be. "Jake", I said through gritted teeth, "I thought you had checked all these jackets. You said they were all in working order" I asked him. It was evident that he had not inspected any of the five jackets. What kind of lifeguard was he? There was nothing lifesaving about his life jacket inspection skills.

"Oh, sorry Sharon", he mumbled, "I didn't think to check the zippers". What? So what did he inspect? Did he just check they were all orange in colour and had some form of padding? If anything happened here in the middle of the ocean it would be like the Titanic all over again. Well, in this case, not even one useable life jacket. Again, Ali and Jake were oblivious to the potential risks now inflicted upon us by Jake's lack of life saving skills. "Sharon, this is not a problem", advised our skipper who look bemused by the whole life saving jacket dilemma. "I have a ball of string. I will secure the jacket with some string". String? I'm going to be strung up like a piece of meat ready for roasting. Our skipper, pleased with himself for his quick zipper improvisation, had started to rummage in his cabin before proudly holding up a ball of string. "Look! It even matches the colour of your jacket". Great! At least I was colour co-ordinated for the police pathologist that would be examining me after I had been dragged out of the water. Our skipper set to work with the ball of string. I was instructed to put my arms in the air while he tightly wrapped the string around my torso trapping the life jacket to my body. Round and round he went with the orange string while Ali and Jake were laughing in hysterics at the makeshift zipper. "You look like a parcel wrapped up with string. It's hilarious!" laughed Ali as she took a photo of my well-strung lifesaving sheath.

Surprisingly it did feel secure and I now felt confident to grab some snorkelling gear and climb down the boat ladder to gingerly lower myself into the water. With mask in place, snorkel attached and in my mouth, I donned my flippers at the very last moment. Whoa it was choppy. I had no control over the turbulent waves as they tossed my body up and down like I was on a rollercoaster ride. I must've looked like an orange buoy bobbing on top of the water, a warning marker for other swimmers. Luckily, the only other swimmers anywhere near me in this big ocean were Ali, Jake and our skipper. I saw some colourful fish in between gulps of rancid saltwater that poured into my snorkel when I was slammed down by a wave to then be pounded in the face by another. It was exhilarating but petrifying at the same time. The string continued to remain around my chest, however, the spacing of the loops was decreasing, pushing the jacket off my shoulders onto my neck and head. Our skipper stayed with me the whole time I was "snorkelling" which, considering the fuss I made over the life jackets, was understandable and I was extremely grateful.

Exhausted by the continual battering from the waves and my now, loose fitting life jacket, I decided it was time to get back onto the boat which was easier said than done. The continual churning of the waves while clinging onto the ladder with one hand and trying to peel off my flippers with the other saw me being continually dunked in and out of the water. In spite of all the obstacles the ocean threw at me, I negotiated the waves and executed my final heave onto the deck with about as much finesse as a beached whale, albeit, a fluorescent orange beached whale.

The second and final activity of the day was deep sea fishing. This meant no salty water up my nose and down my mouth as we would stay on the boat for this one. How hard could deep sea fishing be? We had the basic tools required to catch fish, a fishing rod, bait and a big ocean with lots of fish. As there were only two rods we had to take turns; remember, you get what you pay for. The thrill of the catch was surprisingly exciting, but I'm not sure the thrill would last for hours and hours of waiting. After a very brief lesson for dummies in how to cast off it wasn't long before something started tugging on my line. "Oh my god! Something's tugging on my rod!" I shouted over to Ali. She turned round and looked at me like I was an idiot which I undoubtedly was when it came to my expertise in fishing. "Quick! Sharon! Don't just sit there like a lemon. Start reeling it in. Quick! You'll lose it otherwise." In my shock at such an aggressive tug I just sat there clinging onto the rod. With the prompt from Ali I jumped into action, reeling and winding the spool device as fast as I could. The frantic clicking sound of the spindle sent me into a frenzy. Whatever was on the end of my fishing line was heavy, well, it was compared to the tiny Australian Bream which is the only fishing experience I have had. A Great White Shark did cross my mind, over 25 feet in length, the size of a double decker bus – which is what this fish felt like. The bursts of metallic clicking continued for what seemed like an eternity as I wound the spool, slowly reeling in my catch. Our skipper was there to assist with the final reel and there it was. My catch! "It's a King Fish", he announced, "Not a bad catch for a first attempt". I beamed with pride. This is not word of a lie; the fish must've been about 25 inches long! The jubilation I felt was absurd. It was just a poor fish that had an unfortunate encounter with my fishing rod. There was no skill whatsoever on my part as I sat there dangling the fishing line into the water. It made me think of a funny saying someone once told me "a fisherman is a jerk on one end of the line waiting for a jerk on the other". How true is that? Really? Our big fishing day ended up with Ali catching another King Fish. Jake regrettably caught none, his fishing skills evidently as good as his lifesaving jacket inspection techniques.

Ali's fish boning prowess was displayed that evening as she skilfully removed the heads and tails before opening the fish like a book. Next was the removal of the backbone, rib cage and skin. Another one of Ali's many skills was negotiating which she had also done for us. She had secured the use of a kitchen knife to bone the fish, a chef to season and cook the fish pieces and a restaurant to eat it at with the proviso that we purchase side orders to be served with our fish. Perfect. That night a fish banquet was prepared and lots of our fellow Intrepid travellers joined us. Fenella and Georgie looked even more stunning that night, bungalows and white sand beaches had undoubtedly agreed with them. Note to one's self, get Fenella and Georgie's beachwear tips. Not urgent.

This was our last night together on the island of Zanzibar, which is a fascinating place, with the exception of the stringent Immigration and Customs bureaucracy that you have to endure before stepping onto the island. Well worth a visit if you venture around East Africa, but for us it was the end. Tomorrow was a big day of bus rides and ferries to take us back to the mainland where we all went our separate ways in the world with some people going home and others to continuing travelling.

Another plan had formed in my head since my Kilimanjaro experience. I needed another trekking challenge and I had just the one in mind. Everest Base Camp. Not quite as high as Kilimanjaro, nonetheless near enough to possibly develop high altitude pulmonary oedema. Twelve days trekking in the Himalayan Mountains. It was time to work and save some money to bolster my dwindling travel fund.

Chapter 13

Everest Base Camp

Twelve months on I had worked and saved hard, my travel fund was well and truly beefed up again for my next journey to Everest Base Camp. Neither my near death experience nor the risk of developing high altitude pulmonary oedema was high on my list of concerns. The thrill and adventure I experienced from the Kilimanjaro climb was far more rewarding than working nine to five, sitting at a desk, in a stuffy office, looking at other people's finances. The world was beckoning me to go exploring again. So it was that I found myself planning to expand the Everest Base Camp trek to include the 'Stans in Central Asia, which are notoriously bad when it comes to red tape and excessive bureaucracy. I had meticulously catalogued every tourist visa that I would require prior to entering the various countries. Every entry date, exit date, duration of stay, every single requirement was chronicled on an excel spreadsheet. I was determined not to face any visa issues on my next journey, even it if meant being slightly OCD about the whole subject. My heedful attention to detail and regimented documentation would certainly ensure I was not subjected to accusation at any border crossing.

My flight and entry into Nepal were uneventful, there were no arrests or immigration officials accusing me of illegally entering their country. I'd forgotten, from my last visit to Kathmandu, how manic the city taxi drivers drove as I hurtled along the potholed roads, clinging onto the headrest in front of me in an attempt not to be thrown around the back of the car like a ball in a pinball machine. The seatbelt that would have kept me anchored to the seat in an upright position was unmistakably absent from the rear of the vehicle. The windscreen was a roadmap of cracks as though suffering from an acute case of varicose veins. Threadbare fabric covered the seats along with many layers of grime that had accumulated from countless bodies smearing an assortment of substances such as ice cream drips to fried food grease. The polluted air blew in from the open windows stinging my eyes. My incessant blinking delivered no respite from the noxious fumes. A local guy I befriended during my last visit to Kathmandu was genuinely shocked when my answer to his question, "Why aren't you wearing a face mask?" was "Because I don't have one". He insisted we should immediately find a shop that sells them to protect me from inhaling the toxic fumes. He was being deadly serious. There is a global air quality ranking called the Environmental Performance Index (EPI) which is environmental data collected each year by Yale and the International Earth Science Information Network. The 2014 air quality index shows Nepal ranking 177th out of 178 countries, managing to beat only Bangladesh. Not surprisingly, China is third from the bottom ranking. The best air quality rankings are Switzerland, Luxemburg and Australia. Britain comes in at number twelve. So there you have it, any respiratory issues that may arise during my Everest trek could be nothing to do with altitude mountain sickness, but simply the effects of air pollution.

At the pre-trek gathering I met my fellow Everest Base Camp hikers and the lead guide, Asouk. I find it strange that you 'climb' Kilimanjaro without getting out your ropes, crampons and ice axes, yet you only 'trek' to Everest Base Camp. I understand that Kilimanjaro is the only mountain you can climb to the summit without climbing aids, whereas with Everest Base Camp you are not even reaching the summit of a mountain. If you were to reach the very summit of Everest then you most certainly would have climbed but with using the ropes, crampons, ice axes and maybe an oxygen tank or two wouldn't go amiss. There were twelve of us attempting the trek.

'Team America' consisted of five law students, two girls and three guys, all from different parts of the United States, but friends from all studying at the same university. I cannot remember any of their names as they were one entity, like the Oompa Loompas from Willy Wonka's chocolate factory or the dance cast from Michael Jackson's Thriller, with their all-American, clean cut looks and wearing their conservative clothes with a sporty edge. Saying that, I do remember being envious of their Rab down jackets and Moleskin blister plasters when the climate was getting harsher.

Then there were three Australians, Cassie, Joe and Mike, who all worked together in Brisbane and thought it would be a bonzer idea to take bush walking to a much higher level, literally.

There were two Irish firemen, Neil and John, who said they were climbing the big hill just for the craic. I wonder if their firefighting training included aiding persons suffering from the effects of high altitude pulmonary oedema. Note to one's self – check Phil and John's first aid skills.

Finally, there was Marc, a Chinese Australian from Sydney. I dubbed him the walking pharmacist. His doctor had prescribed him enough Diamox to supply the Nepalese army. He had hundreds of the little white pills. Perhaps he was a drug dealer supplying them to the locals in the little mountains villages? I made another note to myself to find out how much John was charging for his drugs, just in case.

Our guide, Asouk, was a local man from Kathmandu, slightly built with short dark hair and a cheeky twinkle in his eyes. He was a joker.

Cassie was nominated as my teahouse roomie as we were the only females along with Team America #1 and #2. Although Cassie was only 20 years old she had a wise head on her shoulders. She was actually due to turn 21 years during the trek. How many people can say on their 21st birthday they were trekking to Everest Base Camp? My 21st birthday celebration was a party at the small terraced house that I had just taken out a mortgage for. Drinks were flowing, Taboo and lemonades, Bacardi and cokes, dancing to Cher's 'The Shoop Shoop Song' and Right Said Fred's 'I'm too Sexy'. My friends thought I was barmy buying a house four days before I turned 21 years old. Committing myself to mortgage repayments and never ending house repairs. As it happens, it was the most sensible thing I have ever done. My now diminutive mortgage and low outgoings mean I can indulge in a world of travel and adventure without being tied down with debt.

This world of travel meant I had to meet my fellow trekkers at the guesthouse reception at the ungodly hour of four o'clock in the morning. Our first destination was Kathmandu airport to catch the early morning flight to Lukla, the official starting point of the Everest Base Camp trek. Lukla airport is infamous and is said to be the world's most dangerous airport for planes to land and take-off. This piece of knowledge did not bode well with any of us, knowing that we were about to experience firsthand the terrifying landing strip which is a mere 460 metres in length and 20 metres wide (1,500 feet x 65 feet) more of a garden path than a runway. Compare that to a standard international airport runway which is over six times that length at around 3,048 metres (10,000 feet). Add to that the altitude at Lukla of 2,860 metres (9,380 feet) which effectively reduces the plane's life and engine power thus a longer runway is needed at higher altitudes. One silver lining is they built the runway on a steep grade, twelve percent, to try and help slow the planes down quickly, perhaps they should have also thought of location? Oh, did I also mention the 2,800 metre (9,200 feet) sheer drop at the end of the runway? Then we saw the plane. Our hearts sank. It was a 15 seater propeller plane that had clearly seen better days.

As we boarded the 'Tara' plane, an immaculately dressed flight attendant greeted us, which was a difficult task in itself as the plane was so small. She had her back pressed against the seats and breathed in to enable us to shuffle past her. The inside of the plane had suffered even more abuse over the years than the exterior. The emergency exit signs were detached from the sides of the plane and were hanging by an electrical wire obstructing the views from the windows below. The seats were tiny and not a headrest in sight which meant no in-flight entertainment. Once we had all squeezed past the flight attendant and wedged into a seat, we had a clear view of the pilots. The cockpit had a dividing wall with a domed entrance cut out of the middle through which I could see the entire control panel; an array of dials and switches that provided the pilots with important information such as altitude, speed and direction. The pilots were already on the plane in their starched shirts and big green headsets. Team America #3 was from New York and his demeanour was very camp with his tiny body frame, tiny rectangular glasses and effeminate walk. He was terror-stricken by the poor quality of the plane. "Oh my god!" he cried "this pile of metal will never get us to Lukla! Look at it? Oh my god! What am I doing? I detest flying in normal, modern planes but this...?" He promptly started to chew his fingernails in a desperate attempt to focus his mind on something else.

The flight attendant then sucked in her breath in preparation for her shuffle down the plane. She had in her hand a tiny straw basket. Well, let's face it, nothing could be big on this plane. One side of her basket was filled with boiled sweets and the other with cotton wool. Cotton wool? Was this to muffle the noise of the airplane engine? Good grief! How loud was it going to be? Were engine mufflers not invented in the 1960s? Maybe I should have invested in some sound blocking earmuffs. Or even better, a parachute! Cassie and I are grinning at each other like imbeciles not knowing whether to laugh or cry. "It was nice to know you even if it was only brief" I joked to Cassie though I'm not sure she was particularly impressed by my humour. The plane spluttered into life and started to position itself on the runway for take-off. This was the easy part. It was the other end that terrified us all. With cotton wool crammed in my ears and what I concluded was a barley sugar sweet in my mouth we were finally in the air heading for Lukla. Forty five minutes of apprehension and dread. There was no room for pilot error during the landing or else we would end up crashing into the side of the mountains.

The views of the snow-capped mountains were stunning as we all stared out of the tiny windows. Our hearts pounding with the excitement of what the next twelve days would bring. Well, the next twelve minutes was pretty daunting too with the imminent landing from hell at the world's scariest airport. "I think I'm going to be sick" declared Team America #3 "this has to be the worst flight I have ever taken". With my attention diverted from the views I began to examine the cockpit control panel and to my horror, I could see that none of the dials were moving. I nudged Cassie "Psst – have you seen the pilot's dials?" She studied the dials and her jaw dropped. "They're not moving" gasped Cassie. The pilots were now navigating a very tight, constricted route through the Himalayas, high mountains towered either side of us, without any computerised assistance. They were relying solely on the view from their cockpit window which was now fogging over with condensation. Oh my god! They now couldn't see out of the window. In a flash the co-pilot had picked up a blue paper roll from the floor of the cockpit, the type that you get at a garage or a petrol station, and after tearing several sheets off the roll, he stretched over the useless control panel and started to wipe the condensation from the cockpit window. Cassie and I looked on in horror as the co-pilot continued to wipe the glass, his attempt futile as every blue paper towelled wipe seemed to smear the condensation to another part of the cockpit window. How on earth the pilot missed crashing into the mountains I do not know. Maybe, seeing that there was no functioning radar equipment on board the plane, he had some form of inner physic ability to 'see' his way through the mountains. The smeared window was now as useful as the non-moving control panel. As we approached the runway I did spare a thought for the glow in the dark Jesus from the Rwandan mission and said a silent prayer for the condensation difficulties to end and that the brakes had recently been serviced. I glanced again at the emergency exit sign hanging by an electrical wire and reluctantly admitted to myself that maintenance checkups were probably not a priority for the Tara airline. Clearly more effort was put into selecting a nice outfit for the flight attendant than fixing the radar equipment.

Team America's #3 knuckles had turned white as he gripped the arm rests in anticipation of a crash landing. The runway was consistent with the plane, tiny! As the plane started to descend we could see the cliff edge where the tarred runway abruptly ended into thin air. The delight of taking off from the edge of the cliff is, thankfully, delayed for twelve days, however, our current predicament was the wall of mountains facing us. We were flying low into a cul-de-sac of rugged mountains, the 460 metre runway led directly into some buildings that sat at the foothill of the mountains. Surrounded by mountains, the pilot only gets one chance to land. There is no room for the pilot if he is not happy with the initial descent to stop descending and turn around for a second attempt. This was all or nothing, land or crash. Thankfully my prayer to the glow in the dark Jesus came up trumps again as the pilot skilfully lowered the plane onto the tarmac with the smallest of bumps before slamming on the brakes for the hair-raising finale. I cringed as the buildings inflated from dots to life size in just seconds. At the very last second the pilot veered sharply to the right into a tiny airplane 'car park' which had six miniature bays for the tiny planes to park up. Team America #3 had his eyes tightly squeezed shut. "Is everyone still alive? Have we landed okay? Oh my god! I can't believe I have to go through all that again in twelve days' time" he wailed. I had to agree with him. The thought of the tiny plane racing, as fast as 460 metres would allow, off the end of the cliff was daunting to say the least.

Our first priority was breakfast as we all trudged up the hill to a local teahouse; the climb in altitude from 1,400 metres in Kathmandu to 2,860 metres in Lukla was already having an impact as we puffed and panted. Flashbacks of Kilimanjaro came to mind; Fetaeli barking "pole, pole" and biscuit crumb trails that turned into vomit tracks. I was optimistic that the twelve day acclimatisation during the Everest trek would ensure no repeat performances of any form of trails or the onset of high altitude pulmonary oedema.

Asouk introduced us to our porters who had the arduous task of carrying our sleeping bags, thermarests and sleeping mats, limited clothing and underwear, not to mention evening footwear and socks. Evening footwear was not the latest pink 3" block heel strappy shoes but a pair of reef sandals with adjustable Velcro straps to accommodate bulky walking socks. Comfort outweighs fashion when trekking, nevertheless, I still refuse to do the flip flops with socks thing. Horrible look. Asouk also had two junior guides to help him during the trek, Parsons and Suresh. Parsons was a tiny, stocky man with rosy, chubby cheeks and an entertaining Nepali humour. Suresh was young with dark, floppy hair that hung over his youthful and unblemished face and he too was blessed with the Nepali humour.

As we began trekking on day one, it immediately became clear that the Nepalese 'flat' was unlike the rest of the world 'flat'. This 'flat' was hilly. Up and down steep mountains, not an inch of horizontal ground to be seen. It took eight days to reach Everest Base Camp and each day brought with it challenges. The main obstacle without a doubt was the high altitude, every day the air got thinner and thinner. The familiar sucking in a large amount of air to have only a tiny fraction enter your lungs returned. The continual effort of breathing was relentless and tiring.

Most days involved 6-10 hours trekking through the Nepalese 'flat' terrain taking in some of the most incredible scenery I have ever seen. It started with lush, green valleys with gentle streams trickling down the hillsides. We were surrounded by huge rocky mountains and clusters of pine trees. Suspension bridges were also a common feature in the landscape due to the many valleys and rivers to cross. It was like being in an Indiana Jones movie striding over the swinging bridges, only these were made from metal slatted sheets to walk on and thick chicken wire sides to protect people from falling off. The slight flaw was that you couldn't hold onto the steel cable handrail unless you wanted to shred your fingers on the jagged edging of the chicken wire which was like barbed wire.

Colourful Buddha prayer flags were strewn in the most bizarre spots, fluttering in the wind over raging rivers, draped around the 'barbed wire' on the suspension bridges and even in the ice and snow between rock piles. They quietly spread harmony through the mountainside, creating happiness and good fortune to all who pass through. Farmland was divided by low, dry stone walls with small outhouse buildings, which reminded me a little of the Yorkshire Dales. With altitude the landscape gradually changed to white rocky hills and barren valleys filled with floating clouds. Snowy mountains encompassed us. Everywhere you looked there were white mountains and low lying clouds. White rock turned into grey stone where giant craters had formed, filled with melted glacier water the vivid colour of jade green.

We had two 'acclimatisation' days at the villages of Namche Bazaar and Dingboche. These days involved a small hike, Nepalese 'flat', up a further 100 metres or so in altitude where we would just 'hang out' for around thirty minutes and then walk back down. For Aussie Joe and lead guide Asouk, 'hanging out' usually meant hopping around on one leg with their hands behind their backs trying to barge each other over with their body weight. The first one to fall over lost the game. Tricky game when the simple task of breathing was an effort but it kept us all entertained during the waiting period. Another way to pass the time was to find the biggest rock, climb to the top, take a photo while on top of the rock, then scramble back down. It was amazing what you could find to do to keep you amused while 'acclimatising'. The remainder of these days were like a mini break in the mountains, strolling around the villages, exploring the back alleys and pathways and, if you had a Pringles and gambling addiction like me, you would just kick back in the teahouse and play the card game 'Switch' to win individual Pringles. The sole aim of the game of Switch is to discard all your cards and the first person to have no cards is the winner. It is similar to UNO and Crazy Eights.

Another challenge we faced was an unexpected encounter which took place on day six, as we were trekking on the Nepalese 'flat' which was a steep, narrow and rocky path that had been chiselled and formed from the side of a mountain. Rustic steps had been chipped out from the mountain stone. One side of us was the rugged rock wall of the mountain and the other a sheer drop to the ground which, as we climbed, was getting further and further away from us. At what seemed to be the most tapered section of rocky path we could hear what sounded like the jangle of Swiss cow bells. It was as if we had been transported to the Swiss Alps. The different tones created by the bells were like a symphony of clangs but instead of cows, we came face to face with a herd of yaks. The first one appeared from around one of the many 'brows' of the hillside and loomed over us like a giant yeti with horns. Yak attack! These heavy animals have huge, bulky frames with stumpy, but sturdy, legs. They have lovely shaggy hair to keep them warm with a not so nice looking hunch on their backs. Even uglier was the pair of horns which looked like giant, pointed boomerangs, attached to the sides of their heads. The yak filled the narrow ledge with its bulky frame making it impossible for us to pass. You could tell by the steely look in his eyes that the path was his for the taking, not ours. The only option we had, other than to throw ourselves off the edge of the mountainside, was to scale the rock wall and clamber far enough up to avoid being trampled by a herd of yaks.

Yak also appeared on the menu each night at every teahouse in every village. It was as if each chef had stolen the recipes from the village down the hill and had replicated the dishes, or perhaps there was a special offer on at the printing shop, order 50 menus get 50 free. A teahouse menu consisted of a basic and repetitive selection. Hot drinks included coffee or tea, black or white, hot chocolate, hot lemon, lemon tea, ginger tea and boiled water. There were three sizes on offer; a cup, small pot or big pot.

Breakfast was either toast with jam, 'chapatti' with jam, Tibetan bread with jam, pancake with jam, porridge or a tuna sandwich. Undoubtedly there was some kind of special offer on jam supplies. Eggs came in every style; boiled, fried, scrambled, cheese omelette, onion omelette or vegetable omelette. Dinner was mainly a rice, noodle or potato dish with flavourings of vegetables, eggs, tuna or cheese. There was even was a fried noodle with cheese dish. Soup or sherpa stew were also a popular choice. To add a dose of international flair there was also a small selection of spring rolls and pizzas, cheese or vegetable of course, together with 'macaroni cheese' and fried spaghetti. The Nepali speciality on offer were 'momos' which are stuffed dumplings that can be served steamed or fried and, you guessed it, the fillings on the menu were cheese, vegetable or tuna. They were delicious. I'm referring to the unhealthy deep fried dumplings and not the healthy steamed ones. For those trekkers with a sweet tooth there were 'chocolate rools' which turned out to be deep fried Mars Bar or Snickers. There had plainly been some guidance from celebrity chef, Heston Blumenthal, considering some of the curious styles of cooking, in particular the fried spaghetti and cheese combo.

It was like Groundhog Day. Every menu was the same every night of the twelve day trek. The only variation was the price, the higher the altitude, the more expensive it became. Highly understandable seeing as how some poor bugger has had to carry the yak steaks and tins of tuna further up the mountain. Even at the highest altitude the prices were still cheaper than buying a Marks and Spencer club sandwich at Leeds train station.

The teahouses were constructed from old stone with timber doors and window frames. No double glazing on the Everest trek. It looked bad enough for the locals carrying huge slabs of wood balanced on their back which is how they get the materials up the 'flat' terrain to build new houses. Most buildings were only two storey and they were very basic. Some internal walls actually felt like thin hardboard. In every dining room, single paned glass windows covered every wall to enable all diners to have 360 degree views of the mountains. The tables and benches with cushions were always positioned against the walls in a big square around the room with the fire in the middle. Simple but effective. The dining hall was the only room with a fire to keep you warm from the freezing temperatures outside. Not quite so toasty in the sleeping quarters. I don't believe my thermal trousers were even taken off after passing a certain level of altitude.

After dinner playing cards would come out and the games would commence. "So who's for a game of Switch?" offered Neil, the Irish fireman who looked like a bit of a card shark to me. "None of this playing for the fun of it. We can play for Pringles" said Neil. Pringles were an expensive and highly sought after commodity on the Everest trek. At the highest altitude the cost of a tube shot up to four Euros. The 'pop til you drop' slogan took on a whole new meaning up in the Himalayan Mountains than it did at sea level. "Count me in" confirmed Cassie whilst digging into her pocket for a Euro. Firefighter John and I quickly followed suit and soon we had a tube of sour cream and onion Pringles on the table. "Four Pringles per win?" suggested Neil, clearly no newcomer to this betting business. We all solemnly agreed and it was game on. The game of Switch became quite an obsession with us. Pringles never tasted so good. We even played it seated around a rock at Everest Base Camp, the prize for winning at such an elite location was the remainder of half a tube of Original Pringles. That equated to roughly fifty Pringles give or take some broken bits. I think perhaps addiction may be a more suitable description for our Switch playing Pringle winning games.

Day eight was our day to reach Everest Base Camp although Mount Everest at this stage had remained elusive and was still an unknown sight for us all. Were we actually on the correct track? I had serious doubts. Surely we should've at least had a glimpse of the mountain who's Base Camp we were heading for? At numerous sections of the trek Asouk would say "today we will be able to see Mount Everest in the distance" but all we saw were clouds. Cassie had also gotten rather annoyed at not seeing Mount Everest. "This is ridiculous. We have spent eight days hiking towards the bloody mountain, you'd think we'd at least have seen it once". I had to agree. Making it to Everest Base Camp would be a huge achievement, but not actually seeing the world's tallest mountain you have just trekked to would be verging on unbelievable. How can you spend eight days trekking towards the base of the world's tallest mountain and not see it? It just doesn't make sense. To top it off, you can't even see what we now believe to be a mythical mountain from the Base Camp. Day nine would be our last chance to see the mountain when we ascend to the highest point at Kala Patthar. Note to one's self; make sure I say a prayer to the glow in the dark Jesus tomorrow. Hopefully I hadn't used up all my prayers.

On the way to Everest Base Camp we were treated to snowfall as we trekked through the grey, rocky terrain past the water filled craters. There was even a yellow signpost wedged into the rocks confirming 'WAY TO mt EVEREST BC' which, considering my serious doubts that we were on the right track, assured me that we were. For the momentous occasion Cassie and I had brought with us a packet of Oreos and Mars Bars. Team America had brought their special knitted animal hats to put on for the EBC photos making them even more homogeneous. All of them now had either tiger or panda ears sticking out of their heads like something out of The Muppet Show. Everest was so different from Kilimanjaro. The weather was positively balmy compared to the freezing temperatures at the Kili summit. No frozen hair. No frozen water or backpack. Not one biscuit crumb or vomit trail. Then, on the other hand, I was still only at 5,364 metres and tomorrow, there was a climb of 186 metres to 5,550 metres so there was still a chance of the dreaded high altitude pulmonary oedema.

Day nine was the biggest challenge so far. Destination: Kala Patthar. Altitude: 5,550 metres. Compared to Kilimanjaro it was a late start at 3.30am when we all donned our warmest clothes and headlamps for the final ascent. It was exciting as we set off in the pitch black with our headlamps twinkling in the dark. Our strategy was to reach the summit of Kala Patthar with enough time to watch the sun rise over Mount Everest. This was our last pitch to lay eyes on the damn thing. Breathing had gotten tricky. The recognisable lack of oxygen symptoms returned as I kept trying to suck in some air into my lungs. We were all exhausted from the big trek to the Base Camp the day before. The deprivation of oxygen was crippling me again as I shuffled along. Asouk then stopped us. "Guys, we are half way to the summit and I can see that many of you are struggling" he declared "even though you can't see it now, Everest is just over the hills and when the sun rises and the clouds hopefully disappear you will see it from here". A likely story I thought. How many times had we been told this over the last nine days? "If you want to stay here", continued Asouk, "that's fine. I will stay here with you. For those of you that still wish to climb to the summit, Parsons and Suresh will go with you". I didn't think we looked that bad. Perhaps Joe and John looked a bit worse for wear but no-one looks their best when they are trekking in freezing temperatures and unable to suck in enough air to breathe properly. I was stunned when five of the twelve Everest trekkers decided not to climb to the summit. Good grief, I hadn't even vomited yet. There was no way I was going to stay here and sit on my butt in arctic conditions waiting for sunrise. I'd rather be shuffling on the Nepalese 'flat' being unable to breathe enough oxygen into my lungs. Who wouldn't? The seven of us, Team America #3, #4 and #5, Aussie and roomie Cassie plus her mate Mike and fireman Neil all continued up the mountain.

Over an hour of shuffling and wheezing my rhythm near the summit was three steps. Stop. Hopelessly trying to suck air into my oxygen deprived lungs, three steps, stop. Parsons stayed with me, imitating my rhythm. I was last again but as my mother always used to say, it's not the winning that counts but the taking part. Parsons, even though being super supportive, was not in the same ranking as Heaven. If they were chocolates Heaven would be Lindt and Parsons would be Cadbury's. That sentiment is in all likelihood to do with my physical condition while climbing Kilimanjaro. Let's be honest, I was on the verge of developing high altitude pulmonary oedema as a result of my severe AMS. Not here. Nine days of acclimatising had ensured no excruciating headaches or vomit trails. I was at the summit of Kala Patthar and what a view! Kala Patthar had a 360 degree view of all the Himalayan Mountains. I felt like I was on the 'roof of Asia'.

The sun was rising but there were so many mountains. Which one was Everest? I decided, even at the risk of sounding foolish, to ask Parsons. "Parsons, which one is Everest?" I managed, after finally inhaling enough oxygen to utter those five words. "Over there" he pointed. "See the mountain between those two big ones?" I could see a small mountain in the distance between two nearer mountains. Was that it? The tallest mountain in the world? It looked insignificant compared to all the other mountains surrounding us. This must be wrong. Fireman Neil stood next to me with his camera pointed in the direction of the small mountain and was happily taking pictures. "Neil, is that it?" "Yeah it's the small peak between the two big ones" he confirmed. Finally convinced the tiny pinnacle was indeed Everest, I began taking photos too, using my zoom lens in an attempt to capture some of its shape. This was a huge disappointment. The claims that Everest is the tallest mountain in the world must be inaccurate. Neil was also nonplussed by the unveiling of the mythical mountain. "I thought it would look a bit bigger than that," he grumbled "I'm definitely going to have to get my photos enlarged when I get home". Cassie sidled across to us. "What are you guys taking photos of?" she asked, clearly puzzled as to what we were so captivated by. "Duh! Everest of course," was my smart response. Cassie then went into hysterical laugher. What was so amusing I thought? "That's not Everest. It's over there," said Cassie, pointing to another mountain. A big mountain! Neil and I sheepishly redirected our camera lenses to the big mountain. "Thanks Cass," I mumbled. "Thank fuck for that!" exclaimed Neil "the folks back home would've had a field day looking at photos of the other puny mountain." Finally we were looking at Mount Everest in all its glory with its snow covered peak proudly protruding into the sky.

It was an unforgettable experience. Towering, majestic mountains could be seen from every angle. With snow and rock everywhere you looked it was a black and white monochrome landscape. If it wasn't for the splash of colour on our hiking jackets and a small show of blue sky, the photos I had taken could be mistaken for black and white ones. The hike down the mountain was gratifying as the simple action of breathing became normal again. Oxygen levels increased into the lungs. Wheezing ceased. It took us three hours to reach the summit and only thirty minutes to walk back down to the teahouse for some breakfast. It's surprising what a bit of oxygen can do for your walking abilities. I was a bit disconcerted when Cassie told me, that to her disgust, when chatting to Parsons on the way down, he informed her that what we had just climbed wasn't even a mountain. In Nepal, mountains are only considered to be proper mountains if they are 6,000 metres or higher. Anything less is classified as a hill. So, using that theory, Kilimanjaro is also just a mere hill at 5,985 metres, only 15 metres short of making the grade.

Chapter 14

Earthquake!

From that point on we commenced our descent back to Lukla and on day eleven we did a five hour trek back to a mountain village called Phakding, which we had also stayed at on the way up to Base Camp. Phakding was one of those tiny villages that just appeared on the mountainside with old stone houses perched on ledges, dotted on the steep incline of the mountain. The teahouse was just at the side of the old cobbled road with the usual single paned glass windows along the long expanse of two of the dining room walls. Along the side of one of the walls was a narrow footpath leading to some small wooden cabins at the back. There were six cabins in one long row with a narrow veranda running the full length for access to each individual cabin. There were even two tiny sinks on the veranda for us to clean our teeth and wash our faces. The cabins were on the edge of a sheer drop into a grassy field below. Thin wooden stilts were attached to the rear and into the ground so over half the cabins were suspended in mid air, hanging over a grassy field. Cassie and I had the cabin nearest to the teahouse building which we were pretty smug about as it meant less distance to walk from the dining room to our abode in the dark.

The evening started with the familiar menu of rice, noodle or potato dishes – which were getting as dull as dishwater. After eating our usual fare we all lounged on the dining hall floor and watched a DVD of 'Touching the Void', convinced, of course, that we were all now qualified to make judgement on the film having just completed the Everest Base Camp trek. After we had finished reviewing the film, the gamblers and Pringle addicts, being myself, Cassie and firemen Neil and John, decided that we should play cards on our penultimate night before arriving back at the start point in Lukla tomorrow.

It was 6.30pm and dark outside the teahouse so, with headlamp positioned on my forehead making me look like a deformed dalek, I ventured outside onto the narrow footpath at the side of the teahouse to the stilted cabins. Having bagged the nearest room, my door was the first one off the tiny wooden veranda. As I stood rummaging through my backpack searching for the tiny pack of playing cards, the cabin suddenly started violently shaking which made me immediately topple and fall to the floor. It was like being on a fairground ride with the entire cabin precariously teetering on its fragile stilts. The primitive glass windows were rattling against the wooden frames, the noise was deafening. The thought of the glass smashing and shards flying into my face panicked me. Incredibly, my immediate thought was that it was big Aussie joker, Joe, who had spent the previous stay here, stamping and jumping on the frangible structure as a wake-up call. The weight of his heavy body thumping down on the wooden veranda made the whole framework shudder and shake. But not like this. He may be a big guy, nonetheless, even his body mass could not achieve this amount of disturbance. Oh my god! Earthquake! The realisation that it was an earthquake petrified me. I felt sheer horror that I was experiencing such an intense natural phenomenon and more importantly, that I was lying on the floor of a scanty cabin, suspended over a steep drop, with just giant matchsticks keeping me and the cabin from crashing down onto the ground way below.

I used the bed frame as leverage to get onto my feet and as I let go to make a dash for the doorway the cabin swayed from side to side. It felt like I was drunk. I tried to put one foot in front of the other but it was impossible. I eventually lurched for the door and ran outside and down the narrow footpath to the front of the teahouse. The ground was thrusting back and forth like a DJ mixing a vinyl record on a turntable. As I turned the corner to the front of the teahouse everyone had congregated outside on the flagstone paving, huddling together. Cassie saw me immediately and grabbed me. "You're ok!" she shouted, dragging me towards the others. Cassie had to shout over the deafening cacophony of rumbling buildings and screaming people. The mountain was a disaster zone. The teahouse alone was creaking and groaning as the earth pushed it from side to side. The loose glass panes ferociously vibrated in their frames creating a thunderous clatter. From above, the mountain now shrouded in darkness, we would hear locals running out of their houses screaming hysterically. Panic was bubbling up inside me. Were we going to survive this? Buildings were swaying dangerously on the steep mountain edges. Someone kept shouting "cover your heads... cover your heads!" So I hurriedly placed my forearms over my head but quickly realised that this shield was not going to protect me from collapsing buildings and rubble that might come crashing down from the mountain above us. It was terrifying. I believed at one point that this was where my life was going to end, in this tiny village on a cliff side. No high altitude pulmonary oedema for me. My life was going to be extinguished by falling rocks and debris from the crumbling houses above me.

Then the shaking stopped and there was an eerie silence. A whimper here or there was heard, and a rumble or two from the top of the mountain. It was dark and we had nowhere to run. We were stuck in a tiny village in the middle of a mountainside in Nepal. No electricity. No mobile network. No teahouse roof, although thankfully, we weren't aware of that until the morning. Asouk immediately took charge and assured us he would try his best to find out the extent of the situation. He tried to ring his contacts but the networks were overloaded with callers undoubtedly trying to ring their loved ones to make sure they were alive and safe, and had jammed. All his attempts were futile. At this point we were all oblivious to the magnitude of the earthquake and just how much damage it had caused. We were cut off from the entire world, marooned in a tiny village on the side of a mountain. Asouk's face was grave. It was cold and dark. We had no means of communication with the outside world. Our lives were at risk, not from the earthquake which had now stopped, but from the aftermath. In all probability, the impact of such a major earthquake on a mountainside will generate landslides and of course, there was also the possibility of the occurrence of aftershocks. Landslides were Anouk's main concern, the result of which could mean we ended up being crushed by falling rubble and debris. "Guys, please stay calm," pleaded Anouk "All mobile phone networks are down. I cannot contact anyone at the moment. We cannot go back into the teahouse as there is structural damage to the walls". The roof did not even get a mention and even though I am not a qualified structural engineer, I would hazard a guess that the collapsing of an entire roof would also be categorised as major structural damage.

Convinced we were still in danger Asouk wanted to have a designated rendezvous point that we should run to in the event of ensuing landslides. Consequently, we ended up stumbling in the dark with our headlamps lighting the way through what looked like a freshly ploughed farmer's field. This led to a grassy area, in the middle of nowhere, on the side of a mountain. "This is the place you should all come to if there are any aftershocks or landslides" instructed Asouk. "Just get here as fast as you can". As we trudged back to our cabins Cassie was shaken up, as we all were. "If there is a landslide I'm not sure we will make it to the field" she said "God, this is scary". I agreed. I was still stunned by the power and force of the earthquake. The ground was actually thrusting back and forth. I knew that one of the secondary effects of earthquakes was indeed landslides, especially in steep river valleys and areas of weak rocks.

Mine and Cassie's cabin was deemed unsafe, not because it was teetering on fragile wooden stilts, but because it was next to the bowing teahouse wall with giant cracks. Asouk instructed us to move out of our cabin and share with someone else. Cassie went into the cabin of her friends, Joe and Mike, and I ended up with my mattress on the tiny bit of floor between the two beds of Neil and John, the Irish firemen. Now if anyone knew how to respond in an emergency it should be a fireman! They train for these situations every day. Gosh, my glow in the dark Jesus was surely working overtime!

None of us particularly wanted to, or would've been capable of, sleeping at that moment so we all piled into one cabin, myself, Cassie, Joe, Mike and firemen Neil and John for a nervous game of cards. This was more to take our minds off thinking about our sorry plight than for fun. Isolated from the rest of the world in a rickety wood cabin with landslides imminent, I think my mind just went into autopilot. There was absolutely nothing anyone of us could do to stop a landslide. Even so, we all kept our boots firmly tied up on the assumption that we may just have to make a mad dash for the landslide rendezvous point. All at once the cabin began to shake and we could hear a loud, thunderous rumble. My calming thoughts were quickly replaced by terror. We all looked at each other wildly, and within seconds we had jumped to our booted feet and ran out of the cabin. My heart was racing as fast as my feet. We were engulfed in darkness as we all stumbled through the mud, our headlamps flickering manically around the field of dirt. Fuck. I was wading in some bushes. Where did they come from? Where was I heading? Panic set in. Everyone seemed to be ahead of me, as usual. The roaring rumbling was deafening as it elevated around us. Oh my god! My breathing became irregular as I got myself into a frenzy. Where had the damn mud gone? Where the hell was I running? My sense of direction was seriously amiss. I saw a white jersey in front of me. It was fireman John! "John!" I screamed. I caught another glimpse of his jersey with a flicker of my headlamp. "Wait! Pleeaasse!" With flailing legs I ran through the bushes towards him. John grabbed my hand "quick" he urged and we ran together, now in the right direction, to the landslide rendezvous point.

We huddled together at the rendezvous point until the ground stopped vibrating and the deafening rumble subsided. We learnt there had indeed been a landslide; however, this was on the other side of the river. Exhausted, we walked back to the cabins and tried to sleep. Even in my fortunate position of lying snugly between two firemen, sleep evaded me for most of the night. The threat of another landslide on this side of the river not too far from my thoughts.

The morning of day twelve brought even more challenges than the major earthquake the day before. A daylight view of the teahouse shocked us all as we saw the immense damage to the building. The entire roof had collapsed down onto the rooms below. Huge grey rocks, some even looked like boulders, and splintered timber filled the bedrooms, the beds nowhere to be seen underneath the destruction. Luckily, there was only one other trekker staying at the teahouse, a Japanese guy, who chose to sleep in the one bed that was untouched by the demolition. Maybe he has a glow in the dark Jesus looking over him too.

There were three porters who had families in Lukla and, unbeknownst to us, they had set off in the dark, post earthquake, in an attempt to reach their loved ones in Lukla. All mobile networks were down and they had no way of knowing if they were safe. As we began walking back to Lukla, it was horrifying to see the damage the earthquake had inflicted on the mountain villages. Some houses were now dangerously leaning with collapsed gables. Rubble and beams of timber lay in great piles on the ground. Cobbled pathways had disappeared into deep crevices; the jigsaw edging of the stone path, once in the middle, now formed the rim of a sheer drop into the dirt and stones below. Everywhere you looked there were fallen tree branches and debris. We walked in silence for a short while as we took in the havoc and devastation. How many people had been injured or died? What scale was the earthquake? Had there been tsunamis like what the 2004 Indonesian earthquake triggered? As these unspoken questions went through our minds, the three porters who had set off trekking last night in the pitch black had reappeared and were talking excitedly to Asouk. They were extremely agitated about something. Asouk kept nodding then asking questions, his face pensive. "Do you think they made it back to Lukla?" whispered Cassie. "I'm not sure" I responded "but something is bothering them. They keep pointing to further up the track. Something's not good". Incredibly, they were heading back to Phakding to pick up our backpacks which was way above and beyond the call of a porter's duty. They had made it to Lukla but not the accustomed way. Their families were uninjured; however, Parson's house had collapsed and was now unliveable.

Asouk then relayed another crucial piece of information. There had been countless landslides all over the mountain and one of them had destroyed a suspension bridge that we needed to cross to get back to Lukla. It didn't take us long to reach where the suspension bridge had been. A mass of earth and rock had moved down the mountain with such force that everything in its path had been destroyed. The bridge now drooped loosely across the river, all the wire sides completely destroyed. Asouk was grim-faced again as he contemplated our options. We couldn't go down the mountain as firstly, it was too steep, and secondly, there was a raging river at the bottom. As Asouk pondered with Parsons, we all wondered if we were actually going to make it back to Lukla that day. It didn't look good. Asouk finally had a plan. We go up. What could possibly go wrong with such a plan? A big branch was Asouk's makeshift machete to clobber the vegetation around us and make a primitive 'opening' for us to walk through.

We started to climb up the steep mountain face which had never before been 'trekked'. We were truly now off the beaten track and in the middle of thick vegetation on the vertical edge of a Himalayan mountain. It was tricky. No worn track to place your feet onto. Leaves, branches and twigs were in our faces. Then there was another choice to be made. I felt like Bear Grylls. A right turn would take us to a cliff edge formed by the landslide or continue up the mountain face via a waterfall scramble. The clearest and most direct route was the cliff edge, yet Asouk was not convinced this was safe. The landslide made it impossible for Asouk to know whether or not the ground at the edge would take our weight. A few metres in and we could end up dropping like flies, the floor crumbling beneath us. The waterfall also had its dangers. The constant water flow had made the rocks perilous. A slippery film covered them all and they were highly unstable. Scrambling up them could easily send an avalanche of rocks hammering down on the heads of the climbers behind causing everyone falling like dominoes down the vertical, rocky waterfall.

Asouk chose the waterfall scramble. His reasoning, I expect was that at least we could try and dodge a falling boulder, whereas, if the cliff edge crumbled beneath your feet there was only one outcome. As we started to climb I immediately slipped on a rock. This didn't bode well for the vertical section near the top which, at that moment, looked so far away as it loomed above us. If you weren't skidding on rocks and losing your balance with every step, you were diving out of the path of falling rocks. The person in front forever shouting "Sorry!" each time they dislodged a stone, causing it to plummet down on the person behind. I was Bear Grylls. Sadly, there was no entourage of cameramen to capture the feat on film. Asouk's choice of route proved successful as, in spite of all the obstacles, we all reached the top of the waterfall. The mood was jubilant as we hugged and patted each other on the back congratulating each other on our triumphant endeavour. It was no mean feat scrambling up the waterfall, with rocks that were even more slippery than my ex-buddy, Gary from the Pekanbaru school.

In spite of our victory, Asouk's face remained grave. It was an immense responsibility on his shoulders. He had twelve people to try and keep alive; twelve inexperienced Everest Base Camp trekkers. A hard task when a major earthquake had just generated hundreds of landslides. We continued through the dense bush. Asouk pounded the vegetation with his makeshift machete until we reached our next impasse – another cliff edge. This time it wasn't formed by a landslide. This one was a long established cliff edge with thick, green vegetation that covered the steep ground. Twisted vines hung loosely around the foliage like a spider's web. There was a small 'ledge' that had naturally formed along the cliff which was no more than a foot deep. In most places! A mere 30 centimetres to place our feet! My walking boots are a UK size 6.5 which meant the ledge was more or less the same width as my foot. In some parts it was even less.

"Guys listen up" ordered a grim-faced Asouk. "We have no option but to walk across this cliff edge. You must go very slowly and tread very carefully". Holy shit! "This wasn't mentioned in the brochure", I joked to fireman Neil, who agreed. "An added bonus with no extra cost! You can't get more off the beaten track than this!" replied Neil. Both of us tried to make light of a very serious situation. In line again we set off. It was more of a shuffle than a walk as we inched our way across the mountain edge. It was treacherous. This was like a game of Russian roulette. Instead of one bullet in the chamber there was one tiny section of ledge that could collapse under your weight sending you hurtling down the vertical mountain side. Thank goodness for the vines that we could grab along the way that kept us upright when we slipped. There were also some obliging branches here and there to help with the awkward terrain. With my head down, concentrating on my feet and the lack of ground to place them on, I hadn't seen the line stop as I crashed into Cassie. "Oh my god! Sorry! I didn't realise you had stopped" I exclaimed as I clung onto a vine to keep my body upright. Only the balls of my feet were on the narrow ledge. "What's the problem? Why have we stopped?" I couldn't see past Cassie and certainly wasn't going to hang out over the ledge like Tarzan. The puny vine I was grasping didn't look particularly substantial and certainly not enough to take my whole body weight. Like a game of Chinese whispers word got back to Cassie. "There's a big gap. There is nothing to walk on" reported Cassie. Good grief. What do we do now? The village of Lukla seemed even more unreachable as we faced yet another obstacle.

As we crept closer to the gap I could see Parsons in front of Cassie and, across the void, Asouk. Then I noticed a man clinging to a vine, looking like a Nepali version of Spiderman, between us and Asouk. How on earth could he grasp a vine and stick his feet to the foliage? Where had he come from? What was his name? Perhaps my glow in the dark Jesus had sent him to us.

It was tricky as we approached the void, each of us grasping onto Parsons as if performing a waltz, into the hands of this miraculous stranger. His strength was incredible as he somehow clung to the mountainside, allowing us to use his hands and body to keep us upright as we performed an intimate shuffle into the waiting hands of Asouk. The horrifying thought crossed my mind that if Spiderman's super power failed, then we were both doomed to a very long, terrifying, fall. With my heart pounding, I stepped out onto a vine to start the awkward manoeuvre across the void. With my leg outstretched trying to find a foothold while reaching for another vine to hang onto I threw myself over to Asouk who grabbed me to safety. Holy shit, I did it! It was miraculous that we all came through the gap safely and uninjured. Even more bizarre, the stranger, after helping Parsons who was the last person to cross the void, went on his way, to where or to whom none of us knew. I am forever indebted to our guides Asouk, Parsons and the mysterious Spiderman, who put their own lives at risk to ensure twelve tourists made it back to Lukla on their own two feet and not in a wooden box.

With no further obstacles after the cliff edge adventure we made it back to Lukla late that afternoon. It was only later we discovered that the earthquake measured 6.9 on the Richter scale, killing at least 100 people. It struck near the border of Nepal and the Indian state of Sikkim. Within 30 minutes there had been two aftershocks and it also triggered hundreds of landslides, resulting in considerable damage to buildings and infrastructure. Even two men and a child were crushed to death outside the British Embassy in Kathmandu when a wall collapsed. We were so lucky not to have been in the bedrooms upstairs in the teahouse when the roof caved in, covering the entire room, bar the Japanese trekker's bed, in huge rocks and timber.

As I sat in the mock "Starbucks" cafe in Lukla I sent an e-mail to my parents, a quick one liner to let them know that their daughter had survived the major earthquake and was alive. The "Starbucks" cafe was hilarious and clearly a fake. Just one look at the logo confirmed this, instead of the weird mermaid with two tails there is an image of Mount Everest. The bogus latte was actually better than the genuine thing. It was much cheaper too. I'm surprised the Starbucks enterprise hasn't slapped a huge lawsuit on the owner for using their international branding; perhaps they are unaware of its existence?

The eventual response from my parents was 'What earthquake? We haven't heard of any earthquakes but glad you are okay'. Then it was the hair-raising flight back from Lukla to Kathmandu. The short distance from the airplane parking bay to the edge of the cliff took seconds before we soared off the 9,200 feet drop into the air. Team America #3 screamed in terror, his knuckles white as they gripped the armrests for one last time. We all survived the earthquake and the dodgy flight back to Kathmandu with lots of stories to tell our friends and family. I would like to thank again, Asouk, Parsons and the Himalayan mountain man for putting our lives before their own. They are truly remarkable people. Oh, and a little thank you to the glow in the dark Jesus who surely must've had some influence over our choice of bed that night in the teahouse.

Chapter 15

Chinese Invasion

Having climbed two big mountains, classified as 'hills' by the Nepalese, and surviving a major earthquake, I felt good. Well, mentally good. Physically I had a raging headache and felt nauseous from the previous night's celebrations in Kathmandu. I lost count of the number of Everest beers I was downing and the glasses of wine at the restaurant seemed never ending. Today I was setting off on a new journey that would take me to four of the 'stan' countries. There are a total of seven 'Stan countries in Central Asia which means 'place of' in Persian and 'settlement' in Russian. Five of the 'Stans were part of the former Soviet Union; Kyrgyzstan, Kazakhstan, Uzbekistan, Turkmenistan and Tajikistan. They all became independent countries in 1991 when the U.S.S.R. dissolved. Afghanistan and Pakistan are the other two 'Stans that make up the seven.

In world terms, Kyrgyzstan is very near to Nepal. There is a little bit of northern India and western China that separates them. The most direct route is just over 1,200 miles which is the same distance as travelling from Leeds, England to Krakow in Poland. Be that as it may, there are no direct flights from Kathmandu to Bishkek, the capital city of Kyrgyzstan. As a result I had booked a flight from Kathmandu to Guangzhou which is a whopping 1,766 miles right over to the eastern bottom corner of China. Then a flight from Guangzhou all the way up to the top of China to a city called

Urumqi. That journey was a ridiculous 2,040 miles. The final leg, Urumqi to Bishkek was a mere 650 miles. With such a mammoth journey, I had arranged an overnight stop at Urumqi. I had researched the city and found that it was a major industrial hub within the Xinjiang region in north western China. There was not a great deal to see there and the fact I was arriving late afternoon made me decide not to attempt any 'tourist sites' but to book myself into a swanky hotel. It was a treat to myself for completing the Everest Base Camp trek and surviving a major earthquake. I deserved it. The hotel I found online was the opulent 'Tian Yuan Hotel'. The online pictures of the rooms oozed extravagance and luxury, all tastefully decorated in neutral shades with giant king size beds covered in crisp, white cotton linen. After sleeping on hardboard beds and squat toilets located a good distance away from the room, this is just what I needed for one night.

After a fond farewell to my fellow Everest Base Camp trekkers I caught my first flight. Eleven hours later, with stiff legs and throbbing ears, I arrived at Urumqi airport. The seats on the plane seemed so small or maybe it was just Southern China Airlines. Chinese people tend to be small. Perhaps that was the reason. It didn't help having an overweight man squashed into the seat next to me, his rolls of soft flesh poking through the gap and invading my seat space. Not to mention the arm that protruded substantially over the armrest making it impossible for me to lift my fork to my mouth at meal times. I had to adapt my Nivea body wipe Houdini act by twisting my arm and elbow in front of my face as if doing an impression of an elephant's trunk, in order to get some food onto my plastic fork and into my mouth. The effort didn't seem worth it when I eventually tasted the food, which stated it was chicken on the menu card, but I had my doubts that the lumps in my meal originated from any form of poultry.

The thought of my flash hotel room brought a smile to my face as I exited the plane. A young Chinese woman in a China Southern Airlines uniform stood just outside the plane door with a big white board. On that board, in big, bold, black letters was my name '**SHARON CRACKNELL**'. I was taken aback. Why did this woman have my name on a board? No-one knew I was here. Had someone died? All these thoughts raced through my mind as I approached the woman. "Hello. I'm Sharon Cracknell" I introduced myself to the woman expecting an explanation in return for my candid disclosure. Instead I got a flow of rapid Chinese. Vowels and consonants streaming from her mouth in a musical mien. Did I look like I could speak Chinese? My curly blonde hair and blue eyes should be a clear indication that my origin is not Asian. I looked at her blankly. She quickly hinted that I should follow her through the telescoping corridor into the airport. I followed her, clueless as to where she was taking me and why. What about my checked in backpack? I needed to retrieve it from the baggage reclaim area. Was I being arrested? The woman eventually found an English speaking colleague, although Pidgin English would be a more accurate description. It was difficult to translate; nonetheless, I discovered they were offering me a hotel room for the night. Free of charge. My connecting flight to Bishkek was not until the morning and it turned out that China Southern Airlines always offer free overnight accommodation to those travellers. Oh dear. What about the opulent Tian Yuan Hotel? My indulgence? But this was free. The effort taken to meet me from the plane and have a hotel room prepared for me was a unique experience. In my years of travelling I had never received this level of courtesy from an airline. I decided to take the free room. My indulgence could wait.

I was led to a minivan together with three businessmen who turned out to be United Nations diplomats from Pakistan who had just been to a conference in Beijing. The hotel was in downtown Urumqi which looked neglected and uncared for. The streets were dusty and depressing. The diplomats were first to check in at the hotel reception desk which soon turned awkward as they were told they would be sharing a triple bed room. "We are United Nations diplomats from Pakistan. We do not share rooms like backpackers and we do not take kindly to being treated as such", demanded one of the diplomats. He turned to me "This is mad. To expect three grown men to share one room". I agreed. They certainly didn't look like backpackers in their Armani suits and Gucci shoes. Another man appeared who was summoned to the hotel by the United Nations co-ordinator in Urumqi. He was the 'fixer'. He effortlessly organised for them to have separate rooms in another, more upmarket hotel and had made dinner reservations for them all at a top restaurant. The 'fixer' was good. I was impressed. As I was a solo traveller I was given a room to myself. After depositing my bags in my room I headed down to the restaurant to order some food only to be told that they do not accept US Dollars or international credit cards. Where was a 'fixer' when you needed one? Exhausted and hungry I went back to my room, too tired to explore the city and find a restaurant. My bowels had become overactive so it was pills and bed. However, I was excited. I was off to Kyrgyzstan tomorrow morning which was famous for its walnut-fruit forests and glaciers.

At 12.55am I was abruptly woken by my room door banging and the penetrating shrill of a Chinese woman. What was happening? Luckily, I had flicked down the hotel door safety latch before heading to bed. Someone had used a key card for my room and opened the door only to be blocked by my safety latch. The door could only open a few inches and was being aggressively pushed back and forth in a frenzied anger. What the hell was going on? It was 1 o'clock in the morning! Who on earth was trying to break into my room? My heart was pounding. A strident voice was screaming rapid Chinese through the opening. I ran to the door and peered through the small opening to find two Chinese women stood outside scowling at me. One was young, with hair tied back in a ponytail and looked like she may have been a hotel employee with her navy blouse and skirt. The older woman had short cropped hair to match her short temper. Her eyes were cold and accusing as she glowered at me. Her 'A' line coat hung from her small frame and looked like it was made from carpet; similar to a Wilton carpet with a gaudy pattern that you could perhaps find on the floor of a casino or an airport lounge. At her side was a huge brown suitcase which made me realise that she had probably just come off a plane too. The loud and unpleasant shrilling continued as they incessantly pounded and punched at my door. "Whoa! Stop it! Stop now!" I shouted over their screeches. "Go away. What are you doing?"

Now that I knew I was dealing with only two kooky Chinese women and not an axe wielding madman, I released the safely latch to confront them face to face rather than just my one eye through the crack of the door. In an instant, the carpet woman had picked up her large suitcase and was barging into me. Her luggage had now been transformed into a wacker plate compressor and was being rammed into my body. She was determined to get into my room. What was wrong with this woman? A tidal wave of high pitched trilling flowed from her mouth. Her sequence of tones was alien to me. This was the most bizarre situation. Did she really expect me to let her into my room? Using her suitcase as leverage I pushed hard and sent her reeling back into the corridor. "No!" I yelled over her shrieking. "You are not coming into my room". I was waving my hands from left to right to gesture what I believe to be the international sign for 'no'. I felt like shouting "piss off you batty old woman" but what would be the point? They couldn't speak English and I couldn't speak Chinese. After what seemed an age the two women reluctantly left. Good grief. What a kerfuffle!

Concerned they would reappear I slipped on my walking boots and headed down the stairs to the hotel reception to sort this fiasco out. It was a complicated task. The woman on reception could not speak a word of English, but via some ingenious sign language and a glance at a China Southern Airline list, it became evident that the airline expected passengers to share rooms with complete strangers who arrive at 1 o'clock in the morning. The courtesy offered by the airline that I was initially so impressed with, was a sham. Personal space is not a concept that Chinese people are familiar with. They believe that it is completely reasonable for a stranger to hammer on your hotel door in the early hours of the morning and to give them a key to let themselves into your room, irrelevant that I am a lone female traveller. By 2am I was back in my room but sleep evaded me. The expectation of another encounter with the carpet woman kept me awake until 5 o'clock when I needed to catch my transport back to the airport.

Having safely arrived at Urumqi airport, which was a miracle considering it had been arranged by China Southern Airlines, I checked in my trusted backpack and made my way to the immigration desk. One chaotic night in China was enough for me. So began my adventures in the 'stans'. I finally made it to the front of the immigration line and was beckoned over by one of the officials who was seated in his little box. As he flicked through my passport to find the Kyrgyzstan visa and check my China entry stamp, my thoughts were with glaciers and walnut-fruit forests. Ninety percent of Kyrgyzstan is made up of mountains, glaciers, gorges and ice-blue lakes. Just think of all the hiking I could do! My thoughts were abruptly interrupted by the immigration officer. "Please Miss. Wait here" he ordered while passing my passport to a colleague. The second official proceeded to scrutinise my passport pages. "Come with me", the second official indicated for me to follow him behind the box to a seating area. "Miss, your Kyrgyzstan visa is not valid until the 25th of September and today is only the 23rd. You have another two days until this visa can be used". I looked blankly at him. This can't be right. I had fastidiously catalogued every visa required. Chronicled them on an excel spreadsheet. It had been a painstaking process. How could this be? He must be wrong. All at once the realisation of my oversight hit me. Oh my goodness. He was right. A few weeks prior to leaving home, all three flights were changed by the ever efficient China Southern Airlines, from the 25th September to the 23rd September. Following the date change I arranged for my accommodation to be changed from two nights in Kathmandu to two nights in Bishkek. I didn't even spare a thought for my visa. How could I be so stupid? Me of all people? What idiot can't learn their lesson after being arrested twice? Mentally I was kicking myself so hard.

"What can I do?" I asked him rather sheepishly. "We will allow you to exit China but I cannot say whether or not you would be let into Kyrgyzstan. They may put you back on a flight to China with a fine, or they may let you in. I only know the rules for China not Kyrgyzstan" he politely informed me. "What would the China rules be if I tried to enter on an invalid visa?" I wasn't sure what good the answer would do but I thought it was a prudent question at the time. "We would fine the passenger $4000 US dollars and send them back to where they flew in from. But that is here. I do not know what the Kyrgyzstan rules are". He was very sympathetic to my predicament. Undoubtedly he saw me as a dumb blonde, and why not? Who tries to enter a country on a tourist visa that isn't yet valid? Duh! "What would you do?" I asked, which surely made me sound even more foolish. "I can't say. This is your decision. You need to decide before the flight is boarded". Again, he gave me a pitying look. What options did I have? I could exit China on the plane to Kyrgyzstan only to be fined and thrown on the next flight back to China. The second option would be to stay in China another two nights and get another flight out to Kyrgyzstan on the 25th September, my visa entry date. The thought of being detained in a room with no toilet facilities at Bishkek airport was not an appealing one, especially with my current untrustworthy bowel. That scenario could turn messy very fast. I knew former Soviet Union countries were renowned for their red tape. Excessive bureaucratic formalities and routines are applied before any official action can be taken. I could be detained for hours, even days. "Please Miss. I need your decision", urged the official. "Your plane is about to be boarded". No brainer. I was staying in China. I couldn't risk another arrest. "I'm going to stay in China", I informed him. His expressionless face gave me no clues as to whether he thought I had made the right decision. He ushered me to the China Southern Airlines desk and in a rapid burst of Chinese he instructed the attendant to get my trusty backpack off the plane. She grabbed her walkie talkie and after another deluge of Chinese, the rush to get my backpack from the plane commenced. Knowing the efficiency track record of China Southern Airlines, I had my doubts as to whether I would see my trusty backpack again. As I waited, I thought of the opulent Tian Yuan Hotel. Didn't the online blurb state it was close to the airport? My delayed night of indulgence beckoned. Two nights would not just be an indulgence, it would be sheer decadence.

Surprisingly, my backpack was retrieved by the airline and after a short taxi ride I stood outside the grand entrance of the Tian Yuan Hotel. Wow. The foyer was gigantic. Bellboys were rushing everywhere, attending to the guests and their luggage. Every surface was immaculate. There was not a finger print or dust layer to be seen. With the credit card transaction successfully completed, I was escorted by a young bellboy to my room. Apartment would be more of an appropriate description. There was nothing cluttered about this spacious room as it sprawled from the door to the window. As promised on the website photo there was a king size bed with crisp white linen. A chaise longue stood at the bottom of the bed which faced a 42" flat screen television mounted on the wall. Near the window was the 'study' which comprised a desk, reading lamp and computer for limitless use by the hotel guest. The ensuite bathroom was the size of my living room back home, with two gigantic sinks and enough big, white, fluffy towels to dry a whole rugby team. The shower was cordoned off by a floor to ceiling glass wall and I swear you could have fitted at least twenty standing people in there. The showerhead was the size of Texas. Two nights in my palatial pad was the perfect end to my China stopover and with my indulgence now accomplished, I was refreshed and fit to face the 'Stans. More importantly, my visa was now valid.

Chapter 16

The Land of Mountains and Gingerbread Houses

Having survived the hospitality of China Southern Airlines and through Kyrgyzstan immigration, I finally made it to Bishkek. Every road in Bishkek is wide and spacious, lined with trees and walkways. Extensive parks are scattered around the city. It is such a relaxed and laid-back capital city where the local people look more European than Kyrgyz. I had booked my journey through the Stans with an overland truck company based in the UK called Dragoman, and that morning, at the beautiful Asia Mountain Hotel, which looked more like a Swiss alpine lodge, I met my fellow travellers. There were seventeen 'Stan passengers on 'Archie', which was the name of the truck we would be travelling in.

There was Matt from Sydney who was gay in every sense of the word. He lived with his partner, Jason, and he was such a hoot to travel with. Another fun Aussie was Catherine who was a qualified pharmacist. This was a godsend when my untrustworthy bowel decided to resume its overactive status. Canadians, Yvette and Jim were a divorced couple who, even though they appeared not to particularly like each other, decided to travel together for seven weeks. Perhaps they were trying to punish each other for their failings or indiscretions during their marriage; a final act of retribution? Who knows, but it made for a few uncomfortable 'I really don't know what to say' moments. Trying to maintain neutrality was, at times, difficult. Julie and Norbo were doctors from Norway and she was very precious. So precious, in fact, that she gained the nickname 'Princess Norway' on the truck for her narcissistic and self-absorbed behaviour. Her partner in crime, Nyla, an English girl, was also egotistical. Their running sessions through the cities and towns in what looked like Kylie hot pants was shameful. Eighty percent of the population in Kyrgyzstan is Muslim and as such there is a very strict dress code, especially for women. The expression 'when in Rome' had clearly not registered with them. Then there was Mick, an accountant from Sydney, who we never failed to make envious with our 'Stan antics. Teasing him with photos of our adventures including, strangely, our many wedding party invites. To make up the remaining passengers there was American Sara – a geologist, Jacob from Denmark, Aussie Lorraine from Perth, Steve from Bolton, Ed – a retired Dutchman living in Thailand, and fellow Brits Geoff and a couple from London who seemed to continuously offer McVitie's Hob Nob biscuits when we were travelling on the truck. I wondered if they had room to pack any clothes amongst the hundreds of packets of biscuits.

Luca was the truck leader, a small flirtatious man from Italy, who I swear must have had some female genes. The effortless way in which he coped with the tedious red tape and could perform multiple tasks at the same time was impressive. He also had to suffer being paired with fellow Brit, Noel, who was a lovely man to chat and joke with, however, he seemed to have overlooked the fact that he was not a paying passenger. He should've been working alongside Luca instead of drinking and partying every night. The fact that he got behind the steering wheel in the morning to drive us onto our next destination was worrying. Did they not have breathalyser testing in Kyrgyzstan? They must do, surely?

The most popular item I had seen so far in Kyrgyzstan wasn't walnut-fruit trees but 'Morrisons' plastic carrier bags. The Yorkshire based supermarket chain is a well known establishment in Kyrgyzstan. There are no stores or home brand products, no Market Street butcher or fishmonger, just plastic bags. They are used all over, more notably though, in the markets. You would think if they were going to print an

English supermarket logo onto their plastic bags they would've chosen a more upmarket brand like Waitrose or Sainsbury's. At least it wasn't Aldi.

The next day we set off on the road to Ala-Archa canyon where I did my first Kyrgyz trek up what I now know to be a hill and not a mountain. Matt, Boltonian Steve and I were determined to reach the snow and ice which could be seen in the distance. This must be the starting point of the Adygene glacier. Nothing was going to stop us from reaching the glacier. The views of the Adygene valley were stunning. Huge mountains surrounded us, the sun creating a light and dark shadowed side on all the peaks and troughs. Snow had settled on the very tips of the mountains and speckled down the sides of the coldest ones. Plantations of green fir trees rose high in clusters in the valley whilst the ground was quite yellow and dry. The hike, if I'm honest, turned into something like an episode of the 'Amazing Race'. Luca had raced up the hill and disappeared into the distance reminding me of Irmi, the ultimate driving machine, my fellow German Kili climber. What is it with these small Europeans? They're like whippets. Now you see them, now you don't. Sara and Catherine were hot on our heels. We caught glimpses of them on the track as we climbed higher. Luca was never to be seen again until we returned to our campsite. Matt couldn't contain his excitement when finally we reached the snow. "How cool is this!" he exclaimed "I haven't seen snow since my last visit to the Snowy Mountains a couple of years ago. Take a picture... take a picture!" He thrust his camera into my hand as he pondered which pose to use for the snow photo. I've noticed when travelling, that stance is incredibly crucial when taking that all important photograph. It is imperative not to use the same old pose; you know the one, standing stiff and straight, hands by your side, smiling at the camera, looking rather like you have a rocket up your bottom. The hundreds and hundreds of photos that are taken over a three month period need diversity; the plethora of pictures that friends and family are to be subjected to, will be overkill, no matter how much gusto and zeal you inject into the narrative. At least an array of alternating postures will offer some respite for the, more than likely, comatose viewers. Some of the varying poses I have tried are: a rotation from 'rocket up the bottom' (stood stiffly, smiling directly at the camera); the 'star' (arms and legs open with hands in the air); 'contemplative' (looking slightly away from the camera at a 45 degree angle and appearing to be looking at a distant object); 'jump' (more for group photos when you all joyfully jump in the air and pray the camera operator has pressed the shoot button at the correct time), and finally, the 'word' pose (again, for group photos where you all lie on the floor and create letters with your bodies to spell out a word, i.e. 'Spain' if visiting Spain).

Matt chose the 'sitting on a rock' pose and after our snow photo shoot had finished we headed back to camp for dinner before retiring to our tents for the night. The temperature had dropped dramatically since our afternoon hike. Poor Matt had brought no thermal clothing, not even a fleece to keep him warm. Luckily, I had all my Everest gear which I dug out to ward off the bitter air as it enveloped our tents. My blow up Thermarest floor mat kept the cold, hard ground at bay. Nonetheless, it was still freezing. When morning finally arrived I saw Matt crawl from his tent. His lips were blue, his teeth were chattering and he was uncontrollably shaking. "Quite frankly that was the coldest night I have ever experienced. It was soooooo cold!" he wailed "I had no fleece, no Thermarest or sleeping mat and my sleeping bag was too thin!" Yesterday we had climbed in altitude from 800 metres in Bishkek to 2,150 metres, from a heated hotel room to a canvas tent which would explain why it felt so cold for everyone, especially Matt who was more used to the hot Australian sun. It's a shame there wasn't a Marangu Hotel storeroom that Matt could visit to 'loan' some more appropriate camping gear and a full winter wardrobe.

What we did do back in Bishkek that afternoon, which included every single person on the truck, was purchase a Kyrgyz blanket. These were no ordinary blankets, these were polyester and acrylic knitted, quick-dry, dirt repellent blankets. Thick, chunky blankets to keep us warm at night.

Designs varied from big gaudy flowers to Spiderman and Hello Kitty. Bishkek market was gigantic and had a whole section dedicated to blankets. They were all hung from hinged metal hangers and could be viewed like reading a book. It was so difficult to choose from such an overabundance of colour, size and pattern. Everyone was taking their final choice extremely seriously. Colour schemes back home had to be considered together with the size and whether it would look right in their rooms when they took them back home. After much debate I decided on a gaudy red flower pattern which would match my red leather sofa. Not that I have ever got the thing out since returning, but the thought was there. It also came in a cute plastic zip up bag with handles which ripped before I even stepped foot off the truck.

With blankets purchased and passports lodged with the Uzbekistan embassy for the required visas we set off again, this time into the Chong-Kemin valley which was more of the same stunning mountainous scenery and a very warm, toasty night in our tents with our new Kyrgyz blankets. No complaints about frost bite or other 'cold' ailments that night. The Kyrgyz certainly know how to make warm blankets and without even using a thread of wool. Matt was in debating whether or not to buy two blankets to keep warm at night but finally opted on a super-sized one instead.

Lake Issyk-Kul is said to be the second largest Alpine (elevated) lake and the world's second largest navigable lake after Lake Titicaca on the borders of Peru and Bolivia in South America. The lake changes colour depending on the time of day and sun position, from pale green to turquoise blue. It is surrounded by the imposing snow-capped Tian Shan Mountains making it a perfect lunch stop for the 'Stan travellers. The time of day and sun position must have been off kilter the day we visited as its colour was anything but vibrant. It was blue. Be that as it may, the impressive size and location of the lake was stunning. It sits 1,600 metres above sea level and its deepest point reaches 663 metres. In size it is around 180 kilometres long by 70 kilometres wide. Basically, it is a massive lake. With lunch over we drove further east to the peaceful town of Karakol.

Karakol, despite being the fourth largest town in Kyrgyzstan, is a sleepy town which hasn't yet been spoilt by high rise buildings. The backstreets are lined with Russian gingerbread houses boasting decorative, colourful patterns that have been painted around the elegant, tall windows. Some had grand shutters framing the windows; others had intricate carved woodwork lining the eaves painted in pastel colours of sky blue and green. Another common feature was a tied up goat outside the front of houses, possibly the family pet.

The following morning, Matt and I went walkabout. Our mission was to find the AKB Bank which was an agent for the Western Union. Matt needed Kyrgyzstan Soms, but not one ATM in Karakol accepted foreign credit cards. A money transfer was needed. As we walked along the streets admiring the handsome gingerbread houses, we also had to make sure we had one eye on the ground to avoid disappearing down one of the many random holes. They appeared at any location, footpath or road, and swallow you up in seconds. Some of them were so deep that if you stood inside one, the sides would come up to your chest. Never take your eye off the ground when walking in the 'Stans; a valuable lesson learned by Matt later in Uzbekistan.

Having successfully manoeuvred around the haphazard holes we located the AKB bank and entered the old building. After some clever hand gestures and flashing the Western Union logo, a lady directed us to a room at the top of some stairs. It looked like someone's office with a desk and some chairs. An antiquated computer monitor sat on the desk, its bulky frame filling most of the wooden surface like an old-fashioned television. It looked like it would have the ancient green and black interface with instructions like 'Press <F3> to Exit' After loitering for twenty minutes in some unknown bank worker's office, a woman came in and ushered us to yet another room. Maybe it was her office and she wanted to make a personal call or perhaps eat her breakfast. The second room promised more as it appeared to have a very primitive teller counter along one wall. This was not your typical teller counter with a person seated behind a transparent screen, smiling as you approached and communicating both visually and verbally. No. The AKB Bank teller person could not be seen. A vast white wall faced the customer with a waist high wooden ledge. A small semi-circle had been cut out of the wall, no bigger than half a dinner plate, which was positioned in the middle of the ledge like a rising sun. Years of customers pressing their heads against the top of the half moon hole, straining to communicate, had left layers of grubby marks and grease stains on the wall. "Strewth! I will have to double over just to speak through the hole" exclaimed Matt, giggling at the thought of trying to communicate to the unknown person through the hole. It was hilarious.

We could hear muffled voices behind the wall, talking to each other and then there was a new voice that spoke very near to the wall. "Hello" responded Matt to the wall while bending down in an attempt to peer through the half moon opening. Then followed the money transfer transaction with Matt doubled over as if in chronic pain while chatting to a wall. Eventually, the transaction was complete and Matt had his Kyrgyzstani Soms and a backache.

I was brimming with excitement for the next destination. Beautiful mountain scenery, natural hot springs and some of the best hiking in Kyrgyzstan is what awaited us in Altyn Arashan. To get to this stunning alpine valley our transport was to be an old Soviet army truck. It was essentially a metal box attached to a drivers cabin and painted in green military camouflage. The front of the drivers cabin looked similar to the old-style Volkswagen Campervan with its small round headlights like little piercing eyes watching the road. I'm surprised the vehicle was still operating after years of traversing the rocky terrain that we were about to experience.

But the Soviet army truck was robust and strong as it bounced off rocks and boulders. It was full to the brim with our food for two days, daypacks with essentials such as thermals and Nivea body wipes, not to mention sleeping bags and our new must have accessories, the Kyrgyz blankets. A portable stove and gas cylinder were also crammed into the army truck with pots, pans, plates, mugs and cutlery. The 'resort' next to the hot springs was clearly just a shelter and not a self-contained mountain chalet. It was an organ churning ride as the wheels ricocheted from stone to stone. As we drove further into the valley we were repeatedly deflecting rocks and veering from side to side. I definitely selected the 'thrill seekers' side of the army truck as I peered out of the window and saw the sheer drop into the river valley that was inches away from the truck. The savvy driver knew exactly how to tackle this terrain. The skill with which he manipulated the aged army truck was impressive, that being said, I still decided to hop off and trek the remainder of the distance to the 'resort'. Matt, Catherine and Sara also chose to hike rather than continue the bone rattling ordeal. With hindsight, possibly not the best option to take as we tramped through wind, rain and hailstones, my emergency plastic poncho flailing in the wind like a discarded Morrisons plastic bag. Through the wind and rain we eventually caught a glimpse of the 'resort' tucked away in a valley. At that moment I exhibited a moment of nostalgia, the green mountains with speckles of grey limestone rocks reminded me of the Yorkshire Dales. "Gosh. I could be home in the Dales looking at these hills. It's uncanny". I shared my feelings with the others. "Bet the rain reminds you of back home too eh?" muttered Matt as we continued to fight against the bitter wind and rain. We couldn't see much of the surrounding scenery as the mist rolled in. On approaching the 'resort' we immediately saw how primitive it actually was. An effort had been made, clearly some time ago, by painting the building white and the old window frames a pastel blue. There was an annex to the side constructed of wood and painted the same pastel blue. It was more like a conservatory with slatted wood at the bottom and from the middle to the roof it was single paned glass split into multiple tiny squares replicating the Georgian period. The hot springs were located just a short distance away, two bathing areas outside and a hut that housed two more. We could see the army truck parked by the side of the building.

"Looks like we'll definitely be using our Kyrgyz blankets tonight", said Catherine as we approached what I would now downgrade from a 'resort' to a shack. The shack entrance opened to a cooking room. I cannot call it a kitchen as we brought that with us. Thinking about it we even brought the kitchen sink which was basically three plastic washing up bowls, which was just as well as there was no sink in this kitchen. To wash our dirty pots and plates there was an outside tap. A door from the cooking room led into a sitting-cum-dining room with two rows of wooden tables and benches. Thankfully, there was a wood burner to keep this room warm while we ate. There were two dormitories, one in the main shack and the other in the annex. It had been decided that the men would use the shack dorm and the females the annex. After a candlelit dinner, nothing romantic about this setting – purely a necessity on the account that there was no electricity or gas, we all retired to our designated dorms.

"It's bloody freezing in here" moaned Sara who was full of cold and now blowing her nose like a trumpeter. We were now all lying under our layers of sleeping bags, sleeping sheets, Kyrgyz blankets and anything else that we could dig out of our daypacks. "We definitely drew the short straw. This entire room is constructed of single paned glass. The guys will be much warmer in their enclosed shack room", I declared. "I can't feel my nose" mumbled Catherine. Remarkably, we all managed to get some sleep in the icy annex that night in between blowing of noses and dashes to the outside toilet.

"Psst... are you awake?" I opened one eye to see Sara sat up in bed. "Check out the view. It's awesome!" she exclaimed. I opened my other eye and sat up. "Wow!" was my short response as I took in the spectacular scenery that had eluded us yesterday under a blanket of mist. We were surrounded by snow-capped mountains, green rolling hills and alpine forests. "These views are unbelievable", I exclaimed. This was accompanied by condensation from my warm breath against the cold air, which had produced a fog around my mouth making it look like I was smoking a cigarette. "Fuck its freezing!" I muttered as I continued to admire the magnificent view. We had a 270 degree view of the stunning Altyn Arashan valley.

Following a quick breakfast, Matt and I were ready to set off on yet another Kyrgyzstan hike. We were at 3,000 metres in the Altyn Arashan valley and at the southern end of the valley was the glacier, Mt Palatka at 4,260 metres. To reach the summit it takes six days of hiking, however, there was a five to six hour hike up a wooded valley to the top of a much nearer mountain. We were told by the shack caretaker that this was a great trek and his only instructions were to climb on a steep track beside the Arashan River, ensuring we keep left of the river, through a pine canyon which would take us to the mountain. He warned us that there was deep snow at the moment, nearly a couple of feet, starting at the foot of the mountain.

"Shall we give it a go?" challenged Matt, who in shorts and trainers, was not in the least prepared for a big hike. "If we reach the snowy bit and it's too deep then we'll just turn around and come back down", I suggested, giving his attire a "god help you if we do reach snow" look. Matt was up for the risk and we commenced our hike by initially crossing a rickety old bridge. We had been warned by the caretaker that this section was extremely muddy and he wasn't exaggerating. It took us nearly twenty minutes to gingerly cross the mud patch without sinking too far into the sludgy mess. With the mud obstacle behind us we continued uphill making sure we stayed to the left of the river. We climbed for quite some time through a forest filled with tall alpine trees. The scent of the pines interlaced with the crisp cold morning air was invigorating as we climbed steeper up the hill. We passed through grassed valleys dotted with pine trees and a backdrop of imposing snow-capped mountains. It was like a scene out of 'The Sound of Music' as the Von Trapp family make their escape from Nazi-occupied Austria across the Alps into Switzerland. It was breathtaking.

Then came the snow. At this point we were still left of the river as instructed, yet we hadn't seen a well-trodden path for quite some time. Inches of snow disguised any footpath that might have been there. Any traces of grass had disappeared. Not a tree in sight as we crunched through the snow. It was a gradual ascent up the mountain. At times, the river transformed into a micro waterfall as fresh water tumbled over large boulders that appeared regularly on the hillside. In only shorts and trainers, Matt was feeling the bitter cold of the snow. "Fuck! My sneakers are soaked, my body is so cold I'm constantly shivering and to top it all I really do need the toilet!" groaned Matt who had already suffered a couple of days of the trots prior to our hike. This created a slight quandary as Matt was subject to an embarrassing handicap. Without the aid of something to hold onto or walls to place his hands for balance, his ability to squat was lousy. He just couldn't keep his balance, which was problematic when being in a country that uses mainly the squat toilet. "I really need to go but I'll fall over if I have nothing to hold onto. This is not good". We could see some large boulders ahead which looked ideal for Matt to use as handrails to steady his balance when bending his knees. "Perfect restroom stop," I said and left Matt to shuffle over to the rocks where he managed to squeeze his body between two large rocks.

Shortly afterwards we set off uphill again, determined to reach the top of the mountain. We had only been walking for another ten minutes when Matt cried out "Oh my god! Sharon, look". He pointed across the river and to my surprise there was a man. We had seen no other people since leaving the shack and here, in the middle of nowhere, was a man. A stocky man dressed from head to toe in military combat dress with a long barrelled rifle slung across his back. His camouflage peaked cap matched his camouflage jacket that matched his camouflage trousers, finished off with a pair of black gumboots. In his right hand he held what looked like a detachable rifle scope. Perhaps it was a day and night vision scope? Was he a military man? Maybe he was a hunter. "He's got a telescope in his hand. Oh no! He must've seen me between the rocks. This is so embarrassing", cried Matt. I tried to suppress a giggle and failed. "He won't have seen you. He'll be looking for deer or rabbits. I'm sure of it", I said in an attempt to console him. The military man started to wave at us and gestured for us to come over to him. "What do you think he wants?" I asked Matt. "There's a wide river between us. Does he expect us to wade through the river for a little chat?" The man continued to beckon us over, pointing up the mountain and shaking his head in a 'no' gesture. "Do you think he is trying to tell us we shouldn't go up the mountain?" asked Matt. We were somewhat bewildered by this solitary man dressed in a full combat outfit. The military man then started wading into the river towards us signalling for us to use the rocks near our side of the river as stepping stones. We now grasped that he was quite serious about not letting us walk any further and for us to cross to the other side of the river. But that would mean we were on the right side of the river and not the left. The shack caretaker specifically instructed us to stay on the left of the river. "We should go across I reckon", confirmed Matt. I agreed. Military man was waiting in the middle of the river to assist us over to the other side. After precariously balancing on the first few rocks, military man took my hand and guided me across the second half of the river. Matt followed, his shoes already drenched.

Once again there was the language barrier, but after some innovative hand gestures, we discovered the mountain we were climbing was the wrong one. The man's name was Oscar and he was out hunting for the day, although from what I would gather, clearly not a good hunter as he had no 'kill' to take home. Having exhausted our sign language repertoire, we trailed behind Oscar back down the mountain and alpine forest. "Did you see the way he looked at me?" whispered a red-faced Matt. "He definitely saw me between the rocks. This is so embarrassing. I can't look him in the eye". Oscar never did let on whether or not he saw Matt squatting in the distance as he kindly walked us back to our shack. After dinner that night, Matt and I sneaked into one of the huts that housed the hot springs and had a candlelit soak in the dreamy warm water. The unattractive grey cement block that masqueraded as a bath was undoubtedly an old Soviet construction. In spite of that, the flickering candlelight and hot steamy air made for a relaxing, and more importantly, a warm end to the day.

The following morning, after scraping ice from the dinner pots which had been left out overnight, we made our way back to Karakol for the Sunday animal market due to take place the next day. On the edge of town, on a derelict piece of land, the Karakol traditional Sunday animal market is a mammoth event. Roads in all directions are jammed with cars and trailers full of sheep, goats, pigs, cows, you name a farm animal and it was there.

The next day we arrived at 7.30am and already it was chaotic. Everywhere you looked there were traders walking groups of bleating animals with a piece of rope as a makeshift lead. They reminded me of the New York dog walkers with their leads splayed out like a fan but instead of a dog, there was a sheep on the end of each one. Walking through you needed to be alert. Dodging large sheep with matted dreadlocks that looked infested with parasites, to jumping over piles of dung, made for an interesting morning. The earthy smell of cow manure mixed with the wet fur of livestock and horse sweat filled my lungs. As I brushed past goats and sheep I made a mental note to myself. *Put clothes into laundry bag when back in town.* "Shit. I've just stood in a pile of it!" I wailed. Matt just grinned "Well love, we are in an animal market. Expect more". Behind the hundreds of sheep and goats we found ourselves facing an arena full of horses and cows. There were hundreds of them all in rows. Metal bars ran along the enclosure to allow the traders to tie their livestock. There were also hundreds of locals in the enclosure near their vendibles. The men wore their traditional Kalpak hats which sat tall on their heads and are made up of four panels of white felt with a turned up brim. Traditional patterns are embroidered on them for decoration. According to Kyrgyz tradition there are three rules when wearing a kalpak; you must not kill a man with a kalpak on, kalpaks should not be put on the ground, and lastly, kalpaks are laid next to your head at night, never by your feet. Women are not offered a ladies version and instead they tended to favour headscarves on top of their thermal beanies. More of a practical and sensible headwear I reckon.

Under what looked like total chaos there appeared to be some semblance of order as animals were grouped into sections; horses at the front of the arena and cows at the back kind of order. Amazingly, by 10 o'clock in the morning it was all over and the traders were packing up. Taking home their live purchases or, if not, a pocketful of Kyrgyzstani Soms. That left the rest of the day for us to explore the sleepy town of Karakol before heading to our next destination, Jeti-Oghuz.

Twenty five kilometres south west of Karakol is the Jeti-Oghuz canyon with some impressive red sandstone rock formations. The name means 'Seven Bulls' which, as with every rock formation I have visited in the world, there is a tale behind the name. Legend has it that one day a king stole a wife of another. The king of the stolen wife was obviously not happy and wanted the other king to suffer. He consulted a wise old man who advised him to kill his wife and give him her corpse. "Let him own a dead wife, not a living one". The king carried out the killing at a funeral feast, and as the last of the bulls were being slaughtered as part of the ritual, he stabbed her. Blood and other mysterious fluids gushed from her heart into the valley below taking the dead bulls and the murderous king with them. The seven bulls formed into seven mountains thus the name, Jeti-Oghuz. Pretty gruesome seeing that the rock formations are red in colour to match the wife's blood.

There is also a huge rock that is splintered in two which is named the 'Broken Heart' and, of course, there is a story here too. Legend says that this is the heart of a beautiful woman who died of a broken heart after two suitors killed each other fighting over her. I find that most rock legends are very depressing and have no happy endings but the rocks themselves are very striking to look at. The unromantic reality is that the rocks will have taken thousands of years to form by the compression of grains of sand, and with the aid of water and minerals, left undisturbed for long enough, it will cement to form sandstone.

Matt was so excited about how much hiking we were doing that for the Jeti-Oghuz trek that he had now activated his iPhone pedometer, which was linked to a 'James Bond style' chip in his trainer. He recorded a whopping forty two kilometres. The Olympic trek was again, packed with beautiful panoramas of snow-capped mountains, glaciers and ridges. There were a couple of minor incidents. I lost my sunglasses that were perched on my head when precariously balancing on a log. The incriminating log crossed over a fast flowing river and as Canadian Jim stuck his arm in to rescue my glasses, he forgot his watch on his waterlogged arm. From that day on his watch failed to tell the correct time and my sunglasses were never to be seen again.

Our tents were to remain rolled up over the next two days as we upgraded to a homestay accommodation in Bokonbayevo. The main attraction in Bokonbayevo is the eagle hunter. Hunting with golden eagles is an ancient Kyrgyz tradition that dates back to the 13th century when the country was under Mongol rule. In their day, Berkutchi, the hunter, and his bird, were highly respected within society as they provided much needed fresh meat for their families and fellow villagers. Call me naive, perhaps stupid, however, I had imagined seeing an eagle hunter release his big bird into the sky for it to gracefully glide around. I was also being realistic and knew that the eagle could possibly spot a field mouse and swoop for the kill. I was psyching myself up to deal with this. I do find it upsetting to see any animals being hurt in anyway, real or acting. I can't even watch 'Turner & Hooch' or '101 Dalmatians' without bursting into floods of tears. My interpretation of what the day would bring couldn't have been further off the mark.

We drove Archie (the truck) into the middle of nowhere. It was a hot sunny day and there were rolling hills around us almost yellow in colour in parts, with the Tien Shan mountain range in the distance. The arrangement was to meet the eagle hunter here and it wasn't long before, what looked like an old Skoda, pulled up beside us. The eagle hunter had arrived. He was dressed for the occasion in his traditional Kyrgyz outfit –

black buttoned jacket and boot cut trousers. Golden swirling embroidery covered the bottom of his trousers and the front of his jacket. His grey furry hat was twice the size of his own head which sat like a fuzzy spare tyre around his forehead. His partner, the golden eagle, looked majestic as it perched on the arm of its owner. A giant leather glove protected the eagle hunter's arm from the razor sharp talons. A leather hood covered the eagle's face. This masks its eyes which has a calming effect on the eagle. There was a line of stitching on either side of the hood that resembled slit eyes with a brass stud beneath each one. This created a particularly menacing look. I did initially mistake the brass studs for its eyes but soon realised my error when they remained static. Two stiff leather ties were knotted at the tip of the hood, protruding like an old television aerial. It looked sinister. Not much difference when the hood was taken off to be honest. Its yellow and grey bill resembled an industrial pincer, large in size and very strong. I kept getting glimpses of its rather generous pink tongue which looked out of place against the muted browns and blacks of his feathered body.

"It has got a hood on hasn't it?" I asked Matt for final clarification. It did seem to blend extremely well with the colourings of the eagle. "Of course it has. Did you think the brass studs were its golden eyes?" laughed Matt. "Ha ha. As if I would think that" I mumbled sheepishly. The eagle experience began with everyone having a go of holding the eagle on our arms using the leather glove. With strict instructions to keep my elbow in and the glove in place, the eagle was placed onto my arm. It was so heavy that my arm soon started to shake from the strain of the weight. The average weight of a golden eagle is 5-6 kilograms so it was like having six bags of sugar resting on my arm. "Quick, Matt. Grab my camera. Can you take a photo of me please?" I asked, knowing that I would not be capable of holding the bird for much longer. With what felt like a weight training session over, it was now time to release the golden eagle for a demonstration. But the man was walking to his car. How strange! Had he forgotten something? It seemed he had as he opened the boot of the car to reveal a cute fluffy white rabbit with big floppy ears. Oh no! Surely not! All I could feel was horror. This was cheating. The poor bunny didn't stand a chance. "Oh my god, this is awful", I exclaimed. "What kind of demonstration is this?" Fighting back tears I declared I was not watching this horrific show. There was nothing 'natural' about this. The sacrificial rabbit had been placed in a field a short distance from us and the eagle hunter was walking up the nearest hill to release the eagle. "I'm not staying to watch this either" announced Ed, the Dutchman and we both walked to the truck, our backs to the whole charade.

With the show over and the rabbit now dead, they all came back onto the truck smiling. How could they smile when they've just, for fun, watched an innocent little rabbit being torn apart by a golden eagle. Matt was contrite as he sat next to me. "That was horrible", he admitted. "The rabbit was ripped to shreds in seconds. I don't know why I watched it. Poor little thing". He then turned around and went on proudly to play his movie clip to the others of the horrific slaughter. The flashes I caught of white fur against red blood made me look out of the window to blink away my tears without anyone watching.

The next day involved building a yurt which was much more fun as there were no animals harmed during the making of it. This was in another sleepy little village called Kochkor. We had travelled back around Lake Issyk-Kul towards Bishkek. We were now only 185 kilometres south west of Bishkek. There was nothing else much to do in Kochkor other than to build a yurt. It was fun as we got to watch a yurt being built from scratch. Layers of felt are stretched around a collapsible wooden frame which they assembled in front of us. We had to hold onto long poles that reached up to the roof of the yurt while the locals secured them. A small opening is left in the middle of the roof to allow air and light into the enclosed space and also let smoke from the fire to escape. The red flag of Kyrgyzstan has a yellow sun in the middle and inside the sun is the circular emblem of a yurt. If you look up to the roof you can see the wheel with the three-ply struts that is portrayed on the flag.

There were also two beautiful older Kyrgyz ladies demonstrating how to make felt; which is an ancient craft with a long history in Central Asia. They both wore headscarves that looked like they were originally used as handkerchiefs. The Kyrgyz women certainly get a raw deal when it comes to headwear. They are not offered any form of grand traditional bonnets like the men and their kalpak hats. Over their regular clothes they wore floor-length velvet gowns, deep crimson in colour, with the typical gold swirling embroidered edges.

No machinery is required as felt is a non-woven cloth that is made by matting, condensing and pressing fibres. There is no interlocking thread when felt making. These two women were making felt from wool that had been dyed to make a nice pattern. The wool initially looked just like regular cotton wool you buy from a chemist or supermarket, only theirs was dyed red and brown. Kneeling on the grass they made a square the size of a cushion cover from the brown wool and a typical Kyrgyz swirling design was created by using the red wool. This square was sitting on a straw mat that resembled the straw window blinds that students favour, as they only cost a fiver and it doesn't matter if you can't even roll them up without one side being higher than the other. They then brought a pan of hot water and using a metal sieve, they poured the water over the wool square. This was then tightly rolled in the straw blind and tied together with rope. Then the fun part began, they started to roll it on the floor and stand on it and, in typical tourist style, we all had a stand on it. With the condensing and pressing well and truly complete, the straw blind was unravelled to reveal a flat square piece of patterned felt. It was so simple but effective. No wonder this form of textile has been around for thousands of years.

It was then back to Bishkek to collect our passports from the Uzbekistan Embassy. Yet again, my meticulous planning had failed, as my visa dates on the Uzbekistan tourist visa I had purchased from home were incorrect. This resulted in having to spend an additional $105 US dollars for a second visa. I had come to the conclusion that whatever painstaking steps I took to ensure I obtained the correct visa were inconsequential. No wonder I have to renew my passport regularly. I often have many years left before it expires, yet due to my stupidity; two whole pages are being used for just one country's visa.

Our fleeting visit to Kazakhstan included just one full day for a trek in the Aksu National Park. The accommodation was a homestay in the village of Zhabagly, a lovely house full of colourful rugs and curtains. Each bedroom had two or three beds covered in vibrant blankets and cushions. The family served up a warming dinner of vegetable stew that evening, which was needed due to the falling night temperature. The following morning, after a breakfast of homemade jams and cakes, we were driven to the Aksu National Park where we were met by our guide Vladimir, who wore a very conspicuous bamboo shoot camouflage outfit which was very strange seeing that there was not one stick of bamboo to be seen in the National Park.

Aksu is the oldest National Park in Central Asia which is full of mountains and valleys with many rivers and lakes. There are many species of animals living in the park including snow leopards, marmots and the Tien Shan bears. As we hiked through the National Park, images of being mauled by the cute, furry giants, their long claws ripping our bodies to shreds filled our heads. American Sara was very familiar with wild bears and soon she was on all fours inspecting a pile of poo on the ground. "Hey guys – this here is definitely bear poo", she proudly confirmed. Great! Having survived being eaten by a lion in the unfenced Serengeti campsite, I was now faced with the possibility of encountering a big, brown bear armoured with long white claws. "Oh, and look here", she exclaimed. "This is a bear footprint!" Matt and I exchanged a worried glance. There were just five of us hiking on what was turning out to be a bear hunt; all the others had stayed with Vladimir. His constant order for us to "walk as a group, within my vision and do not detour from the paths", had made us do just that, bored with his persistent demands and very slow pace. After eating our packed lunches, while tentatively on the lookout for bears, we decided it was best to head back onto the proper track to rejoin the others. When we did eventually catch up, Vladimir was extremely annoyed by our insubordination and insisted that we stay on the track until leaving the park. Duly chided, we hiked the remainder of the walk; slow pace, on the designated footpath, not a piece of bear poo in sight. What we were seeing however, were rolling hills and impressive rocky mountain ranges with the occasional flash of canvas bamboo.

Back at the homestay, what started as a kick-a-round with a football turned into the 'Zhabagly Village Cup' match with all the local children joining in. Team International versus Team Zhabagly. The kids were pros! They knew all the football kicks and tricks. My position, unfortunately, was goalkeeper, my goal posts substituted with rocks. The competitive streak in me, clearly inherited from my Dad, had me diving left and right onto the hard tarmac in a futile attempt to save some goals. "Come on Sharon! Get saving!", yelled Luca, who, being Italian, surprisingly didn't seem to be diving or playing 'injured' during the match. "I'm trying!" I responded while watching the ball fly past my ear. After much fun and bruising, the match ended with a win for Team Zhabagly; the prize? The football, of course!

The following morning, after devouring more homemade jam and cake, we left our Zhabagly family and headed for the Uzbekistan border.

Chapter 17

The Land of Weddings and Vodka

From the Kazakhstan border we travelled to Tashkent, the capital city of Uzbekistan. Tashkent is Central Asia's largest city and is surprisingly very modern and cosmopolitan. Then when you read the history of the place you realise why. Most of the old buildings were destroyed in 1966 by a major earthquake. It measured only 5.2 on the Richter scale; however, due to the seismic activity being so deep (from 3 to 8 kilometres underground) it ranked over 8 on the surface bringing the city to ruins. Incredibly, it was reported that only 8 people died. 300,000 people were made homeless. The epicentre point is now the location of a moving memorial which shows the time and date, 5.23am on the 26th April 1966. A new Tashkent was rebuilt using the 'model Soviet city' which comprises wide streets, expansive parks, lots of monuments and concrete apartment blocks.

"I really want to see a Russian cabaret" gushed Matt. He had been mentioning the Russian cabaret since day one in Bishkek and we were finally in Tashkent to, hopefully, see a show. Matt continued, "They are supposed to be amazing, lots of dancers and lavish costumes. I've been told it's similar to Burlesque shows". "Sounds great count me in", I replied enthusiastically. The whole idea of going out that night to see a show sounded like fun to me. After a small amount of searching on his iPhone a theatre was found providing, what we believed to be, a Russian cabaret show. "Too easy", was the typical Aussie comment from Matt as he wrote down the theatre name and address. By evening there was a group of us dressed in our 'posh' clothes ready to hit the theatre. My 'posh' outfit was a pair of combat trousers and a long-sleeved white cotton top, slightly smarter than my usual shabby knee length shorts and T-shirt that had misshaped slightly from being washed and dried incorrectly. Matt had recruited fellow Aussie, Catherine, American Sara, and Jim and Yvette the Canadian divorcees for our night out.

"Wow! This is awesome" raved Matt as we all stood outside the rather grand theatre building. "Didn't expect it to be so grandiose" said Jim. We all stood at the bottom of the theatrical steps that led up to the imposing entrance of the theatre looking in awe at our surroundings. "Come on. Let's go in", I said as I tackled the steps. The main entrance led into the theatre foyer which strangely had a seaside board at the foot of the stairs like the kind of "Carry On" cartoon face board that you see at Blackpool beach where you poke your head through a hole. This one was what looked like a Sultan and a belly dancer. The Sultan had the rolled turban and a fancy smock. The belly dancer had not much on apart from a bra, pants with a veil and also a head veil. Her arms were posed above her head in that belly dancing kind of stance. In true tourist style we all had our photos taken with our new bodies before heading into the main hall.

We were greeted by a young male waiter who escorted us to a table. The whole floor of the spacious room was filled with tables and chairs. Every table had a white linen tablecloth draped over it with candles that flickered and provided muted lighting for the guests. You know you are in a classy establishment when the tablecloths aren't made of plastic or paper. The stage was unoccupied with the standard thick red curtains drawn. Our attentive waiter quickly lit our candles and provided us with a drinks menu. The choice was a bottle of spirits or an even bigger bottle of spirits. The Uzbeks don't mess with piddling little vodka shots. If you're going to have a proper drink then anything smaller than a bottle, quite frankly, is pointless. With our bottle of vodka ordered we excitedly waited for the cabaret to begin. The lights dimmed and a suited man walked onto the stage in front of the red curtain and started to sing. "This is a bit boring", whispered Catherine "where are the dancers?" Oh dear. Perhaps our understanding of the term 'Russian cabaret' was lost in Uzbek translation.

Several vodka swigs later the singing man had exited the stage and the red curtains were drawn to reveal an array of elegant ladies dressed in short A-line dresses with fitted bodices speckled with shiny sequins. The music started and I was taken aback to recognise a form of Irish dance music. "Watch it", I whispered to Matt "they're going to suddenly start jigging and imitating a Riverdance number". Sure enough, they started with the military style kicking and flicking, arms straight by their side as they attempted to mimic a Riverdance routine. It was surreal. Here we were, in Tashkent – Uzbekistan – Central Asia in a grand theatre watching Uzbek dancers perform a routine from the Irish dance group, Riverdance. "This is awesome", gasped Yvette "I can't believe they are doing Riverdance!" It was a rather tame version of the genuine article but fun to watch. They were on and off the stage like yoyos. There was a different costume for every dance routine they performed. Some of the outfits were breathtaking with flowing veils, glittered bodices, gold tassels, silk, jewels and silver stiletto shoes all of pure glitz and glamour. Each dance routine had a theme, from mermaids to oriental and belly dancing to regal, it was fun to watch. "I don't think that was the Russian cabaret that I was expecting, more of a family friendly version of what I was anticipating. Mind you, I feel a bit left out that they didn't perform a corroboree" joked Matt as we finished off our vodka bottle. A corroboree is an aboriginal dance with music and painted bodies. Maybe it was too earthy for the ladies to perform? "It was so good. I really enjoyed all the extravagant costumes and dance routines", I said as we started to make our way out of the theatre.

Our focus was now on finding a taxi to take us back to the hotel. Tashkent has an unusual custom. Every car being driven in the city is a potential taxi for anyone needing transport. If you just look like you are hailing a taxi or hover near the kerb, you will be offered a taxi ride by a stranger who is driving a car. No need for licences or liability insurance, as long as you have a moving vehicle then you can be a taxi. As we loitered outside the theatre, it was very evident that we had just seen a show and needed transport to get back to our hotel. As promised in the guidebook, a random driver stopped his car and asked us if we needed a taxi. His car was a pocket-sized Nissan Micra which couldn't even fit three people in the back never mind six of us. But the man wasn't going to let a simple obstacle such as not enough car seats to stop him from earning a cab fare. Having convinced us that his miniature car could indeed accommodate six adults including two males, one over six feet tall, we began the tricky task of squeezing into the tiny space. The best configuration we could muster at such short notice was Sara and Yvette squashed into the passenger front seat with Matt, Jim and Catherine jammed tightly into the back seats. I then laid across their laps in a semi-foetal position and prayed it would not be a bumpy ride as it could prove painful for Matt or Jim should I jolt and land awkwardly. With the fare already negotiated our 'taxi' set off to the hotel. With chaffed legs and bruised elbows the faux taxi successfully delivered us to our destination.

Sydney based accountant, Mick, felt his first pangs of jealousy when he browsed through our vibrant dancing photos the next morning. "Oh this looks amazing you lucky buggers. I wish I had come now", he groaned. Instead, he had chosen to spend the night on the truck, which was parked up in the hotel grounds, to drink himself silly with Princess Norway and her flock. Today we explored the stylish city of Tashkent. Of the many statues and monuments, there were two that we particularly wanted to visit.

The first was the large crying mother statue in the sprawling Independence Square. This monument is a memorial to those who died during the Second World War and curiously, a backdrop for newlyweds and their photographers. They come in convoys of limousines for the bride and groom to pose for their 'happy wedding day' pictures, in front of a statue depicting a grieving mother crying over the loss of her son. Very bizarre, I thought. Why not choose another leafy area within the park to remember the joyful day? The second monument was the 1966 earthquake 'Courage' memorial which is a simple message but it had a powerful effect. Two huge bronze statues stand together, a man shielding a woman holding a child, her arm outstretched as if to ward something off. From the base of the plinth there is a deep zigzag cleft portraying the earthquake and the courage of the inhabitants of Tashkent. The gorge leads to a cracked stone cube which has the date '26 April 1966' on one side and a clock dial stopped at 5.23 on the other. In yet again, true tourist style, and don't forget the all important varying photo poses, seven of us did a 'falling over but looks more like surfing' stance to give respite to our potential photo viewers.

"We have to use the underground trains while we are here, I've heard the stations are amazing to see" said Matt. "Would that be just like your Burlesque Russian cabaret?" I joked. "Ha ha. Very funny. Perhaps it was the Uzbek family version of a Russian cabaret?" laughed Matt. We both knew the Tashkent Metro was a 'must see' and made our way to the subway. The Metro was built by the Russians after the 1966 earthquake as an underground city transport system and is one of only two underground transport systems in the whole of Central Asia; the other being in Almaty, Kazakhstan. We bought our tickets, which were blue plastic tokens, and headed through the barrier into the station. I was astounded by the scale of the grand architecture. "This is unbelievable", I exclaimed. "Friggin' awesome", responded Matt. Ornate and lavish, the station oozed style and sophistication. Each station had its own theme and design. There were marbled tiles, granite, ceramic, stone and even carved artworks etched into the walls. There was an abundance of light fittings. Some were elegant and regal in style, others were cleverly hidden in crevices and glass features creating a theatrical atmosphere using light and shade. High ceilings and vast platforms created a feeling of airiness and amplitude. The floors were immaculate. Not a piece of litter in sight. But where were the bins?

This experience is all but a memory, no photos to recall the flamboyant platforms. It is illegal to take any photographs inside any of the stations as they are considered to be military installations. Policemen patrol every platform, so there is no opportunity to sneak out your phone and take a cheeky photo.

Moving south east to the ancient and exotic town of Samarkand, this place is one of Central Asia's oldest settlements, founded in the 7th century. It was the key Silk Road city seated at the crossroads leading to China, India and Persia. We arrived early afternoon which meant time for a walk around the town. Matt, Catherine, Yvette and I went on an exploration to see what Samarkand had to offer us for three days. On our agenda we had lots of medressas, mosques and mausoleums to visit over the next few days where we would encounter magnificent buildings covered in decorative blue tile work. The town had a good vibe as we wandered through the quiet streets, taking in the many clothes shops; in particular, wedding dress shops. We also passed the Uzbek mock version of McDonalds, with the identical red and yellow logo, only the big 'M' was for 'Marokand'. We then stumbled across a crying mother monument in a big square and it was a hub of activity. There were lots of locals gathered by the entrance to the square, dressed very smartly, women in nice dresses and men in suits. Everyone was chatting excitedly. "Something's going on here" stated Matt "I wonder what all these people are waiting for. They look like they're dressed for a wedding. They look too happy for it to be a funeral", he said.

More and more people flocked to the square and the crying mother monument. The four of us attempted to look nonchalant as we perched on the wall boundary of the square, but being the only westerners for miles, we stood out like a gaping sore on the landscape. Then, to our surprise, a convoy of six limousines cruised down the road and stopped beside the square. "What's going on? Do you think it is some famous

Uzbek movie star coming to do some filming?" joked Catherine. "I reckon it's the Uzbek President coming into town for his 'Marokand' cheeseburger", I joked back. "This is exciting", gushed Matt. The limo doors opened and out stepped six sets of brides and grooms. The brides were kitted out in full, western style, white wedding dresses. The grooms in slick suits looked gallant as they escorted their new wives from the cars. The procession of brides and grooms were then drawn to the crying mother monument like magnets. Each joyous couple wanting that all important wedding photo in front of the mother grieving for the death of her son. As we watched a young lad, dressed in a dapper suit who was clearly a member of one of the wedding parties, approached us. "Hi there. I'm Zaf. Where are you all from?" he asked in perfect English with what sounded like a slight London accent. "Hello Zaf. We're from all over", explained Matt "I'm Matt and I'm from Sydney, Australia". Catherine and Yvette introduced themselves and then me. "Hi Zaf. I'm Sharon and I'm from Leeds which is in the north of England. Is that a London accent I am hearing?" I asked. "Yes. I've just come back home from spending six years studying in London", Zaf confirmed my suspicions. He went on to tell us how much he enjoyed his time in England and would love to go back one day. He pointed to one of the brides. "That's my cousin and these are also my cousins", he said gesturing to a group of young guys behind him. They all smiled and waved at us. "Later this evening there's a big wedding party for my cousin and her new husband. You must come and celebrate with us", he unexpectedly offered. "Oh, no! We couldn't possibly intrude. The guest numbers will already be catered for and we really wouldn't want to infringe on your cousin's special day. But thanks for the offer. It was really nice of you to ask", said Matt. We all agreed with his sentiment but Zaf was having none of it. "Nonsense! Here in Uzbekistan it is considered good luck for a foreigner to attend someone's wedding celebrations. My cousin will be delighted to have two Aussies, a Canadian and an English girl at her wedding party". And that was that. He wrote down the venue address and arranged

225

to meet us outside the building at 7 o'clock. Zaf then left to continue the wedding party walk about town.

"I'm so excited! This is so cool. To get invited to an Uzbek wedding party!" enthused Yvette. "We have to get back to the hotel to get ready". She was right. It didn't leave us much time so we quickened our pace through the town back to our hotel. Out came the 'posh' outfit comprising combat trousers and long-sleeved cotton top. The finishing touches were a plastic bead bracelet and a pair of pink flip flops. The taxi ride was short and soon we had arrived at the venue with Zaf and his friend waiting for us on the steps of the building. "You came! Great!" said Zaf. "A table has been laid out for you. Come on!" I glanced at Matt with an 'I can't believe this is happening' look as we walked into the wedding party.

I was immediately overwhelmed by the scale of the celebration. Extravagant and flamboyant summed up the decor and the mountain of food that faced us. There were easily over three hundred guests seated in groups around circular tables. Old fashioned wooden chairs upholstered with silk embroidered fabric completed each table setting. The ceiling was painted with blue swirls like ocean waves and glitter balls hung like Christmas baubles ready for the disco beat. The wedding top table was ostentatious and, I thought, on the verge of being garish. A mammoth star, covered in cheap silver glitter, had been erected behind the seats of the bride and groom. The top table had white roses strewn along the front edge which looked nice, but the wedding photos would have been spoilt by the array of vodka bottles and plastic coke bottles that were lined up from one end to the other. Two television monitors were mounted on the wall at either end of the top table just in case guests were missing out on what was happening.

Zaf escorted us to our table where the volume of food could have fed the entire population of Ethiopia. Each table setting had a bowl of fruit which was probably more for decoration than for healthy eating. Platters of cheese and cold meats, roast chicken, salads, feta cubes and olives, breads, were just some of the food on offer. Hot dishes kept arriving, replacing empty platters. It was lavish. Zaf and his friends sat at the table with us as we joined in the celebrations. Bottles of vodka were flowing but not so much the coca cola. Zaf pooh-poohed our request for drinking vessels other than shot glasses informing us that in Uzbekistan no-one taints their vodka with fizzy drinks. With the bigger glasses dismissed we took on the 'when in Uzbekistan' stance and knocked back the shots.

After much food and too many vodka shots the festivities then took on a disco vibe as the lights dimmed and the DJ took up his spot. "Come on guys. You have to dance" urged Zaf who jumped out of his seat. His friends took our cameras. "They will take pictures of you dancing!" We made our way to the dance floor and joined the crowd that had very quickly formed after the newlyweds finished their shuffle. A popular dance move that everyone seemed to be performing involved shaking the whole body, as though being electrocuted, with your arms in the air. Easy, I thought. Much easier than 'shuffling' or attempting Beyoncé's 'Single Ladies' dance which no normal person could possibly perform without looking like a total idiot. Zaf's friends were like paparazzi circling us and taking photos of our shaky, shaky dancing. There were even professional cameramen with bulky cameras resting on their shoulders as they roamed the room searching for victims to film.

After some vigorous dancing where I nearly dislocated my pelvis, Zaf then took us to meet his mother. As we approached her table she smiled at us, proudly revealing a full set of gold teeth. She looked like 'Jaws' the James Bond villain. In Uzbekistan and in other 'Stan countries, gold teeth are regarded as symbol of success and wealth; nothing to do with decaying teeth. By the look of Zaf's mother's golden smile she must've been a millionaire.

The next day, over breakfast, accountant Mick let out another groan of envy as he flicked through our photos of the wedding festivities from the previous night. "How on earth did you get invited to such a big wedding reception?" he asked, clearly impressed with our experience. "Just go hover near a crying mother statue and wait for the brides and grooms!" I told him. I went onto inform him that October is the favoured month for Uzbeks to tie the knot and that they like to have their photos taken in front of monuments, especially the sad, crying mother.

Despite fuzzy heads from too many vodka shots, we set off to see the Gur-i-Amir mausoleum where the tomb of the conqueror, Timur is located. Timur, also known as Tamerlane, was a 14th century conqueror of West, South and Central Asia. He built a powerful empire before he died unexpectedly in 1404 of pneumonia. Decorated inside with blue gilded artwork, Timur's tomb is actually very plain looking, made from a block of dark green jade. Next to him, in marble tombs, are his two sons and two grandsons, including Ulughbek.

Ulughbek was Timur's favourite grandson and became ruler of Central Asia. It was his observatory that we visited next. More famous for being an astronomer than a ruler, during the 15th century Ulughbek constructed an observatory that was far advanced for its time. He discovered over two hundred previously unknown stars and he also did his own calculations of the stellar year with such exactness, that he was only incorrect by one minute compared to modern electronic calculations. Resentful of his preference to science, in 1449 his own son arranged for him to be beheaded.

Close to Ulughbek's observatory is a museum which exhibits copies of Ulughbek's star charts. However, on the day we visited there was a power cut and with no windows in the museum our poor guide had to search for a torch, which proved difficult in the dark but once found he directed the single beam at the various star charts, while we stumbled behind him, praying we wouldn't crash into any of the cabinets containing ancient documents.

Onto the Shah-i-Zinda, the visually stunning avenue of mausoleums full of intricate rich blue and turquoise tile work that sparkled in the sunshine. The densely packed and towering mausoleums made for some tight squeezes in the avenue. The name Shah-i-Zinda means "the living king" which refers to Quasm ibn-Abbas, a cousin of the Prophet Mohammed. Legend has it that he brought Islam to the area and was beheaded for his faith. This is where his tomb is said to be and is now an important place of pilgrimage. Timur's relatives are said to be entombed here as well as other prominent families and aristocracy. Matt and I decided to spice up the all important pose for some of our pictures here, perhaps in bad taste seeing that it is considered a holy shrine. We opted for the 'Pulp Fiction' eye dance pose which involved doing the two finger 'V' sign that you sweep across your eyes and made some pretty awesome photos if I do say so myself.

Registan Square was the ancient centre of Samarkand and an amazing site to visit. The ensemble of imposing buildings consists of three medressas. Medressa is the name for an Islamic school. Only the rich families could afford to send their sons there. Girls were not allowed as they have to study separately from the boys. The main discipline was for them all to learn the Quran. The rest of the subjects could be selected by the students. The Ulughbek medressa is the oldest, having been built in the 15th century, and Ulughbek is said to have taught mathematics there. Sher Dor medressa, built in the 17th century, is decorated in tiled lions with a sun rising from their backs. The lions looked more like a crossbreed of a tiger and a lizard to me! Their bodies were orange tiled with black stripes and they had a long tongue darting out of their open jaws. They did have a mane, but still it wasn't enough to make them resemble lions. Lastly, the Tilla-Kari (Gold-Covered) medressa was also completed in the 17th century. The intricate tiles of blue, turquoise, white and orange must have taken years to complete. Delicate patterns from flowers and circles to huge geometric designs and of course, the supposed lions. Turquoise tiles also covered the roof domes which glistened in the sun and the whole courtyard floor central to the medressas was also tiled. It must have taken thousands of painted tiles to create the beautiful intricate designs on such imposing buildings. Hundreds of different patterns adorned the giant canopies that surrounded each entrance that had been sculpted into the vast square facades.

The scale of the buildings was imposing, with the three medressas dominating the square. The giant doorways were characterised by the distinguishable Islamic arch. The corners of these majestic buildings are flanked by high minarets that just about reach the lofty height of the medressas. As Matt and I wandered around the square Catherine came running up. "Guys, word has it that if you pay one of the policemen guarding the minarets he will lead you to where you can climb up the stairs. The views are supposed to be awesome". Accountant Mick had been unexpectedly resourceful and had already paid his 8,000 som, which at that time, converted into around five US dollars, "Would you like to see my photos for a change?" joked Mick. "The views from the top of the minaret are amazing". With a trace of smugness he pointed us to the direction of where to find the policeman. My competitive streak had now kicked in making the current 'score'; one point to Team Mick versus two points to Team 'Lucky Buggers'. We found the policeman sitting in a chair next to a locked gate and as we neared we were not quite sure of what to say. The most direct approach would be "Hello Sir. Are you the officer who takes backhanders from tourists who wish to climb up the minaret?" The more subtle method would be just to smile and show him your 8,000 som notes which is what we opted for. This worked. The policeman just took our soms and unlocked the gate. This opened up to what I could only be described as a building site. There was rubble and bricks covering the ground, with tools discarded in every direction. The policeman led us to an opening in the bottom of the minaret which looked like someone had taken a sledgehammer to it. There were loose bricks around the patchy doorway with a rugged and misshaped opening for us to enter the minaret.

The policeman then left us to do our 'sightseeing'. "This is so dangerous. It's a building site", exclaimed Matt, as a hanging electrical wire caught on his head. We had to duck and dive as we made our way up the tight, spiralling staircase.

Dust was on every surface. We encountered more electrical cables that were left swaying loosely down the minaret. With much trepidation I pushed them aside to make way for my journey up the brick tower. "I've reached the top!" gushed Matt, "this is hilarious. The 'observation platform' is a hole in the roof!" Through the electrical cables and scaffolding I peeped around the narrow corner to see Matt's legs and bottom, the rest of his body had disappeared out of a jagged hole in the roof. "The views are awesome", he shouted down at me. He must have looked like a meerkat from below, with his straight torso and head moving from side to side. When Matt had taken his all important photos and taken in the views, it was a tricky manoeuvre for us to switch places. The confining minaret resulted in a tight shuffle and squeeze to get me at the top. As I stuck my head out of the roof I was in awe of how much I could see. If I pirouetted on the tiny top step I had a 360 degree view of Registan Square and the surrounding area. It was stunning. Well worth the 8,000 som.

The following day, having seen the impressive three 'M's, mausoleums, mosques and medressas, we thought it only fair to visit the fourth 'M', Marokand. The Uzbek 'McDonalds'. Matt and Jim, after checking what fast food was on offer, chose the quarter pounder with fries. Unlike the real McDonalds, Marokand had pizza on their menu, which is what I chose. Another deviation was beer. Bottled and in the refrigerator to buy with your happy meal. I was disappointed by the Marokand fast food. When my cheese and tomato pizza arrived it looked like it was from the Tesco value range and had a lattice of tomato ketchup squirted on top and what looked like, but didn't taste like, mayonnaise. It was disgusting. Matt and Jim's burgers fared better with them giving their food a score of eight out of ten. I decided in future I would stick to the Uzbek dish, lagman which is a tasty soup with meat (I don't even question what type as I really don't wish to know), vegetables and noodles. Spiced with cumin, coriander and chillies – it is delicious.

While at Marokand, Matt, who seemed to be the only person who had a mobile phone, received a call from our new friend, Zaf. "He's invited us to another wedding party tonight! He says it's his close friend that's getting married and before inviting us he wanted to check with the family, who have said they are delighted for us to come. How cool is this? It's an Iranian wedding apparently". This was so exciting, another wedding party. My 'posh' outfit was taking a hammering.

That night all four of us got a taxi to the second wedding party. We were becoming professional wedding party guests. We arrived just in time to see the Iranian bride step out of the wedding car and make her way up the steps of the building. Fireworks were exploding at either side of her in an, "I'm a Celebrity Get me Out of Here', style when the evicted contestant has to leave the jungle via the suspension bridge. Her western style white wedding dress was full of ruffles and on her head sat a tiara that spangled with every movement. Having survived third degree burns from the fireworks she disappeared into the building. Zaf was nowhere to be seen so we decided to enter the building and hoped that we were not going to be escorted out by angry bouncers. Luckily we found him inside and we were again given a table with mountains of food and vodka. Zaf was in top form pouring the vodka shots. He was more boisterous and flirtatious that night which I put down to his mother, with the formidable gold teeth, not being there.

The groom's family came to meet us, as the special multi-national wedding guests, and the mother beamed with pride at having such important guests. To my horror, we were then ushered to the main dance area and handed microphones to give a wedding speech! I know we might be mistaken for professional wedding party guests but this was taking it a tad too far. "Oh my god Matt, I can't do a speech. There are over 300 people here! We don't even know the bride and groom! What are we supposed to say?" Panic had set in. This could end up being extremely embarrassing. "Just say you wish the bride and groom many years of wedded bliss... blah... blah... blah that kind of thing", whispered Matt. As we stood on the dance floor with the microphone in my hand, I could feel my face burning up. The embarrassment of the whole situation was making me blush. "Ahemm", was the start of my wedding speech as I cleared my throat. "Thank you so much for ermmm....including us in your celebrations...errmm...I would like to wish the bride and groom much happiness and I hope they have many happy years together. Thank you". A quick bow and I thrust the microphone into Matt's hands like a pass the parcel. With the speeches completed, we were directed off the dance floor where the groom's family were waiting to thank us for our speeches. I needed vodka.

Several vodka shots later we could see tea light candles being lit and arranged on the dance floor area in the shape of a heart. The happy bride and groom then did a smoochy shuffle in the middle of the flickering heart. I say happy bride, however, during the whole celebrations she did not smile once. She looked very unhappy about the whole situation. Her head remained slightly bowed and her eyelids lowered. Even when they shuffled inside the heart of candles her eyes remained fixed on his elbow. "It is Iranian custom", confirmed Zaf, "she is not allowed to look happy". I'm not sure how true this is. Perhaps she wasn't happy and it had been an arranged marriage. All I know is she looked as miserable as hell.

Then the extravagant show began. Russian dancers came out wearing emerald green satin shirts with black trousers and high boots. The women dancers wore matching cropped tops with loose trousers puckered at the ankles and gold edged chiffon veils. The dance show was amazing with much knee bending, leg kicking and stomping. Then came the inevitable disco with more shaky, shaky dancing. If I survived these wedding parties without dislocating my pelvis, or developing alcohol induced liver failure, it would be a miracle.

There was, however, an injury that night as we walked back from the party. The night lighting on the streets of Uzbek towns is very subdued and one minute I was chatting to Matt, the next he had disappeared down a manhole. It was a huge hole in the middle of the road, unmarked, not a traffic cone in sight to warn vehicles and more importantly, pedestrians. "Oh my god!" wailed Matt, "that bloody hurt. I've really hurt my leg". Like something out of "Til the World Ends' music video by Britney Spears, Matt clambered out of the manhole and revealed to us his bruised leg. "Shit. That looks bad", commented Catherine. Poor Matt limped back to the hotel. He was lucky to have all that vodka in his body to act as a temporary anaesthetic. God help him in the morning.

I have since read that the mayor of Tashkent has brought in a new decree to impose limits on the number of guests that can attend a wedding and a curfew is to be applied to the length of time festivities can continue for. Instead of the normal 300 plus guests the new act limits this to just 100 and set times of the day have been established under the new act. The extravagant, wasteful and over lavish-weddings are often unaffordable, leaving families in serious debt. Considering the two wedding parties we experienced, I reckon the mayor of Samarkand should introduce the similar laws to tone down the over indulgent and extravagant weddings being held there.

The next day, Accountant Mick let out another groan of envy as he yet again, saw our photos showing the lavish wedding party with Russian dancers and glitter balls. He paused at one photo. "Why are you holding a microphone on the dance floor? Did they have karaoke?" he asked. "Oh, no. We were guests of honour and the groom's family asked us to do a speech. Can you believe it?" I asked followed by my face burning up with embarrassment at the recollection of it. "I wish I'd been there. I don't know how you guys do it, getting invited to all these wedding parties", mumbled Mick. Team 'Lucky Buggers' Three versus Team Mick One.

A visit to Central Asia is not complete without an overnight stay in a yurt, and what better place to fulfil the experience than in the middle of the desert – the Kyzylkum desert to be precise. It is one of the most extensive deserts in Asia, the majority of which is located in Uzbekistan and a small area in Kazakhstan. We were staying at a yurt camp in Nurata and what better way to see the desert than from the top of a camel's back? When we arrived we were more or less thrown on the backs of smelly camels to have a trot around the sandy dunes. It was tricky. The swaying movement of my camel was quite exaggerated and my fingers initially strained from squeezing onto the saddle which appeared to be some old rags. Matt and Catherine were in front of me, no surprise there, I was last again. There was a stench now and then when a camel decided to offload some dung. Soon I found myself mesmerised by the camel's sway, staring at the back of his fluffy button ears and brown fuzzy quiff, listening to his snort. It was relaxing as the sun lowered and we could take in the remoteness of desert. Back at the yurt camp, dismounting the camel was precarious as he veered left and right in order to kneel down in the sand. It was even trickier to avoid placing a foot in a steaming pile of dung which Norbo, Princess Norway's husband, managed to do with great style. Wearing only a flip flop, his foot sank into the wet, gooey mess activating an even stronger odour. Then a quick flap of his flip flop sent dung flying in every direction.

The yurts were incredibly cosy. The round walls were covered in a patchwork of felt patterns. A rainbow of vibrant colours filled the room making it warm and inviting. Quilted blankets and cushions covered the entire floor which made for a soft, warm bed. It was much better than any hotel room in my opinion. The 'bathroom' sinks were an outside affair with a white porcelain sink set in the frame of a chair with a small tap attached to a bar in middle of the back rest. A small mirror was also attached to the top bar of the back rest for anyone who wished to see their 'tent hair'. As you cleaned your teeth or washed your face, whatever water was used disappeared down the plughole straight onto your feet. I would chase the cowboy plumber to demand a refund for that shoddy job.

Later that evening the owner brought out his teapot. He donned a thick moustache with a pair of busy eyebrows to match and he was clearly a bit on the tiddly side. "This is a first. All I seem to have been offered is vodka. A nice cup of tea will make a change", said Matt. Only the owner then started to pour the 'tea' into shot glasses. "Oh no!" groaned Matt "this is Uzbek tea! I should've known". The clear liquid was undoubtedly vodka, their favourite tipple. Again our stance was 'when in Uzbekistan...'.

With yet more thick heads we set off in the morning to Bukhara which is south of Nurata, heading towards the Turkmenistan border. On route we stopped at Lake Aidarkul for a lunch stop. This crystal blue lake is a giant oasis in the middle of the desert. In a landlocked country you don't expect beaches, but there is a perfect beach holiday destination for Uzbeks. It is a manmade saline lake which covers a whopping 3,000 square kilometres (1,158 square miles), apparently, an unintentional by-product of Soviet planning. I was excited to see an unexpected beach. "Wow! Check out the colour of the water. A beach too! I didn't expect to see one of those in my 'Stan travels", I said to Matt, itching to get out onto the sand. "I need to use the facilities" groaned Matt, "I think I may have the runs again". He looked dreadful as he bowed over clutching his stomach. When the truck came to a stop by a beachside building, Matt raced out and dashed through brush and rocks to reach the tiny wooden shack that was the public toilet. That was where Matt stayed for the majority of the lunch stop. My memories are of a sun-drenched beach with the sun glistening on the vibrant blue water of the lake. Matt's recollection is of a soiled wooden toilet hut that smelt so ripe it made him gag. Oh, and there was also the multitude of annoying flies.

Finally, we visited the old town of Bukhara. A UNESCO World Heritage Site with more than 140 architectural monuments making the whole town a museum. Packed full of over a thousand years of history, this old town was mind-blowing. It is the most complete example that remains of a medieval Central Asia town, which demonstrates the level of urban planning and architecture that was around so many years ago. Once again, we encountered the beautiful blue and turquoise tile work, domes and arches. We completed a walking tour which included the Kalon minaret where, for centuries, criminals were executed by being thrown off the top, which is pretty horrific as the tower stands tall at 47 metres. To walk around the bottom of the tower and know you are stepping on ground where men have been smashed to death, is pretty gruesome. We visited the many three 'M's;

mausoleums, medressas and mosques, ending with The Ark which is an old fortress and it was also a royal town within a town. It is Bukhara's oldest structure built in the 5th century.

Feeling slightly overwhelmed by the three 'M's and hankering for something other than architecture, five of us opted to visit a hamman the following morning. Hammans are the oldest form of spa treatments that are native to Central Asia. Myself, Catherine and Yvette booked ourselves into an old bathhouse that was located behind the gruesome Kalon minaret. Matt and Jim were booked into a men only hamman a few streets away. At 9 o'clock in the morning, Catherine, Yvette and I were greeted at the hamman by two old ladies wearing flowery headscarves and bearing gold teeth. The building was over 500 years old and housed many underground chambers. As we stripped off all our clothes Yvette couldn't contain her excitement. "This is going to be awesome. How many people can say they've been to a bathhouse that is over 500 years old". "I know, I need a spa treatment after all this partying and sightseeing", I groaned as I placed the last of my garments into one of the wooden lockers that lined the wall.

Wrapped up in a modest towel, we were led by the old ladies down into the first steam room where we were left for the steam to work its magic on our lungs and pores. It was terribly steamy and as I lay on the heated stone slab, I found it an effort to breathe normally. Not on a Kilimanjaro level, nonetheless I could feel the strain. The chamber resembled a dungeon. The old, grey brickwork was damp with steam. Low stone ledges had been built within bricked archways with the typical Islamic characteristics. "I can't breathe!" exclaimed Catherine. It was becoming a bit of a pea souper I had to agree. I heard one of the old ladies enter and lead Yvette into another chamber followed by Catherine. Finally, I was led into a different chamber where I was given a rather vigorous body scrub by a woman, who looked like David Seaman, the former England goalkeeper, wearing her large white mittens. Just when it felt like she had rubbed every ounce of my skin from my body she started a massage which, at the time, I could not decide on whether it was pleasurable or painful. Next she smothered me in a body mask of ginger, spices, egg and a list of ingredients that she could probably have made a few fruitcakes from. Then she went onto to perform a body wash. Good grief. Now I felt like I was drowning as she squeezed soapy water from a sponge directly over the top of my head. My eyes were tightly shut but still the soapy water still managed to get into my eyes.

After all the treatments I was led into yet another chamber where Yvette was lying naked on a heated slab. I lay on my own stone slab exhausted from the steam. "Hey, Yvette. How was it? Have you seen Catherine?" I whispered. "It was incredible. Didn't you know? Catherine passed out from all the steam and has left" answered Yvette. Gosh. I had no idea. I felt bad that I had been oblivious to the entire goings on but I really couldn't see much through the haze of steam. As we left, the two beautiful old ladies wished us well via some hand gestures and a flash of golden teeth. Our final Uzbek destination was Khiva. The bone rattling ten hour drive to get there was painful. Potholes unexpectedly appeared making the truck jolt and veer. Our bodies were thrown in every direction, including a regular smack of head on the roof of the truck which reminded me of the Kilimanjaro to Nairobi drive. Khiva is another open air city-museum which during the 10th century was a major trading centre on the Silk Road. By the 17th century the city had turned into a busy slave market. Millions of Persians, Russians and Turkmen were brought to Khiva to be sold or forced to work on the construction of buildings in the walled city. A cruel history for such a beautiful city.

It was also a cruel start to my Khiva visit as my untrustworthy bowel returned with much fervour. I managed to shuffle around the ancient city and take the all important photos, but my heart and bowels just weren't into it. Poor Yvette was sharing the hotel room with me those two nights. I apologise Yvette for using all the toilet paper and creating a disgusting odour. The matches helped. Thank you.

Chapter 18

Crater of Fire

It is always sad to leave a country that has amazed you in ways that you weren't expecting. I knew of the ancient cities and fascinating tiled architecture, the beauty of which was captivating. Yet the friendliness of the Uzbek people astounded me. Who invites strangers from the street to their wedding parties? Who showers outsiders with hospitality and feeds them mountains of gourmet food? Who gives foreigners endless shots of vodka which cause them to disappear down manholes in the street? The Uzbek people, that's who.

Today was the border crossing from Uzbekistan to Turkmenistan. First stop, a bush camp in the Karakum desert. Much of the landscape of Turkmenistan is desert and it sits on a relatively untouched abundance of oil and natural gas. Despite its wealth in gas reserves, the country only exports to Russia, China and Iran. For decades there has been talk of building a new pipeline under the Caspian Sea through Turkey into Europe, but nothing as yet has been implemented. It has the smallest population out of the five ex-Soviet 'Stans with a mere 5 million people. Compare that to Uzbekistan's population of nearly 30 million, and both countries are geographically similar in size too.

Our second port of call was Konye-Urgench in the far northern tip of Turkmenistan. Nowadays, there are only a few mausoleums, a mosque and a 60 metre high minaret that remain from the Old Urgench, but in the 12th century it was the capital of the ancient state of Khorezum. It was one of the greatest Islamic cities on the Silk Road. The city was first destroyed in the 13th century by Genghis Khan, in what has been described as a horrific bloody massacre and then again a few centuries later by Timur, who obliterated Old Urgench leaving just the few ruins that can be seen today. The remaining buildings were beautiful, notably the Turabeg Khanym mausoleum which had the typical blue and turquoise tile work on the ceiling representing the days, months and seasons of the calendar year.

But what we found of particular interest was the hill at Kyrk Molla, which is a sacred place where it is said local people held their last stand against the Mongols. It is here, if you time your visit right (which unfortunately we didn't), you can see young women wrapped in thick protective coats, rolling down the hill. This isn't an attempt to enter the Guinness World Records for the 'most women rolled down a hill in thick coats' category. No, this is an old fertility ritual; a popular place for women who want to get pregnant. A Turkmenistan cheap alternative to IVF treatment. "Geez... I wouldn't fancy rolling down this hill. It's so dusty", commented Catherine as we stood at the top peering down the hill, squinting our eyes against the windblown dust particles. "Me neither", agreed Yvette, who added, "I wonder if the men have to perform any rituals to ensure they aren't firing blanks? I bet not".   There were also mascots that had been left amongst piles of rocks; another desperate lucky charm to become pregnant. It was eerie with all the headscarves, dolls, bed pans and miniature rocking cradles all in a heap on the floor like jumble for sale.

Then it was on to the markets to purchase food for our camp nights. I love market shopping. The characters you meet are as colourful as the fresh fruit and vegetables that they have for sale. My job was to buy eggs for breakfast and there, at the entrance to the market, were four egg ladies. They looked exquisite in their flowery headscarves and long patterned coats. The hues of the colours was intense; red, pink turquoise, green and blues. They were certainly of different ages, perhaps a family. Grandmother with her lined face and lack of teeth and perhaps her daughters who were keeping up the family business. They all had trays of eggs stacked high in front of their makeshift upside down plastic laundry basket stools. Across from the lovely egg ladies was CD boy. His CDs filled his wall space, the covers of which looked like eighties bands Depeche Mode or Bucks Fizz but were actually Turkmenistan bands. Marketing was clearly not their strong point. All burnt on his computer at home. CD boy looked like a typical young Turkmen in his fake three stripe 'Adidas' jacket and fake 'Levi' jeans to match his fake CDs. With the grocery shopping completed we were ready for our journey to the much talked about 'Gateway to Hell'.

I know I shouldn't be really excited about this as there was nothing natural about it, but I was. This new addition to the 'tourist attractions' in Turkmenistan isn't of ancient historical interest, but is an embarrassing blunder made by the Soviet Union. Back in the 1950s the Soviet Union sent exploration teams around Central Asia in search of natural gas and oil. In 1971, a natural gas field was discovered near the town of Derweze in the Karakum desert and drilling quickly commenced. But disaster soon struck when the oil rig proved too heavy and the ground collapsed beneath it, creating a huge crater. The geologists, in their panic to stop the poisonous methane gas that had then started to release, set alight the fumes thinking that they would burn off in just a few days. Forty years later it is still burning. Whoops! Slight miscalculation on their part, I believe. Locals have nicknamed the burning crater the 'Door to Hell' and the 'Gas Crater of Darvaza'.

We set up bush camp an hour's walking distance to the crater and as I pitched my tent into the sand I could feel myself bursting with excitement at the thought of seeing the hellish pit. "I'm so excited! I know it's a result of a major bungle by the Soviets but I've never seen a burning crater before", I enthused to Catherine. "I know. You'll have to be careful not to singe your hair or stand too close to the edge" she warned. Being a pharmacist I was sure she would have some kind of burn ointment should I be overzealous near the edge of the crater. I was so giddy. "Come on guys, let's set off", shouted Matt, who was also itching to see the crater. The five of us, myself, Matt, Catherine, Yvette and ex-husband Jim were ready for our Karakum desert hike on the sandy path that would lead us to the burning crater. But no-one else was walking it seemed. Noel, the co-driver, or passenger as he was sometimes mistaken, had decided he would drive the truck to the crater. This was a ten tonne (just my guess again at bloody heavy) truck on a soft sand track in the middle of the desert. It was late afternoon and we were staying at the crater until it started to get dark. Vital for those all important photos and the flames would look more impressive in the dark. Noel intended to drive the truck back in the dark. Now, I know I am no expert on heavy vehicles, but surely there was a high risk that it could sink into the soft sand? In spite of the concerns we voiced to Noel and the others, they were not walking. We were told not to be so stupid. Why would a heavy truck sink into the sand? We left Noel with Princess Norway and her flock and commenced our desert trek.

Over an hour had passed of trudging in the sand when Matt did a sudden turn and yelled, "Welcome to hell!" In front of us was this great big hole in the ground. It just appeared in the flat sand plain below. It was surreal. Flames flickered in patches on the floor and up the deep sides of the crater twenty metres deep to be precise and sixty metres wide. It was like something from another planet. "This is unbelievable! I have never seen anything like this in my entire life", I gushed as we approached the flaming pit. The heat intensified as we closed the gap. "This is fucking awesome!" was all Matt could say as his face got redder and redder from the heat. The closer I got, the more sulphurous fumes filled my nostrils. The wind had picked up too, making the flames dance around in the hole. It was like someone had taken a giant cigarette and stubbed it into flat desert ground, leaving the lit end smouldering in the burnt void. There was not a safety rail or warning sign to be seen. We strolled right up to the cragged edge with our toes practically hanging over the rim. Not for long though, as the heat became unbearable after just one minute.

In Europe, or any Western world country, a Health and Safety Act would have this pit securely barricaded with a fire resistant shatterproof glass shield placed at least a hundred metres from the danger thus ensuring safe viewing. Big ugly signs would have been placed in full view warning visitors of the possible dangers of burning craters. The signs would, of course, be placed at crucial viewing spots ensuring no photo could be taken without the unsightly sign in the forefront. There would also be an extortionate charge imposed, probably around $50 per person plus an extra $10 if you wish to take photos. Finally, don't forget that liability clause confirming they will not be held liable under any circumstances for any injuries or medical conditions that may arise from possible heat or poisonous fumes. Not in Turkmenistan. You could dive into the burning pit if you so wished.

We were the only people and vehicle at the gas crater. The new tourist attraction in Turkmenistan clearly wasn't drawing the crowds that evening. As the sun set, the crater took on a more sinister edge. It really did look like the door to hell. I felt like I should perhaps confess to all my sins and pray to my glow in the dark Jesus for forgiveness. In the near dark, the gas crater had now transformed into the devil's lair. I could just imagine an evil horned devil rising out of the flames carrying his pitch fork. It was eerie and it was also time for us to leave.

The sun had set and we needed to climb up the sand dune to get back onto the track before it was dark. It would be easier tackling the flat track with our torches than the hill. We waved goodbye to Princess Norway and her flock before setting off. It wasn't long before it was dark and our torches were lighting the way. The truck passed us early on and we were offered a lift which we declined. It was fun walking in the dark, the desert all to ourselves. "Is that the truck ahead?" asked Catherine "I think they may have got stuck in the sand. Ha... serves them right. It was a stupid idea to even take the truck." As we got closer it became evident that the truck had indeed got stuck in the sand. Princess Norway's flock were digging sand from around the sunken tyres. The heavy iron sand mats were out, ready to heave in front of the wheels to create a lift and traction out of the loose sand. I've done this procedure before in Africa and it is a back-breaking job, even trickier when performing it in the dark.

"I'm not stopping", declared Catherine, "why should we? We made it perfectly clear that we thought it would get stuck in the sand. The plan was always to walk to the crater. I walked in and I am walking out. Stuff 'em". "I agree but won't it look bad just walking past?" asked Matt who looked a little undecided, not wanting to form any enemies within the Princess's flock. "I'm with Catherine on this. It was all of them that changed their minds not to walk. Now they'll have to deal with the consequences, which might I point out that we did try and warn them of the risk" said Yvette. So, rather sheepishly we walked passed the truck holding back the calls of "told you so" that we were so tempted to do. I knew this move was going to create tensions within the truck but Catherine and Yvette were right. Why should we get covered from head to toe in sand hoisting iron mats when we were not involved in the decision to take the truck and also, more importantly, there were no showers at the bush camp? I know I have become quite the professional contortionist with my Houdini Nivea body wipes but even I couldn't get shed loads of sand off my body with a mere moist handkerchief.

We then stumbled our way back to bush camp. Yvette and I had gone off in front (for once I was in the lead position... hurray!) and with only one working torch between us, we managed to spot our bush camp down in a sand valley without walking straight past and further into the desert. It was cold by the time we reached our tent so we huddled inside one while we waited for Matt and Catherine to arrive. Shortly after, we heard a "Cooee" in the distance. "That's Matt doing his Crocodile Dundee impression. Quick let's get out and wave our torch", I said as I unzipped the tent. Matt's Aussie call is usually used in the Australian bush to attract attention, find missing people or just to let people know your own location. I waved the torch while performing the loud, trilly 'Cooee' in return. It worked, even in the desert. Matt and Catherine came stumbling down the sand dune. "It's freezing", chattered Matt, still dressed in shorts and trainers. We all huddled in one tent while nibbling on chocolate chunks. We were starving. It had been a short-sighted plan to walk past. In our haste to chastise the group by leaving them, we had also walked past the cook group who were supposed to be preparing and cooking our evening meal. What a set of dimwits. Now we had to wait for hours for them to return before even one potato could be peeled. Sadly, all the groceries were also on the sunken truck. By the time the truck, Princess Norway and her flock returned we had eaten five squares of chocolate each, drank all our water and flattened the batteries in our torches.

Tensions were high as the rest of them started to peel potatoes and chop vegetables. The disdainful looks were plentiful and we undoubtedly had created a major camp divide. There was no way we were going to wait for two massive pans of water to boil whilst receiving scornful, killer glances from the cooks, so we retired early to our tents, hungry and unpopular.

After a strained breakfast and a restless sleep from nightmares of Princess Norway ordering her flock to throw us in the blazing pit for our sins – our penance for not stopping to help them, we visited two more gas craters. What a letdown. From the infernal gateway to hell to an insignificant hole in the ground with gas bubbling up through stagnant water, then onto another crater that, granted, was very deep, but was filled with rubble and had a small amount of gas bubbling up through some mud. Not quite the same impact as a hellish pit blazing like the devil's cauldron in the middle of the desert, nonetheless, something you wouldn't see in the Yorkshire Dales or Blackpool beach.

Our final destination in Turkmenistan was the capital city of Ashgabat. Dubbed Central Asia's Dubai, this city is extravagance taken to another level. As Archie, the truck, drove into the city, it was like entering the 'Land of Narnia', only instead of a snowy and fantastical land, there was a wondrous world of white marble. Matt's jaw dropped. "This is unreal", he gasped as we passed building after building fully covered with white marble. "Check out the traffic lights", I shouted. Every single set of traffic lights was set in a white frame with a white post to match the white buildings lining the streets. Thankfully, the red, amber and green sequence had not been whitened, but the colours did look strange against a white background. It was so bright. The white marble reflected the sun, making us all reach for our sunglasses. Every other corner seemed to feature a golden dome or a giant water fountain. Did you know that the city of Ashgabat has made it into the Guinness World Records under the category 'the highest density of white marble-clad buildings'? The winning statistics are an area of 22 kilometre square (18.49 mile square) of 543 new marble-clad buildings. I reckon there's probably not much competition around to beat that world record.

There were also a couple of other interesting world records featuring marble. Did you know that Yaping Zhang from China holds the record for the 'most marbles moved with chopsticks in one minute'? Quite an accomplishment. I wonder how long he spends each day practicing. I could do it with tongs... I wonder if there is a record already set for picking up marbles with tongs. Then there's the 'most marble tiles broken with a glass in one minute'??!! The name had been left blank; clearly they are too embarrassed to admit to that one. Well, wouldn't you be too?

After checking into our mid-range hotel, the five of us, including ex-husband Jim, found a restaurant bar that the Lonely Planet guide assured us was good and transformed into a fun karaoke bar at night. It also told us that the Turkmenistan government place bugs in all the top-range hotels and restaurants where foreigners meet, therefore, you must be careful about what you talk about. The implication being that you may get arrested for talking bad politics, or worse if the English translation is poor. That certainly wouldn't affect us in our mid-range hotel and cheap karaoke eatery. Several vodka shots and mint-flavoured shisha puffs later, we were fuelled for karaoke.

The songbook was full of American and British bands for us to sing. From Michael Jackson's 'Billy Jean' to 'We Will Rock You' by Queen. A drunken Matt was quite giddy about his chosen song. "Hit Me Baby One More Time by Britney Spears is what I'm going to sing. I love it. Pass me the microphone". As Matt wailed through Britney's lyrics, I was choosing my song, but it was difficult. I didn't fancy the soundtrack from 'Grease', nor did I want to sing Madonna's 'Like a Virgin', so I opted for 'Hotel California' by The Eagles. A local woman, who looked like she was a regular and, more importantly, a karaoke veteran, asked if we could do a duet. With vodka shots raging through my bloodstream I thought I was the next Beyoncé and jumped at the opportunity. Four embarrassing minutes later, abashed and shamefaced, I passed the microphone back to the karaoke facilitator and reclaimed my seat. Note to one's self – must cut back on the vodka.

The following day we were given two options by our Turkmen guide, to be driven to the local meat and animal market, or to spend the day doing your own thing. The thought of looking at severed pigs heads and live chickens being hung upside down from poles did not appeal to me much, so, the four of us decided to hit the city centre. Princess Norway and all her flock found the meat market much more appealing and off they went to look at the animals, dead or alive. We hopped in a taxi that took us to Independence Square from where we would walk through the city and take in the sights.

The roads and pavements were deserted. Where was everyone? Then we realised that most of the roads were closed to traffic. "Something big is going on", declared Matt. "You don't put up all these road blocks in a city centre for something small". Next thing we knew we were facing an army military tank with what looked like missiles being displayed on top. We just managed to sneak in that all important photograph before being approached by an army officer requesting that we do not take photos of any military weapons. "Geez, what is going on?" asked Catherine. We were baffled as to what would happen next. That came in the form of planes, military aircraft. In full RAF Red Arrow style, they appeared from behind a golden domed building in 'V' formation, with coloured vapour trails leaving lines of red, white and blue in the sky behind them. "Wow!" I shouted over the engine noise, "this is so cool". As we walked further into the centre we stumbled across a huge square filled with people. Every person was dressed in a white jacket with either black or white trousers and carried a large green Turkmenistan flag. There was a group of people sitting on the roof top terrace of one of the marble buildings facing the square, who were undoubtedly important. Huge cranes moved around with cameramen high in their perches, filming the whole show. Then the parades commenced. We had in fact, stumbled into the Turkmenistan 20 years of independence celebrations. Of course, 1991 was the year the Soviet Union dissolved and Turkmenistan became an independent country. The year today was 2011. The cameramen were filming the whole event including the President, who was one of the spectators on the roof terrace. The most wonderful procession of all different costumes and flags followed. Thousands and thousands of men and women passed us, waving and chatting. They were dressed in contrasting traditional outfits ranging from young men in big white furry telpek hats, older men wearing black ones, women in thick embroidered velvet dresses and girls in turquoise satin dresses with chiffon sleeves and matching headscarves. Giant flags of all colours were being waved as they passed. Everyone was happy and full of smiles. The parade was never ending. A sea of turquoise would pass by, then red, then green. This celebration was on a big scale, nothing small for the President. Our prime spot stood facing the President and his parade was just incredible. I have never seen a celebratory parade on this scale before and I have never seen one since. As Matt would say, "This is fucking awesome!"

Back at the hotel foyer we bumped into Accountant Mick and couldn't resist showing him our new set of photos. "Hey, Mick. How was the animal market?" I asked. "It was alright.

A few too many disgruntled cows for me though", he grumbled. "What did you guys get up to?" Cue the photos. "I don't bloody believe this!" exclaimed Mick "where was this? It's friggin' amazing. I can't believe I chose to go to a stupid livestock market to look at farm animals. I don't know how you guys do it". Team 'Lucky Buggers" Four versus Team Mick One.

Following a note at reception from our leader, Italian stallion Luca, we were all gathered in the foyer for an announcement. "Hey guys I have had some bad news. It seems our rooms have been cancelled for the next two nights. There is a worldwide embassy function going on at the moment and their delegates have taken our rooms. The cheeky buggers! The good news is the only available rooms for us to move to just happens to be at the President Hotel which is a five star hotel" advised Luca, clearly impressed by the new accommodation choice. "This will cost you nothing as it is an error on the part of the hotel which my company will have to sort out with them direct. Get packing guys!"

We were so excited, a posh hotel. Archie, our truck was driven to the President Hotel which had 16 floors of pure luxury. It brought back memories of the Tian Yuan Hotel in China. Spacious, carpeted rooms with a marble tiled bathroom and even a 'living room' area with an upholstered three piece suit that looked like it belonged in a stately home. Pure decadence, again! "This is fucking awesome", was the rave review from Matt.

The following morning was an exciting visit to yet another Iranian Embassy. Back home, when fastidiously up-dating my visa excel spreadsheet with entry and exit dates for the various countries, Iran was the only country that demanded you go to their embassy in person to get your tourist visa. No agent is allowed to submit the application on your behalf. I believe we Brits may have slightly peeved the Iranian government thus encouraging them to make it as hard as possible to obtain a visa.

The British publication of Salman Rushdie's book, The Satanic Verses, is regarded as blasphemous by many

Muslims, which led him to be placed under a fatwa, or religious order, calling for his death from Iran's religious leader, Ayatollah Khomeini. This has now been retracted but the fact that the Queen has since knighted Salman Rushdie for his services to literature does not sit well with the Iranian government. In 2007 the Iranian embassy was telling people not to even bother submitting forms unless they had a sponsor. They have now closed down their London embassy which makes it even more tricky for wannabe Iran visitors to obtain a tourist visa. You now have to fly to another country in order to visit an embassy in person just to get that elusive visa.

My attempt at obtaining a visa back home was futile. I rang the Iranian embassy in London and made an appointment. I bought train tickets that don't come cheap, and used a day's holiday from work to travel down to the embassy. When I arrived with all the correct paperwork and photograph wearing the required headscarf, I was politely told the fingerprint machine had broken and I would have to come back when it was fixed. No, they didn't know when it would be fixed. Have they not heard of the alternative paper and inkpad? Several telephone calls and weeks later I was told that due to the fingerprint machine still being broken, they would temporarily accept postal applications. I swiftly posted my passport and application to the embassy only to be told their Tehran office has not provided the required authorisation number. My passport was returned to me two days prior to my flight without the required visa.

Attempt two. Luca informed me that my authorisation number only arrived at the Ashgabat embassy two days ago. For British nationals the cost of a visa is 210 Euros and for all other nationalities it is 75 Euros....even the cost for Americans is cheaper than us and they have really pissed off the Iranians. Payment must be in Euros. US Dollars are prohibited. God forbid they should touch the notes tainted with embargos. British Sterling is also vetoed. Reason not fully known. That morning four of us went to the embassy with a fixer. Yes, I had my own fixer. Who needs to be a United Nations diplomat from Pakistan to get a fixer when you are in

Turkmenistan? It was a long process. The inkpad had no ink which took an additional hour for an embassy worker to run out to the local WHSmith, or equivalent Turkmen stationary store to purchase. They should let the London embassy know about inkpads and their ingenious use for recording fingerprints. Finally, I had my visa. Well, the following day it would be ready... or so they say...

Obtaining the various visas required for travelling through a number of countries is like cooking an Indian curry. Just like the spices that need to be added at different times during the cooking process, the same finesse applies to the tourist visa process. Some visas are valid for three months from the date of issue, others are six months. Some take 5-10 working days to be issued, others take just 3 days. You have to ensure that all the visas (the 'spices') are applied for in the correct sequence or the visa validity (the curry) will be ruined. If you're not careful, your visa could have expired before you have even set foot in the country. Timing is crucial. Dates are pretty important too. That vital entry date was my big error, which I was unlucky to find out at the Chinese immigration desk.

At least I know how to survive two arrests, a near five year jail sentence and a major earthquake, not to mention avoiding falling down the many manholes in Uzbekistan.

I'm not sure what advice to give when obtaining travel visas other than be more diligent than I was or, when all else has failed, say a little prayer to the glow in the dark Jesus...